INTERMEDIAL THEATRE

INTERMEDIAL THEATRE

Principles and Practice

Edited by Mark Crossley

methuen | drama
LONDON • NEW YORK • OXFORD • NEW DELHI • SYDNEY

METHUEN DRAMA
Bloomsbury Publishing Plc
50 Bedford Square, London, WC1B 3DP, UK
1385 Broadway, New York, NY 10018, USA
29 Earlsfort Terrace, Dublin 2, Ireland

BLOOMSBURY, METHUEN DRAMA and the Diana logo are trademarks of
Bloomsbury Publishing Plc

First published in Great Britain 2019 by Red Globe Press
Reprinted by Methuen Drama 2022

Copyright © Mark Crossley and The Authors, under exclusive licence to Springer
Nature Limited 2019

Mark Crossley has asserted his right under the Copyright, Designs and Patents Act, 1988, to be
identified as Author of this work.

All rights reserved. No part of this publication may be reproduced or transmitted in any form or
by any means, electronic or mechanical, including photocopying, recording, or any information
storage or retrieval system, without prior permission in writing from the publishers.

Bloomsbury Publishing Plc does not have any control over, or responsibility for, any third-party
websites referred to or in this book. All internet addresses given in this book were correct at the
time of going to press. The author and publisher regret any inconvenience caused if addresses
have changed or sites have ceased to exist, but can accept no responsibility for any such changes.

A catalogue record for this book is available from the British Library.

A catalog record for this book is available from the Library of Congress.

ISBN: HB: 978-1-137-61158-1
      PB: 978-1-137-61157-4

To find out more about our authors and books visit www.bloomsbury.com and sign up
for our newsletters.

Contents

List of Illustrations   viii
Acknowledgements   x
Introduction   xi

1 Theatre (and You) as Medium and Intermedium   1
Mark Crossley with original contributions from Lars Elleström

Alone in a Hotel Room, Searching for a Medium   1
Medium: Getting the Message Across   2
Back in the Room: Media at Work   6
Modalities and Modes: Things We Find in Cheap Hotel Rooms   8
Representation: Decoding the Divorcee and the Cowboy   13
Theatre as Hypermedium: When Is a TV Not a TV?   18
Intermediality: The Everyday Kind   20
Intermediality: Evolutions in Thinking   22
Aspects of Theatrical Intermediality   27
In Amongst and Beyond   37

2 Twenty-First-Century Intermediality   43
Andy Lavender

A Journey: From Intermediality to Multimodality   43
Piraeus Heterotopia   48
Evros Walk Water   50
Don't Follow the Wind   52
Sanctuary   57
Landing Points   59

3 The Performer in Intermedial Theatre   62
Joanne Scott and Bruce Barton

Introduction   62
Framing the Discussion (Jo)   64
Framing the Discussion (Bruce)   65
Who Is an Intermedial Performer? (Jo's Perspective)   66

The Status of the Performer in Intermedial Performance Environments
  (Jo's Perspective) 66
The Status of the Performer in Intermedial Performance Environments
  (Bruce's Perspective) 71
Performing Presence in Intermedial Spaces (Jo's Perspective) 73
Performing Presence in Intermedial Spaces (Bruce's Perspective) 77
Intermedial Actions and Interactions (Jo's Perspective) 79
Performer-Media Relationships: Intermediality in Action 83
Conclusion 86

4 Time in Intermedial Theatre 90
Joanne Scott

Introduction 90
Time and Technology 96
Time as a Modality of Media 100
Performing Intermedial Temporalities: *The Encounter* and *Birdie* 104
Emergent Thoughts and Ideas 111

5 Technology and Intermedial Theatre 116
Rosemary Klich

Staging Media Magic 120
Media Materiality 122
Staging Media Materiality 125
Performing a Post-digital Aesthetic 130

6 The Audience in Intermedial Performance 136
Gareth White

The Audience in Intermedial Theatre: Networked Bodies 136
Remote London 138
Invitations, Habitus, Enculturation 139
After the Invitation 141
Zunshine and Mind Reading 142
Manipulated Mind Reading 144
Macondo 146
Affect and Embodied Meaning 147
Mediated Life 149
The Encounter 151
Exoticism and Derangement 153
The God of Ears 154

	Discourse Networks	156
	Conclusion	158
7	**Practitioner Case Studies**	**161**

Introduction by Mark Crossley

Tristan Sharp: Artistic Director, Dreamthinkspeak, UK   163
Absent (2015)

Russell Fewster: University of South Australia   171
Walter Benjamin – A Life in Translation (2016)

Andrew Quick and Peter Brooks: Artistic Directors,
Imitating the Dog, UK   175
The Zero Hour (2013) and *A Farewell to Arms* (2014)

Rosie Garton and Ildikó Rippel: Artistic Directors and
Performers, Zoo Indigo, UK/Germany   179
No Woman's Land (2017)

Dries Verhoeven: The Netherlands   184
Guilty Landscapes (2016)

James Yarker: Artistic Director, Stan's Cafe Theatre Company, UK   188
Time Critical (2016)

Craig Vear: Professor of Digital Performance (Music)   192
De Montfort University, UK
Postcards (2017)

David Pledger: Artistic Director, Not Yet It's Difficult, Australia   197
v: Hotelling (2016)

Bibliographies   202
End Notes   212
Chapter Authors and Contributors   219
Index   221

List of Illustrations

Figure 1.1 Amar Kanwar, *The Sovereign Forest + Other Stories* (2013). Photographer: Jonty Wilde. 31
Figure 1.2 Stan's Cafe, A *Translation of Shadows* (2015). Photographer: Graeme Braidwood. 39
Figure 3.1 Intermedial spaces being constructed live, as part of *re-cite* by Jo Scott (2012). Photographer: Matt Taylor. 69
Figure 4.1 Miniature animals and buildings arranged on the green baize floor in Agrupación Señor Serrano's *Birdie* (2016). Photographer: Roger Costa. 108
Figure 4.2 A performer filming the tiny elements of Agrupación Señor Serrano's *Birdie* set live (2016), with the footage projected behind him. Performer: Àlex Serrano. Photographer: Pasqual Gorriz. 111
Figure 5.1 Michèle Anne De Mey and Jaco Van Dormael, *Kiss and Cry* (2011). Photographer: Maarten Vanden Abeele. 128
Figure 6.1 Rimini Protokol, *Remote X* (2016). Photographer: Mike Vonotkov. 150
Figure 7.1 Dreamthinkspeak, *Absent* (2015). Performer: Pip Mayo. Photographer: Jim Stephenson. 165
Figure 7.2 Dreamthinkspeak, *Absent* (2015). Photographer: Jim Stephenson. 167
Figure 7.3 Dreamthinkspeak, *Absent* (2015). Photographer: Jim Stephenson. 168
Figure 7.4 Dreamthinkspeak, *Absent* (2015). Photographer: Jim Stephenson. 169
Figure 7.5 Dreamthinkspeak, *Absent* (2015). Photographer: Jim Stephenson. 170
Figure 7.6 Russell Fewster, *Walter Benjamin – A Life in Translation* (2016). 175
Figure 7.7 Zoo Indigo, *No Woman's Land*, 'Ildikó, Ilona, Charlie, Rosie, Dylan and Lydia' (2017). Photographer: Tom Walsh. 181
Figure 7.8 Zoo Indigo, *No Woman's Land* rehearsal shot (2017). Photographer: Tom Walsh. 183

Figure 7.9	Dries Verhoeven, *Guilty Landscapes* (2016). Photographer: Willem Popelier.	188
Figure 7.10	Stan's Café, *Time Critical* (2016). Performers: Rochi Rampal and Craig Stephens. Photographer: Graeme Braidwood.	190
Figure 7.11	Not yet it's difficult, *v:Hotelling* (2016). Photograph: Bleached Arts Ltd.	200

All images are reproduced with kind permission.

Acknowledgements

As editor of this book, I am in the fortunate position to overtly thank a number of people for all their hard work and dedication to this text. Firstly, my sincere gratitude goes to all the chapter authors: Andy Lavender, Joanne Scott, Bruce Barton, Rosemary Klich and Gareth White. It has been a great pleasure to collaborate with you, as throughout the process you have embraced the spirit of the text and offered the readership insights into intermedial theatre that are both rigorous yet eminently readable. I would also like to add a specific thanks to Lars Elleström, who has been so generous with his time and encouragement for this text. It has been a real pleasure to 'curate' your ideas within a theatrical context and have the added bonus of your first-hand contributions within the opening chapter. Huge thanks must go to all the esteemed theatre practitioners from across the world who have contributed their thoughts to Chapter 7, 'Practitioner Case Studies': Tristan Sharp, Russell Fewster, Andrew Quick and Pete Brooks, Rosie Garton and Ildikó Rippel, Dries Verhoeven, James Yarker, Craig Vear and David Pledger. Your insights on contemporary intermedial performance are fundamental to the text as, crucially, they ground theory in practice and inspire future theatre-making. Thanks also to the editorial team at Red Globe Press (formerly Palgrave), who have been patient, diligent, kind and supportive throughout this process.

Finally, my personal thanks, as always, go to my wife, Siân; my children, Joseph and Beth; and my parents, Diana and Ray.

The editor and publisher would also like to thank the following for the use of copyright text material in the book:

Complicité/McBurney, S. (2016a) for quotations from *The Encounter* (London: Nick Hern Books) in Chapter 4, Time in Intermedial Theatre.
Henriette Morrison/Theatre of Europe for the email correspondence invitation to Remote London sent to Gareth White in Chapter 6, The Audience in Intermedial Performance.
Professor Simon Biggs for extracts from email correspondence sent to Russell Fewster in Chapter 7, Practitioner Case Studies.
imitating the dog for extracts from their website in Chapter 7, Practitioner Case Studies.

Introduction

Mark Crossley

I am very happy that you've found time to open this book, and will be even happier if you take a while to explore and gain some reward from it, be that an insight into how media correspond and interact within intermedial theatre, how professional intermedial practice is conceived and structured, or perhaps how to enhance your own intermedial theatre-making. It is a book that aims to make complex ideas accessible. This is easier said than done, as this is not the same as making ideas simple. In essence, what the book seeks to achieve is a rigorous insight into key aspects of intermedial theatre principles and practices as they manifest themselves here and now in the first quarter of the twenty-first century, infused as it is with digital media and the new hybrid experiences this creates. Each chapter author addresses sophisticated ideas in relation to intermediality but infuses these with his or her own experiences of making and spectating, speaking to the reader directly throughout. Themes, practices and even certain productions (notably Complicite's *The Encounter*) are revisited by different authors, but with a new perspective each time, dependent on the focus of the chapter. The approachable analytical style is illuminated and grounded with a wide range of clear practitioner examples, selected by the chapter authors or written about by theatre makers themselves in the final chapter. Every chapter (except for the final chapter on case studies) concludes with a **Practical Ideas** section written by each author, offering the reader some thoughts on how to translate the concepts within the text into theatre practice.

Intermediality is dealt with at length in this text, but lest we forget the second word in the title – 'theatre' – this is perhaps best thought of, for our purposes, as a broad church of performance practices with the centrality of the live event, offering some rallying point even when digital technologies suffuse the interactions between performance and audience. Examples in the book are drawn from conventional dramatic-based practice, sound-based performance, dance, site-specific installation, digitally immersed improvisation and many more besides. In Chapter 1, I recalibrate the existing term 'hypermedium' to describe theatre's embrace of multiple media within its bounds, and therefore it's deft evasion in the face of definition. For now, perhaps, step back from any absolute delineation of theatre, and make up your own minds from experience and experimentation.

This text can only cover so much of the vast territory of intermedial theatre, which by its innate hybridity has countless tributaries it may follow. Notably, the book seeks to include some of the more commonplace instances of intermediality in terms of how it manifests itself across a plethora of forms, within but also beyond the overtly digital or technological. It also makes no assumptions as to the inherent usefulness or significance of intermediality, seeking instead to understand where and when it may be justified and to question its application where necessary. By its overt embrace of developments within the current century, there is, in the text, a certain degree of attention placed upon digital technologies and their impact on intermedial theatre. However, several chapter authors and case studies attend to the spectrum of low-tech or post-digital responses that have arisen in contrast or even in resistance to the seemingly omnipresent embrace of digital culture. Likewise, although the text is directed towards the theatre of the present day, acknowledgement is given throughout the chapters to the significance of experimental practices from the seventeenth to the late twentieth century that tested the boundaries and confluences of emergent media in those periods, including masque, film, television and analogue sound, and lineages are traced between these pioneering practices and their influence on the here and now.

The aspirations of this book are perhaps best summated as three-fold: firstly, to decipher the structures of media and the relationships between them within intermedial theatre, using a range of theoretical models; secondly, to investigate the methodologies involved in the practice and spectatorship of contemporary intermedial theatre; and thirdly, to reflect upon the range of experiences these interactions and processes create, from the sensory to the intellectual, the social and the political.

Media and intermedial theories are specifically explored in my own extended **Chapter 1, 'Theatre (and You) as Medium and Intermedium'**, and the key principles from this, notably those of Lars Elleström, who contributes to the chapter, are then revisited and utilised by several of the authors. Andy Lavender, in **Chapter 2, 'Twenty-First-Century Intermediality'**, creates a segue between the two aspirations of the text as he continues the reflection on intermedial relations and the recent development of academic dialogue in this field but, having acknowledged the ubiquity of intermediality, turns his attention to the implications of such pervasiveness. As he says, 'If media mixity is now a norm of cultural production, we become interested not so much in the "what?" and the "how?" of media interrelations, as the "so what?" and "to what end?"

In which case, we are interested in intermediality's *affects*, the *actions* it performs or permits, and its *affordances* – for pleasure, participation, empowerment.'

Lavender's instinct for the experiential potency of theatre practice creates the impetus for Chapters 4 through 8, which are determinedly focused on key aspects of practice within contemporary intermedial theatre. In **Chapter 3, 'The Performer in Intermedial Theatre'**, Joanne Scott and Bruce Barton create a dialogue between themselves as practitioner scholars, tackling the complexities of the embodied experience within intermedial performance, considering notions of status, presence, interaction and intimacy, amongst many others. Joanne Scott then presses on with a solo expedition into the temporal expanses of **Chapter 4, 'Time in Intermedial Theatre'**, exploring the capacity of intermedial practice to 'crystallize, disrupt, reconfigure and even reveal the construction and curation of time', not merely for theatrical effects but also as eloquent modes for creating 'feeling states and meanings' for an audience. In **Chapter 5, 'Technology and Intermedial Theatre'**, Rosemary Klich articulates and then questions the 'wizardry' of contemporary media materiality and its capacity to disappear within our everyday lives. She explores the potential for theatre to exploit these illusions but also to offer 'a resistance to its misdirection'. **Chapter 6, 'The Audience in Intermedial Theatre'**, by Gareth White, offers analyses of modes of spectatorship within intermedial theatre, and the new challenges and opportunities this brings. In light of the proliferating new ways for audiences to participate, he considers how 'performances figure the audience member as tech-user' and then how this then generates new 'human-media relationships in action'. Finally, **Chapter 7, 'Practitioner Case Studies'**, delivers exactly what it promises and draws us back to the heart of the book's intentions by considering the interrelationships of media in theatre and the methodologies used to conjure these hybrids into being. Influential and experimental theatre practitioners from the United Kingdom, Europe and Australia reflect on some of their own most recent work and how they think about and construct such intermedial performance to be both relevant and challenging to a contemporary audience.

We hope you find the book useful and thought-provoking from the start or from whichever page you commence. If not, then take a break, get lost in some pervasive digital media for a while and then try reading some of it again. It might all make sense after *Candy Crush*.

1 Theatre (and You) as Medium and Intermedium

Mark Crossley with original contributions from Lars Elleström

ALONE IN A HOTEL ROOM, SEARCHING FOR A MEDIUM

Picture this scene. Close your eyes if it helps.

You are in a theatre. You can decide what kind – sparse or ornate, open-air arena or intimate basement – whatever works for your imagination. The stage in front of you is dark, but slowly it illuminates to a dimly lit state to reveal a scene set for the opening of a performance. Centre stage is a single bed, covered with the impersonal linen of a cheap hotel chain, upon which sits a solitary figure; the choice of gender is yours, but they are lost in their own world, looking down to the floor. Stage right is the door to the hotel corridor, adorned with an obligatory 'Fire Exit' sign. Stage left is the window, framed by gaudy floral curtains, alongside a battered television set, and on the upstage wall the décor is forlornly embellished by a reproduction painting of a horse and rider, their strident gallop across the wide-open spaces amplifying the claustrophobia of the room. The amber glow from a city street meekly radiates the fringes of the room.

Take time to build this theatrical image, the detail of it. Note the composition of multiple elements within the scenographic whole. Now, slowly let it dissolve from your mind's eye. Let the actor fade away, the set and the lights dissipate into the darkness, until you are sitting in the same theatre, but now the stage in front of you is bare. In the chapter that follows we will, for the purposes of understanding media and intermedia, rebuild this scene, but first notice this new absence, this void, an invitation to place performers, objects, sounds, illumination, images or perhaps nothing at all within its bounds. This is theatre's prerogative, it's unique selling point. It is a capacious host, mutable and generous to whom and what it invites.

MEDIUM: GETTING THE MESSAGE ACROSS

Before we begin in earnest, it might be worth offering a brief insight into why you have been asked to imagine. The intention of this chapter is to offer you a clear, robust and useful conceptual framework for considering the practice of theatrical intermediality. It is simply an opening gambit, as every chapter that follows augments these initial ideas with new and challenging perspectives and practices. However, we need to start somewhere in this elusive and sometimes labyrinthine field. There is a compulsion, therefore, to initially consider what may actually be meant by the terms 'intermedia' and firstly its derivative noun, 'media', as to grasp what is occurring in the confluences and collisions between media, it would seem reasonable to comprehend the notion of a 'medium' in the first place. Part of the task here is to untangle and streamline the crowded lexicon these terms inhabit, although it is essential to avoid a mere thesaurus on media and intermediality. So, inherent within the pursuit of clearer terminology is a more fundamental desire to reveal the distinctiveness of theatrical mediation and theatrical intermediality in its capacity to engage and challenge the devisor, performer and audience, and ultimately to create new meanings that other forms may not articulate. You are sitting in the imaginary theatre, therefore, because whatever ideas are unlocked, they will always be more fully expressed through the reality of theatre as it is actually created and experienced, or at least, for now, through your own imagined vision of these practices. You may wish to seek out a real theatre to experiment in later.

> I wanted to be the conduit for somebody else's experiences, filtered through me, and passed on to other people. Which is the job description, really.
>
> —Juliet Stevenson, actor (*The Guardian*, 2009)

At its most basic level, a medium is a tangible means of communication or realisation, a conduit (to use Stevenson's job description for acting) that enables ideas and/or, more prosaically, types of energy to transmit or transfer from one state to another. The 'one' may be the single mind of an author, and the 'other' may be the imagination of the reader via the medium of a book. Or 'one' could be the collective ideas of a theatre company transmitted to an audience via the various media of a play text, actors, action, speech and so forth, this latter example indicating how media invariably work in tandem or sequences. Media *must* manifest themselves physically in some form, to bring to ground and capture our ephemeral or illusive creations, from the kinetic energy of electric light harnessed in the filament of a bulb to existential or romantic angst anchored into poetic verse. The fundamental communicative and realisatory principle of medium/media, echoed in several of the scholarly definitions that follow, may therefore be simple to encapsulate, yet the discourse over media, their origins, functions, forms and interrelationships within society, has been somewhat more extensive, with the arguments often pursuing divergent trajectories.

There have been many prominent postwar theorisations defining media, with Marshall McLuhan notably proposing in the 1960s that media are extensions of our physical engagement with the world: 'All media are extensions of some human faculty – psychic or physical' (1967, p. 26). A book, he suggested, was an extension of the eye, and such media gave us an enhanced perception of the world around us. He also famously argued that 'the medium is the message' (1964, p. 9), by which he inferred that media are the progenitors and facilitators of content, be that events or the movement of people, products and services. Yet we easily forget or ignore that they are entities in themselves. He uses the instance of the electric light as an example of a *pure* medium that holds no content itself, but facilitates the creation and communication of other media within it; think how light irradiates a stage, a sporting event or a surgical process, but we overlook the illumination itself. Media, he contested, are effectively transparent until they are literally or figuratively revealed through another medium. A book, for example, only really manifests itself through the media of literature or factual documentary which it may contain. McLuhan stated: 'This fact, characteristic of all media, means that the "content" of any media is always another medium' (1964, p. 8). He paid particular attention to the impact of technological developments and the new media of the twentieth century, in reference to which he noted the increasing interrelationship and collaboration amongst media, proposing, for example, that film was a 'collective art form', referring to both the collective personnel required to produce it and the collective elements (colour image, lighting, acting, directing etc.) enfolded with it. These propositions of McLuhan offer a clear contention that media are not absolute entities that can be easily delineated, as they are in a constant state of absorption and redefinition with other media in order to function, a process that would later be categorised as *remediation* by Bolter and Grusin (1999). Remediation was introduced as a concept in their seminal work, *Remediation – Understanding New Media,* in which the term is used to explicate the ongoing renegotiation between media and the interdependence that exists amongst them. They write, 'A medium is that which remediates. It is that which appropriates the techniques, forms, and social significance of other media and attempts to rival or refashion them in the name of the real. A medium in our culture can never operate in isolation, because it must enter into relationships of respect and rivalry with other media' (1999, p. 65) Lars Elleström, however, is somewhat forthright in his opinion of Bolter and Grusin's definition of the term, which he refers to as 'acutely vague' (2014, p. 7) and prefers to delineate remediation as *'repeated* mediation', a type of *transmediation* (p. 14). Using this definition, he goes on to define certain types of remediative intermediality and intramediality (pp. 90–92), some of which are revisited later in the chapter.

In the intervening years since McLuhan's early propositions, there have been many contending media theories which have, at times, because of their divergence, limited the clarity and cohesiveness of any analysis. In 2008, Kati Röttger evaluated the developments in this field and noted the ongoing ambiguity of the terminology: 'There is a problem that is inherent in any historical and any theoretical perspective on media, which is the formulation of a useful and widely applicable definition of media' (2008, pp. 32–33). However, resonant of McLuhan's vision, one common denominating factor, with which many writers in the latter part of the twentieth and early twenty-first centuries concur, is that media are not closed systems that can be essentialised[1] or easily demarcated. They do not operate in isolation and are constantly reconfiguring their structures, fundamentally affecting one another. The structure of one medium is bound up in another and our way of perceiving the meaning of a work of art therefore is bound up with our perception of the mediating context in which it is framed. Robin Nelson writes: 'Mediums come together in various ways. In some instances, they collide and create a frisson in the process; in other instances, one medium is imbricated within another so that they are almost dissolved into each other but the form of one remains just visible in the solution of the other' (2010, p. 18). Such fluid affiliations become particularly pertinent when we begin to frame a range of media within a capacious theatrical context.

In recent years, there has been particular attention given to distinguishing the interrelationships between **modalities**,[2] what we might call the specific and tangible elements through which a medium discloses itself, identifying a complex interplay between what actually manifests itself and how we perceive this manifestation through the lens of our cultural knowledge and experience. Multimodality, as this interrelationship is often referred to, was recently explored by Bateman, Wildfeuer and Hiippala (2017), who use the term 'canvas' to signify the site or situation in which the intentional act of the 'sign producer' is made tangible and decipherable by the 'sign consumer' (2017, pp. 86–87). This 'canvas', or medium, may be as simple as a cross etched on a pebble (the example they proffer) or, in our case, a theatrical event. Bateman et al. go on to emphasise the significance of context and community specificity in the negotiation and intepretation of the 'canvas': 'It is this anchoring in a community that turns that task of understanding what the canvas is carrying from a piece of enlightened guesswork to communication.' (2017, p. 88; emphasis in original). The significance of our perception of media, situated as we are within cultures, communities and conventions, is underlined by Werner Wolf's definition of media when he stated that they were 'conventionally and culturally distinct means of communication, specified . . . primarily by the use of one or more semiotic systems[3] in the public transmission of contents' (2011, p. 2). This emphasis on our culturally informed decoding of media, the deciphering of its 'signs', finds correspondence in Claudia Georgi's definition of media, which she delineates as 'the material quality of a means of communication that can be identified by its characteristic and conventionally established use of specific signs or semiotic systems' (2014, p. 22).

To make this chapter as useful as possible, it draws upon one of the most current and comprehensive explorations of media and intermedial structures and relationships, as developed by Lars Elleström.[4] His theories over the past decade have sought to demystify and rationalise the composition and significance of media and intermedia in a cultural context, as Charles J. Forceville highlights in his review of Elleström's 2010 text, noting that 'his fine-grained distinctions allow for teasing out different dimensions of attributing meaning to (inter)media' (2011, p. 3092). It will be impossible to interrogate all aspects of Elleström's comprehensive study, as detailed in 'The Modalities of Media: A Model for Understanding Intermedial Relations' in *Media Borders, Multimodality and Intermediality* (2010) and developed further in *Media Transformation: The Transfer of Media Characteristics Among Media* (2014), yet we may still aim for a robust interrogation of some of the fundamental terms, definitions and concepts. So, in the context of your imagined theatre, it is predominantly this theory that you are asked to consider.[5] Here is a brief introduction to the subject of intermediality from Lars Elleström himself:

> For me, intermediality and multimodality are everywhere in the world of communication. I simply find it hard to understand how communication, this essential capacity of humans and other living species, can be understood and analysed without the notion that all media products[6] are more or less multimodal and always more or less interrelated. It is thus not the case that we have, on the one hand, "normal" communication, and, on the other hand, multimodal and intermedial communication. I would say that intermediality is a perspective, an analytical angle that can be used successfully for unravelling the complexities of all kinds of communication. Not least, the artistic types of communication, such as theatre and other compound art forms, may be better understood with the aid of such a perspective.

An intermedial viewpoint helps us to see both what is specific with certain media types and what they have in common with others – what is transmedial.

Elleström, unlike some other theorists, makes no distinction between arts and other media as he states that the arts are unequivocally 'aesthetically developed forms of media' (2010, p. 11), yet he *is* keen to delineate between the *materiality* of media and the *perception* of them. Consequently, his deconstruction centralises this distinction. Although Elleström does not focus on theatre to any major extent in his own work, the clarity of his approach makes it pertinent for practitioners, with immediate applicability to the realities of theatre and performance. Elleström himself highlights the need for his theoretical categories to be grounded and of use when he states, 'They are tools for thinking, indicating that their validity is only proven if they turn out to be helpful for discriminating among things that are worth being discriminated among, and if they help avoid confusion and misconceptions' (2014, p. 10) He also offers a word of caution, though, to anyone looking to delve superficially into his work: 'In this study, I attempt to dig deeper. I avoid much of the standard terminology and instead delineate the essential concepts, using technical terms and doing some difficult theoretical work. Readers seeking easy solutions should beware' (2014, p. 2). With this warning duly noted, it is hoped the 'imaginary theatre' approach that you've been encouraged to adopt may serve you well.

BACK IN THE ROOM: MEDIA AT WORK

Your theatre is still empty. Before anything is placed on the stage, look around: take a walk around the auditorium and out into the foyer or whatever constitutes the entrance in your imagination. The space you are in is already in action. It is a *medium*, a 'distinct means for communication', to borrow Wolf's definition, crafted by our cultural practices and conventions to look, sound and feel a certain way; a 'temple of illusion' as the British dramatist Noel Coward referred to it. We arrive in the theatre with expectations of what is to come, a suspension of everyday rules, a different set of codes to interpret, the special signs peculiar to the 'temple'. These appear even before the performance begins, in its décor – perhaps the gold leaf or the matte black walls, the scale of the space, the evocation in the posters of imminent excitement, confrontation or catharsis. We are skilled decoders of the context we are in, and once the performance begins, we are ready to decipher the intricate signs of the content itself – the exaggerated gestures of physical comedy, the direct address and interaction of pantomime, the verse of

Shakespeare, the distillation of time and space as epic narratives are enfolded into the singularity of one time and one space.[7] We have absorbed the rules of engagement with theatre; some of us may have been 'exposed' to its conventions more than others, because of upbringing, income, geography and so forth, but all of us have a sense that theatre requires a different kind of perception to real life. In Elleström's theory, this interplay between what appears before us and the requirement for us to decode these experiences through our learnt cultural lenses leads him to refer to theatre, along with other art forms and socially constructed means of communication, as **qualified media**; only fully realised and understood through the combination of what 'is' and what we interpret the 'is' to be; the context and conventions 'qualify' our understanding of the form and content:

> *Qualified media* is a term that I use to denote media categories – artistic and non-artistic – that are historically and communicatively situated, indicating that their properties differ depending on parameters such as time, culture, aesthetic preferences, and available technologies. Qualified media include classes such as music, painting, television programs, and news articles. A qualified medium is constituted by a cluster of individual media products. (Elleström, 2010, pp. 24–27).

A *qualified* medium can be distinguished from a **basic** medium, which can function and be predominantly registered in basic sensorial and semiotic terms (e.g. still or moving image can be recognised as 'basic' visual, iconic data initially), rather than within cultural and aesthetic contexts, although Ellestrom acknowledges a fine gradation between the two, as a *basic* medium quickly develops interpretative, *qualified* complexity once it manifests itself. In this regard he emphasises that both basic and qualified media are types of media product. The final medium in his taxonomy is **technical**,[8] which, simply put, is the actual physical means through which the *media product* is communicated. He describes it as the 'technical media of distribution of sensory configurations or the technical media of display'[9] (2010). Ellestrom clarifies that a *technical medium* is a means of 'distribution', not merely of production or storage, and as an example he identifies the production of vibrating air from our vocal chords as a *technical medium* as our vocal chords 'disseminate' sound but do not store sense-data (2014, p. 19). A *technical medium* may be epitomised by our television set onstage but also by the actor's body itself (the flesh and bones) before it is articulated and then interpreted as 'performer'. We can best illustrate these distinctions between media types and find the delineations and correlations between manifestation and interpretation by returning to your theatre.

MODALITIES AND MODES: THINGS WE FIND IN CHEAP HOTEL ROOMS

Take your seat in time to witness the actor/performer[10] walking on to the stage. The actor has appeared in front of you, ready to perform, and has learnt some lines. We'll put no more detail on it at present. In this sense the actor has *materialised*, their **material modality** is their body, three-dimensional flesh and blood with the capacity to manifest itself through different **modes**, predominantly movement and, if they start speaking or singing, through sound. This is the conduit (if the staging remains as merely a bare stage and a performer) through which the actor's performance is mediated, whilst what they communicate, and its significance, can be, temporarily, detached.

Mode,[11] it must be acknowledged, is one of the aqueos terms within intermediality. Gunter Kress stated in 2012 that 'mode is a term that allows us to get away from using language for everything. They are resources by which we can make meaning material. . . . They are socially produced and become cultural resources for making meaning. They are material.'[12] Sindoni et al. (2016), amongst several theorists, refer to modes as 'semiotic resources' (p. 3), citing elements such as music, voice and language as examples of these resources. In this context, multimodal media refers to those media which articulate themselves through more than one principle mode. Sindoni et al.'s and Kress's descriptions of modes are certainly worth noting, but I take the view that Elleström's precise definitions are more useful 'in the field', and on that premise, here is Lars Elleström's own clarification of modes and their relationship to modalities:

> Just like 'medium', the term 'mode' can, has and should be used to stand for different notions in diverse contexts. One way of using the term must therefore not necessarily compete or be in conflict with very different ways of using it, and so I realise the pragmatic value of thinking about text, sound, image, music, design, visuals, gesture and so forth as different communicative modes. This is the standard way of operation in the research area of social semiotics in the tradition of Kress and van Leeuwen, and it often works rather fine. However, this way of thinking allows for a shifting and overlapping set of modes that are very difficult to compare with each other in a more systematic way. Additionally, both the term 'mode' and the term 'modality' have been used to represent the same entities. My suggested solution has been to introduce a distinction between two levels to facilitate and sharpen the description and analysis of media products: we have, on the one hand, *the types of traits* that are common for all media

products, without exception, and on the other hand, *the specific traits* of particular media products or types of media products. I call the former *modalities* and the latter *modes*. There are four modalities – four types of basic media traits: all media products must necessarily have some sort of *materiality* and some form of *spatio-temporal* extension, and they must furthermore be *sensorially* perceptible and create meaning through *signs*. This adds up to the material, spatio-temporal, sensorial and semiotic modalities. No media products or media types can exist unless they have at least one mode of each modality. However, most media are multimodal in various ways: they may be materially multimodal, having both solid and liquid modes, for instance; they may be spatio-temporally multimodal, being both, say, two-dimensionally spatial and temporal; they may be sensorially multimodal, being dependent on being both seen and heard; and they may be semiotically multimodal, for instance by way of creating meaning through icons and indexes as well as symbols. This is a much more detailed and specific way of outlining multimodality compared to multimodality understood as the combinations of socially constructed entities such as speech, music and gesture.

Returning to the premise of *material modality,* and that every medium has a material form through which it transmits, envisage the reappearance of the television screen, the simple bed and the painting onstage, as our evocation of a nondescript, down-at-heel hotel room begins to reassemble. The television set, with its flat screen and its projection of light and sound, is the *material* object through which the *qualified medium* of television, with all its cultural conventions, needs to manifest itself. Without the physical screen, the binary soup of digital signals would remain in the ether, indecipherable to an audience. Notice as well how I use terms such as 'light' and 'sound' here, rather than 'TV broadcast' or 'speech', as we are identifying that *basic* and *technical* media exist and function in tangible states independently of how we interpret them. Television programmes and comprehensible speech require a cultural context in which to be given such names and thereby decoded. Simply put, if you left the theatre, the TV would continue to emit light and sound without you, but these emissions would only become significant when you returned or when some other curious soul appeared and sought to make sense of them. Likewise, the painting, in its capturing of a still image on a flat surface, is the material expression of art, a *qualified* medium. So, the *material* modality is the physical interface of the medium, and this can be comprised of several features in tandem. We can, in this context, also recognise a television set and paint on canvas as *technical media*, inert until we wish to encounter them, then interpret and bestow significance. Elleström makes a crucial delineation here between **mediation** and **representation**, identifying the different *modalities* that media manifest themselves through in correlation with, but distinguishable from, the process by which we interpret them:

> As I define it, mediation is a presemiotic[13] phenomenon and should be understood as the physical realisation of entities (with **material, sensorial**, and **spatiotemporal qualities**, and **semiotic**[14] potential) that human sense receptors perceive within a communication context. For instance, one may hear the sound of a voice.
>
> Representation is a semiotic phenomenon and should be understood as the core of signification, . . . As soon as a human agent creates sense, sign functions are activated, and representation is at work. . . . (For instance, one may interpret the sound of a voice as meaningful words. . . . [R]epresentation is the creation of meaning through the perceptual and cognitive acts of reception. I submit that to say that a media product represents something is to say that it triggers a certain type of interpretation. (Elleström, 2014, p. 12)

Standing patiently onstage, the actor begins to talk, reciting a melancholic monologue of loneliness and regret. The TV flickers into life, a low-budget Western appears on screen. The stage lighting increases slightly to reveal our horse and rider, a remediated facsimile found in every room down the corridor. Consider our ability to register the fact that a performer stands before us and speaks, that a television is actually onstage and transmitting, or to recognise a picture as the artefact that it is; it is through our senses. The *sensorial modality*, as Elleström refers to this, concerns itself with physical perception and is subdivided into three elements that work in conjunction: the **sense-data** that are transmitted (sound, image, light etc.), the bodily **receptors** (within the eyes, ears etc.[15]) that translate these data and transmit them to the nervous system and finally the resultant **sensation** itself, which is created partly through our physiological reaction but also affected by our cultural reaction – what a particular sight, smell or sound[16] evokes. In this correlation of sensations, there is a transition to the *representational* stage as we interpret using memory and our own cultural perspective. To revisit our own stage – the bed, simple as it may be, emits light as *sense-data*, illuminated by the amber glow; the *receptors* in our eyes receive this combination of light data, and we respond with a *sensation*, empathy or sympathy perhaps, which may feed from our memory of such dimly lit beds in lonely hotels, or at least our televisual and filmic recognition of them.

The actor, emboldened by their tragic yet stirring monologue, begins to roam the stage for a few minutes – we now have movement through space and time. Elleström refers to this aspect as the *spatio-temporal modality* and identifies all media as having a dimensional framework that may be constituted from a combination of **height, width, depth** and **time**. Our actor, as we can tell by our *receptors*, stands and moves in three dimensions and articulates themselves around the stage so that we know (or at least can be fairly certain) that they are a live, physical body. Likewise, the television has a certain **height, width** and **depth** which distinguishes it as a TV rather than a larger film screen or smaller monitor. Media that 'lack the fourth dimension, time' (2010, p. 19) – in other words have no noticeable changes over time – epitomised by our hotel picture, are defined as **static** in temporal terms. Elleström then demarcates *modes* of **sequentiality** dependent on the level of temporal rigidity or flexibility within a medium, from the **fixed sequentiality** of a film which we can be fairly confident runs for a set duration and in the same sequence anywhere it is screened in the world; to **partially fixed sequentiality**, exemplified by our hotel performer or a stand-up comic, who have a degree of fixed time structure (start/middle/end as constructed by a playwright or comedian's set list) but with some room for digression, changes of pace and audience interaction; through to **non-fixed sequentiality**, perhaps experienced in a fully improvised happening or spontaneous rave, where start, middle and end are all unpredictable and fluid.

Now look again at the television picture or the painting, the images projecting from flat surfaces. This is where a **virtual** quality informs materiality, spatio-temporality and sensoriality as we begin to navigate between the *presemiotic* and *semiotic*. We can only comprehend such flat pictorial images if our perception of them is able to draw on our understanding of *virtual* space and time, which in turn is predicated on our capacity to conceive of the *actual materiality* of the original objects. The images on the screen or canvas have to be comprehended as possessing a *virtual* height, width and depth for us to relate to the characters, objects and settings. We must invest them with a range of literal and figurative dimensions; otherwise, they remain undeciphered spots of colour on a flat surface. Lars Elleström offers his own explanation of virtuality in this context:

> When I first, in 2010, published my ideas on how to conceptualise intermediality and multimodality, I included virtual time and space among the spatiotemporal modes but wrote very little about virtual materialities and virtual sensory perceptions. I now think that was an unfortunate omission and have since then spent many years of researching *cross-modal representation*; the imperative phenomenon that meaning-making very

often goes beyond the media product's actual media modes. For instance, a two-dimensional, static picture may represent something that we perceive to be both three-dimensionally spatial and temporal, such as a body running in a landscape. This is to say that with our eyes we perceive only two actual dimensions but with our mind we perceive, or rather construe, *virtual* third and fourth dimensions. By the same token, we regularly construe virtual materialities and sensory perceptions. A sculpture that is actually made of stone may well be understood to represent a living organism such as a cat, which means that the representation crosses the border between non-organic and organic materiality. When reading a musical score we only actually perceive visual configurations, but they are understood to represent auditory patterns; virtual sound is construed in our minds. All these virtualities, these represented objects and phenomena that are made present to our minds through signs, I would now argue, do not strictly belong to the presemiotic modes but result from semiotic activity.

As we notice a character moving off-screen or scan the inference of physical motion in the picture, we also perceive indirect worlds beyond the limitations of the images, worlds in which the cowboy heads off-screen down the imagined dusty street or the horse gallops across the figmental plain. We create the spatial worlds for the figures and events to occupy. Similarly, we understand that there is a suggestion of virtual temporal realms within these media, a sense of time passing or of concurrent times existing,[17] as the film cuts from one scene to another, or likewise with the horse that we perceive to have galloped for many hours before this moment and likely for many hours hence. The particular modes that certain media adopt encourage us to perceive movement through time, as hours, days, decades or centuries of narrative may transpire within the constraints of a single image or performance. We are similarly adept at distinguishing spatial compression and expansion, whereby multiple locations may be invoked upon one small stage whilst epic vistas can be represented in the confines of pictorial images, or, conversely, the tiniest detail of a facial expression, the curl of a cowboy's lip perhaps, can be amplified on to a vast film screen. Film-space (both what is visually present and what is inferred or imagined) has been analysed at length by many theorists, notably Andre Bazin in *What Is Cinema* (1967). Bordwell and Thompson (2013) distinguish three principles of film-space: *plot space, story space* and *screen space*. In reference to these concepts, Chiao-I Tseng writes: 'Plot space refers to settings in *mise en scene*; story space can include spaces created in the mind of the viewers' imagination associated with the plot space. . . . The third type of space is on-/off-screen space, often akin to camera manipulation of framing' (2017, p. 127).

Virtual sensoriality is also at play in our engagement with *media products*, as our sense memory connects, and often rekindles, sensory experiences beyond the immediate impact of the *sense-data*. The sunset in the hotel picture perhaps creates a thermoceptive recollection of heat, or the cheap bed sheets evoke a tactile memory of similar corporate linen. It may be noted that it was our capacity for sense memory which Konstantin Stanislavski harnessed in his early-twentieth-century acting technique known as 'affective memory' or 'emotion memory', by which actors were encouraged to recall the physical sensations of an emotional event as a conduit to rekindling the emotions themselves, a practice further refined within the postwar 'Method' of Lee Strasberg.

So, at this point we have registered the three *modalities: material, sensorial* and *spatio-temporal* – elements onstage having demonstrable form, enacting upon our senses and functioning in space and time. We have a body near a TV, with a bed and a painting lit by an amber wash, and all having a material form, all sending out *sense-data* predominantly in visual and audible forms. All manifest themselves in physical modalities but are enhanced by our ability to perceive the virtual realms that are inferred. In this alchemy, *mediation* is becoming *representation*.

REPRESENTATION: DECODING THE DIVORCEE AND THE COWBOY

In the same instance that we receive the *sense-data*, we instinctively begin to invest it with significance, moving beyond the *pre-semiotic* stage. All features onstage are starting to coalesce, to *represent* something that has meaning beyond the literal. Theatre, as a generous but not entirely altruistic host, has invited a range of media in but is now representing all of them. Understanding this correlation between the form that something takes and the significance we place upon it leads many theorists, including Elleström, to foreground the importance of **semiotics**, or sign systems, as notably expressed in the works of Ferdinand de Saussure and Charles Sanders Pierce in the late nineteenth and early twentieth centuries. One of the principle correlations explored in semiotics is between what is manifested by the **signifier** (the TV or pictorial image, the written forms on a page and so forth) and what this *signifies*[18] – the *sign* being the combination of the two elements. Ellestöm particularly focuses on Pierce's concepts of **icon, index** and **symbol**, which he considers to be the 'three main types of representation' (2014, p. 13) Here Lars Ellestöm explains their significance:

The functions of icons, indices and symbols – iconicity, indexicality and symbolicity – may be simple and straightforward as well as complex and sometimes difficult to grasp. Again, the importance of **cross-modal representation** should be emphasised. All three sign types may cross the boundaries of the *signifier*, or the *representamen* to use Peirce's terminology, in the respect that something visual can represent something tactile, something static can represent something temporal, and so forth; however, *cross-modal representation* may also mean that something material represents something mental. This capacity of our minds to connect the experience of concrete objects and phenomena with the experience of thinking, feeling, perceiving and imagining is absolutely fundamental for how meaning is created in communication. A visual circle may be an icon for a material, concrete object such as the sun, but it may also be an icon for mental, abstract phenomena such as harmony, satisfaction or eternity because of a perceived similarity between the visual form and the cognitive notions. A visual circle may also function as in index for the former presence of a material object like a pen or a brush that actually created the circle, but it may likewise be understood as an indexical sign for the mental act of wanting to draw a circle: there is a real connection between the producer's intention and the realised circle. The pen *was there*, but also the idea *was there*. Finally, a visual circle may be understood as a symbol, a sign based on habits, for instance the letter O. The written letter O signifies symbolically in at least two different ways: on the one hand, it stands for a certain kind of sound, or rather a group of related sounds, and sound is a material phenomenon that is perceived with our external senses; on the other hand, the letter O stands for something abstract and conceptual in the sense that it represents a linguistic function – to form meaningful words – that can only be realised in conjunction with other letters.

In the context of our stage, begin by considering the bed and the painting – think of these as *iconic* – they bear a physical similarity to images that we have in our mind of those objects in the real world, so we identify them and 'label' them as such. Like Russian dolls this can go on and on, as within the realistic painting, what is represented in paint (the horse, the rider, the landscape, the sunset and so on) is also all *iconic*. If the picture were more abstract, a cheap copy of a Picasso, let's say, this would not necessarily be the case, as shapes might be less identifiable and therefore less able to be matched to our mental library of images. Turn your attention now to the hotel room door and the standard sign reading 'Fire Exit', with an arrow indicating where to go. In this one instance, we see both *index* and *symbolic* signs. The arrow is *indexical*, as it suggests what it means, it is not an image of an exit or a human being exiting, but we approximate what it means, and the arrow is a universal sign communicating a direction of travel. Likewise, the sound of hooves emanating from the TV Western is *indexical*, as it indicates horses on the move, even before we might see them in shot. The words 'Fire Exit', on their own, however, are *symbolic*, a collection of signs that can only be interpreted by those of us who read and speak that specific language. The anguished, lonesome words of our actor are also *symbolic* and therefore 'full of sound and fury, signifying nothing' to appropriate Macbeth, unless we are able to interpret them. *Symbolic* signs, notably words and language, have been developed over millennia and distilled to a point beyond real-world resemblance to any actual meaning. Over time, through habit and convenience, we construct and then connect letters into words, words into sentences, sentences into speeches, and each culture codifies and then decodes these combinations through the *basic* media of sound or mark-making (writing or typing) on a page or screen. These written or spoken words are not just decoded literally of course; we always locate them in a specific cultural context, so within the frame of theatre they may be distinguished as the *qualified media modes* of dramatic dialogue or play script. Multiple, rapid cross-references are made in the process of media *representation*. It may be worth reflecting here on the degree of accelerated **semiotic** decoding we have already used in evoking the hotel scene. Not only is each single word so far part of the code, but also consider the depth of enculturated knowledge we access to instantly interpret such complex, descriptive terms as 'Western', 'cowboy', 'actor' or 'monologue'. Enculturation,[19] as proposed by Phillip Kottak (1994), is the process by which a person learns the cultural norms and values of a society through her experience and interaction with it. He identifies three processes of enculturation, two of which are conscious and one being unconscious. Firstly, we can be taught directly by others about the values, such as from teachers or parents; secondly, we can observe cultural behaviours and then emulate them; and finally, we can absorb behaviours unconsciously and assimilate them into our attitudes and practices.

What must be remembered about sign systems, and therein the relationship between *signifiers* and *signified* within the *sign*, is the fluidity of these relationships and the shifts that occur over time and across cultures. There are no preordained truths to these correspondences, and any specific manifestation can blur or transfer between categorisations.[20] Within any given media, dependant on the specific forms used or the stylistic traits, different semiotic modes may come to the fore in the process that Elleström earlier referred to as *cross-modal representation*. Take the aforementioned Picasso copy for example; both this and our first realistic version may both be classed as pictures and art, but the 'Picasso' becomes more *indexical* (as opposed to *iconic*) in its suggestion, rather than its clear reproduction, of real-world images. Theatre creates particularly mercurial boundaries, often to be exploited, as it 'theatricalises' all that it encompasses. All the *iconic* elements onstage may also simultaneously operate on an *indexical* level, as the heightened context of the theatre leads us to invest them with significance beyond their immediate materiality; the single bed in a sparsely decorated room with one cheap painting of a horse and rider indicates isolation or loneliness as we approximate this experience of seeing such a room to other comparable artistic or real-life examples. In this theatricalised context, 'the other media become "signs of signs" as opposed to "signs of objects"', in the words of Kattenbelt (2006, p. 37).[21] Therefore, even before an actor delineates their role or narrative through action or speech (assuming there is an actor at all), we begin to read a complex layering of what is *signified* by the staged *signifiers*.

Our interpretation of signs is inextricably bound up with our life experiences. We are, as Elleström suggests, 'a perceiving and conceiving subject situated in social circumstances' (2010, p. 21). Having delineated the four *modalities*, therefore, he 'qualifies' these in relation to **pragmatic aspects** that affect our interpretation. Firstly, there is the **contextual qualifying aspect** described as 'the origin, delimitation and use of media in specific historical, cultural and social circumstances'. The second 'aspect' is the **operational qualifying aspect**, referring to the 'aesthetic and communicative aspects of media' (2010, p. 24) As noted earlier, media that are significantly reliant on these two qualifying aspects in their constitution, in particular those media that may be considered art forms such as theatre, are identified as *qualified media*. Here, Lars Elleström explains the differences in his model between basic and qualified media, and the nuances required to articulate qualified media:

> In the end, each media product is unique. However, thinking species such as humans are in dire need of categorising things; otherwise, we would not be able to navigate in the world or communicate efficiently. We hence categorise all media products, and as is often the case with classification in general, our media categories are generally quite fluid. However, some categorisations are more solid and stable than others because they depend on dissimilar factors – and that is why I find it helpful to work with the two complementary notions of *basic media types* and *qualified media types*. Sometimes we mainly pay attention to the most basic features of media products and classify them according to their most salient material, spatiotemporal, sensorial and semiotic properties. We think, for instance, in terms of still images (most often understood as tangible, flat, static, visual and iconic media products). This is what I call a basic medium (a basic type of media product) and it is relatively solid. However,

such a basic classification is sometimes not enough to communicate more specific media properties. What we do then is to qualify the definition of the media type that we are after and add criteria that lie beyond the basic media modalities; we also include all kinds of aspects on how the media products are produced, situated, used and evaluated in the world. We may want to delimit the focus to still images that, say, are handmade by very young persons – children's drawings. This is what I call a qualified medium (a qualified type of media product) and it is more fluid than the basic medium of still image simply because the added criteria are vaguer than those captured by the media modalities. For instance, it may be difficult to agree upon what a handmade drawing actually is: should drawings made on computers or scribble on the wall be included? And when is a child not a child any longer but rather a young adult? The notion of childhood varies significantly among cultures and also changes over time, not to mention the individual differences in maturity. The limits of qualified media are thus bound to be ambivalent, debated and changed much more than the limits of basic media.

To fully engage with the hotel scene in front of you requires a complex and 'debatable' web of contextual knowledge. The *representation* of theatre through 'perceptual and cognitive acts of reception' is only made possible because we are conversant both in its own conventions, which have evolved over centuries, but also in our own wider social circumstances which inform artistic practice and spectatorship. Consider the scene again, its evocation of loneliness, potential separation or divorce, the intimation of a city merely through the use of a specific amber hue. All of these are reliant upon our enculturated experience and knowledge, our attentiveness to the correspondences and inferences between our scene and the practices of our actual societies. We are alert to the symbolic significance of the staged décor, the irony of the expansive subject matter in the painting in contrast to the stagnant urban setting and the subdued body language of the performer. We would, of course, instinctively decipher these if we encountered them in the real world, but through the magnified theatrical lens we are primed to collate their significances. We understand that the staging represents a distilled reduction of *signifiers*, an edited cluster to be interpreted both individually and in unison. Working in concert with this *contextual* knowledge is the *operational qualifying aspect* which encompasses the specific conventions of any qualified medium that allow us to identify it as such. These are in part a combination of the *modalities* and discreet *modes* through which it manifests itself, often constructed and then mutated from existing media from which it has evolved through remediation.[22] The hotel stage we have created suggests a variety of conventions to us, a dramatic and naturalistic genre due to its realistic scenography and a traditional 'fourth wall' distancing, as our actor is performing within a fictional world into which we observe but are not acknowledged. Intriguingly, each medium within the scene operates within its own contexts and conventions; we expect a TV to transmit popular mass entertainment and news, to be a stationary object with a certain domestic scale and a predominantly *fixed sequentiality* of programming, whereas we expect a painting to be *static* in time and potentially to manifest itself in more abstract forms than television. However, we have the capacity to percolate all these discreet conventions through a theatrical filter and acknowledge them both as separate media yet harnessed to a unifying performance objective. This USP of theatre needs some consideration.

THEATRE AS HYPERMEDIUM: WHEN IS A TV NOT A TV?

Here is a simple question: if we took all the elements that appear in our hotel scene – bed, actor, TV, painting, curtains and so forth – and then filmed and screened this performance, what would all of these become? The answer, of course, is film. All these elements with their diverse *modalities* of *materiality*, *sensoriality*, *spatio-temporality* and *semiotics*, not to mention their own *qualifying aspects*, all succumb to the specific and – I use this word carefully – 'limiting' *modalities* and contexts of film; essentially a flat image of light and sound most probably with a *fixed sequentiality* of time and a requirement on our part to envisage virtual space, bound by the cultural and operational conventions of film. Likewise, if we converted our hotel scene into an Edward Hopper–esque painting, all elements would subsume themselves within a flat, *static* image, framed literally and conceptually by the conventions of fine art. The marvellous quirk of theatre is that it allows all media to manifest themselves in their own unique forms, expressed by Claudia Georgi as 'its ability to integrate other media without affecting their respective materiality and mediality' (2014, p. 46) whilst simultaneously representing them as theatrical *signifiers*. The television on our stage is an *actual* television in three dimensions, with its own cultural significance, but it also theatrically signifies the isolation of our protagonist, its indifferent transmission emphasising the absence of another human being. The oblate stillness of the painting and its unending invocation of physical vitality juxtaposes with the hunched physical presence of the performer, who wrestles with the unpredictable, non-fixed, three-dimensional uncertainties of life. We, as skilled directors, scenographers or designers, are aware of this poignancy and consciously place them in correspondence within the scene.

This interrelationship, or mobility, between media materiality and theatrical signification is again reflected upon by Claudia Georgi, who identifies and delineates between 'semiotic' and 'medial' mobility:

> To be precise, 'semiotic mobility' therefore does not mean that the incorporated signs are left unaffected, it should rather be understood as a potential to incorporate any sign, an ability that theatre, however, shares with other plurimedial media such as film, television or video. What is unique to theatre is thus not its semiotic mobility as such, but what could in analogy be termed its 'medial mobility,' i.e. the ability to leave the materiality of the incorporated media intact while their respective signs acquire an additional semiotic quality as theatrical signs. (2014, p. 47)

This property of theatre has led to the sobriquet *hypermedium*, capable of incorporating many other media, as notably elucidated in *Intermediality in Theatre and Performance* (2006). In the introductory chapter, the editors, Freda Chapple and Chiel Kattenbelt, state that 'theatre has become a hypermedium and home to all', within which all media can be sited and remediated to create 'profusions of texts, inter-texts, inter-media and space in between' (p. 24). However, it must be noted that Elleström is not persuaded on this specific argument of theatre as a hypermedium. In 2010, citing Chapple and Kattenbelt, he wrote that theatre is 'definitely extremely multimodal and it integrates many basic and qualified media, but it is an overstatement to say that "theatre is a hypermedium that incorporates all arts and media"' (p. 45). To an extent, I am in agreement, particularly if we remind ourselves of the complexity of a medium and the contexts in which it exists. Whilst the material modality of any medium may be mediated essentially 'intact' within theatre, it will undoubtedly be devoid of some of its own qualifying context and therein the semiotic complexity this carries. The additional layer that Georgi refers to may not be easily distinguished as an addition when the original semiotic signification may be denuded to the point where we actually perceive a hybrid between the original and the theatricalised. Furthermore, the materiality is linked closely to the other modalities: the spatial intimacy of a book in our own hands; the lengthy, temporal experience of an entire film; or the physical touch of a statue or ceramic, which are less likely to be part of a theatre experience. Materiality may be intact, but without the correspondence of other mediating elements, it is arguable how much of a medium remains once theatricalised. Yet, it is not without merit or purpose to suggest that theatre represents other media with *less* material interference or transformation than other plurimedial forms and thereby with more of the innate qualities of the original medium present. Therefore, the term '*hypermedium*' can still be invoked, but perhaps with less vigour and with a little more nuance.

Having established this, it might be observed that such hypermediated 'profusions' undoubtedly create opportunities and challenges for theatre makers and performers as we are constantly able to look beyond *intramedial* options and on to *transmedial* modes for inspiration and actual practical application in the theatrical environment. *Intramedial* refers to specific modal configurations and qualifying aspects conventionally found within a given medium, such as the static temporality of a picture or the acceptance of a jump cut or dissolve in film. *Transmediality*, on the other hand, refers to the crossing of media borders. This may be seen in the manifestation of one media 'product' occurring across media (*Harry Potter* appearing in the form of book, film, jigsaw, theme park, lunchbox, etc.) or in the appearance of one medium's conventions and modalities within other media (the use of direct theatrical address to an audience within film or *static* artistic tableau appropriated within performance art). Elleström's own definition of *transmediation* reads: 'The concept of transmediation involves two ideas. Transmediation is not only *re*-mediation – *repeated* mediation – but also *trans*-mediation: repeated mediation of equivalent sensory configurations by another technical medium' (2014, p. 14).[23] We have the capacity to draw, intramedially, upon the *modalities* and *qualifying aspects* within theatre (use of live performers, co-presence with audience, acting tropes, narrative forms, catharsis and so on) whilst simultaneously appropiating, transmedially, from the *modalities* and *qualifying aspects* of other media, from the acting style of film, the forms and architecture of art installation or the very iconography of art itself, all of these seen respectively in the work of imitating the dog, dreamthinkspeak and Stan's Cafe, all of which are represented in Chapter 7, 'Practitioner Case Studies'.

From a practitioner perspective, there are many challenges inherent in these new performance realms, as it demands a superfluity of knowledge and skills to be both conversant with individual media and modes, but also confidence (or at least courageous enthusiasm) across transmedial boundaries in the construction of contemporary work. Initially this may seem daunting, but we may all be more adept than we think.

INTERMEDIALITY: THE EVERYDAY KIND

Often, when the subject of intermediality is discussed, definitions and typologies begin to cascade like confetti. It can seem, in the worst cases, to be a somewhat desiccated concept disconnected from our actual experiences and thereby having limited relevance to theatrical experimentation. Let us try to redress that by considering our own intermediality, the kind we experience and engage with ubiquitously. Let me suggest that we are all everyday intermedialists, to some degree or other. In fact, it may initially be helpful to suggest that we are also adept hypermedialists. I shall try to explain before the confetti descends.

Look around you in your imagined theatre, closer to hand this time, away from the theatrical stage and down to your own body, the 'stage' you 'set' every day. You arrange diverse media upon it, a plethora of *technical media*, including clothes,[24] accessories such as bags or umbrellas, but also sophisticated *qualified media* such as novels to read on the train or, more ubiquitously now, *technical media*, including smartphones and tablets which are portals into the labyrinthine *qualified media* of the Internet, including online television, radio or film. You physically and intuitively carry these media with you each day; you site them upon yourself and remediate them constantly: vintage clothes refashioned for the twenty-first century, sections of novels recounted in essay quotes, or comments from one web source retweeted through your own Twitter feed in an instant. You are a walking hypermedium, accessorised by distinct media, all with their materiality 'intact' but all reframed and given unique significance through the prism of your personality and social context.

Rapid developments in our technological means of communication and the consequent shifts in our cultural practices have reconfigured the way in which we engage with the world around us. Jack Kerouac captured this shift as far back as 1957 in his seminal novel *On the Road*:

> He came the following Sunday afternoon. I had a television set. We played one ballgame on the TV, another on the radio, and kept switching to a third and kept track of all that was happening every moment. (1998, p. 238)

Sal Paradise and Dean Moriarty, the subjects of this scene, may be identified as erstwhile everyday intermedialists as they encapsulate a cultural condition which we embody in our daily lives. This enculturated intermediality is a state of being, and not merely a conscious act of the mind, but of the whole body, embedded in our 'body schema' as envisaged by the twentieth-century phenomenologist Maurice Merleau-Ponty,[25] who stated that the body is our 'medium for having a world' (2002, p. 169). Paradise and Moriarty, in their visual and tactile engagement with the modern technologies of their day, create a collage of media through which they construct their own interpretation of events. They exist in an intermedial space, confident with multiple strands of *sense-data* expressed through a plethora of *media, modalities* and *modes* and then received via numerous *receptors*. The deluge of *sensations* is both deftly managed but also exhilarating for them in its abundance and diversity. To use Amy Petersen Jensen's terminology, they are 'hybrid subjects' operating in a 'hybrid space, [in which] the participatory spectator prefigures a new type of performance that develops out of the interaction between two mediums' (2007, pp. 122–123). In 1945, Merleau-Ponty gave the following example of an object as the extension of our body schema: 'Once the [blind man's] stick has become a familiar instrument, the world of feel-able things recedes and now begins, not at the outer skin of the hand, but at the end of the stick' (2002, pp. 75–76). Now, in the twenty-first century, the 'body schema' for most of us encompasses mousepads, joysticks, on-demand multiscreen TV and smartphones—the 'extensions of man', to cite McLuhan. This conception of enculturated intermediality foregrounds the premise that our *body-schema* is an ever-expanding web of interrelated, intermedial and intermodal discourses within which technology plays a pivotal role. As technology progresses, our perceptual field adjusts to accommodate and engage with simultaneity, and every generation embraces this a little more.

Consciously and unconsciously, we are bombarded with the technologies (both *technical* and *qualified* media) of a digital world that makes many twentieth- and twenty-first-century media and their content readily available through *remediation*. The Internet houses and re-presents filmic and televisual media from across this century as well as the last, from the epics of the silent film era to kitsch cartoons or the banality or fascination of a live feed from the other side of the globe. Digital broadcasters and platforms store and screen countless channels, programmes and clips that allow us to access seminal work from generations ago or simply the mundane from the day before. The value of retaining knowledge and memory are diminishing as we have instant access to that which we have forgotten or never knew. Of equal significance is that the contemporary body itself has assimilated mediated processes into its automatic, pre-reflective[26] motor and postural functions. I am suggesting that such processes and attitudes become consciously and unconsciously embodied and impact upon performative action and interaction. Additionally, we can distinguish this enculturated state from the notion of body as hypermedium, as we not only can 'house' diverse media within our schema but fuse them: the body as an intermedium itself.

INTERMEDIALITY: EVOLUTIONS IN THINKING

It is worth stating that there is no fixed typology of intermediality in theatre or indeed intermediality in a broader sense. As soon as the term 'intermedia' was coined by the composer and Fluxus artist Dick Higgins in 1965, it was, in his own words: 'picked up; used and misused'. Many people have offered definitions and descriptions for certain manifestations of intermediality, but often these are contested, Many have been redefined over the past few decades, and none of them prohibit further additions to the pantheon of categorisation or indeed the determination to avoid or contest such boundaries. Note that I myself have already offered you 'enculturated intermediality' as a new term, chiselled from my own perspectives and preoccupations, but it is only one of many lenses that may be adopted or ignored. What follows in this section is, firstly, a little context to explain how the notion of intermediality has developed, followed by a specific interpretation of key aspects of theatrical intermediality, drawing on some more of Elleström's most recent ideas of mediality and intermediality. In the spirit of remediation, it is important to highlight that this endeavour is not entirely virgin territory as Elleström is cited as a frame of reference within a number of texts, including Bay-Cheng et al. *Mapping Intermediality in Performance* (2010), Claudia Georgi's *Liveness on Stage: Intermedial Challenges in Contemporary British Theatre and Performance* (2014) and Bateman et al. *Multimodality: Foundations, Research and Analysis – A Problem-Oriented Introduction* (2017). Andy Lavender has also applied specific elements of the theoretical model (particularly *adaptation* and *transformation*) in analysing immersive intermedial theatre, in his article 'Modal Transpositions toward Theatres of Encounte, or, in Praise of "Media Intermultimodality"' (2014). However, this chapter is arguably the most extensive use of his theories in an analysis of theatre. His perspective is interwoven alongside some of the other noteworthy twenty-first-century developments and delineations of intermediality. Perhaps what is most useful to remember is that we will never in writing encompass the endless permutations and expressions of theatrical intermediality, partly due to scale but also to divergences of opinion, as to determine something as intermedial is, in the end, a matter of personal perspective towards what is *mediated* and particularly what is *represented*, let alone a matter of individual interpretation of the term 'intermediality' itself. The field, therefore, is yours to inhabit and define or distort as you wish; the practice will determine the possibilities.

Intermediality in theatre is not a new concept. It may appear to be, as the term is often conjugated with contemporary technology, yet theatre, partly because of its capacity as a hypermedium, has always experimented with technologies accessible in each historical period, as well as perpetually fusing diverse media within its bounds. Opera is often cited as the quintessential intermedial *gesamtkunstwerk*,[27] or 'total work of art', combining music, voice, dramatic performance and complex scenography, but the tradition of colliding, combining or sequencing different media within a theatrical experience can be witnessed across the millennia, well before avant–garde twentieth-century practices, from the ancient Greek chorus, or *dithyramb*, which fused song with dance and subsequently dramatic performance, through to the eclectic acts of music hall and burlesque[28] of the nineteenth and early twentieth centuries.

Over the past fifty or so years, many definitions and invocations of intermediality[29] have arisen, and likewise many attempts to delineate it from other related terms. Within a theatrical context, the debate was, as already indicated, instigated by the British-born, but American-based Dick Higgins in 1965, in his essay, succinctly entitled 'Intermedia', which sought to describe the new hybrid forms of performance that were proliferating at the time. He noted, 'Much of the best work being produced today seems to fall between media' (1965, p. 1). Richard Kostelanetz, writing in the same period, referred to these new hybrid forms as *The Theatre of Mixed Means*, contending that 'the new theatre descends from several arts' (1970, p. 276).

In the last two or three decades, propelled by the exponential rise in such practice, there has been a concerted effort within academia to articulate these intermedial developments. These have flourished in a plethora of texts, from Bolter and Grusin's *Remediation: Understanding New Media* (1999) to Werner Wolf's *The Musicalization of Fiction: A Study in the Theory and History of Intermediality* (1999), through to the notable publications of The International Federation for Theatre Research (IFTR) that established an Intermediality in Theatre and Performance Working Group, out of which came *Intermediality in Theatre and Performance* (2006), edited by Freda Chapple and Chiel Kattenbelt, and *Mapping Intermediality in Performance* (2010), edited by Sarah Bay Cheng et al. At this juncture, therefore, it would be easy to digress at some length into this range of contrasting typologies and definitions of intermediality sent out into the ether since the turn of the last century. However, the very fact that these topics have been alighted upon before, and you may already be conversant with some of them, means that a brief reconnaissance of existing intermedial definitions and distinctions will suffice for now, beginning again with Dick Higgins. In 1981, responding to his initial influential article of 1965, he wrote that the term 'intermedia' referred to those artistic configurations which were 'fused conceptually' (1984), a notion that was returned to by Jürgen Heinrichs and Yvonne Spielmann in their 2002 editorial for the journal *Convergence*, in which they wrote that 'intermediality addresses the merger and the transformation of elements of differing media . . . resulting in the creation of a new (art) form' (2002, pp. 5–6). Irina Rajewsky, in 2005, perceived intermediality as a broad church, but one distinguished by its ability to transgress boundaries, proposing how 'intermediality may serve foremost as a generic term for all those phenomena that (as indicated by the prefix *inter*) in some way take place *between* media. "Intermedial" therefore designates those configurations which have to do with a crossing of borders between media' (p. 46).[30] In 2008, Chiel Kattenbelt offered his own definition of the term 'intermediality' in comparison to 'multimediality' and 'transmediality':

> I focus my attention on three concepts of mediality: multi-, trans- and intermediality. To phrase it very briefly, multimediality refers to the occurrence where there are many media in one and the same object; transmediality refers to the transfer from one medium to another medium (media change); and intermediality refers to the corelation of media in the sense of mutual influences between media. (2008, pp. 20–21)

Certain caveats and clarifications are prompted by Kattenbelt's perspective. The term 'transmediality', for example, has matured and found significant gradations since then, notably from Elleström himself. Some of these have been addressed already, and other variants will be returned to later in the chapter. Likewise, a little more delineation between 'intermediality' and 'multimedia' may be constructive, as the latter term has all too readily been invoked as a catch-all to describe any work in which a variety of media share performance space. Phaedre Bell (2000), in discussing film and live theatre, created her own distinction between two types of mixed-media performance, which she referred to as 'dominant medium' productions (akin to multimedia) and 'dialogic media productions' or 'intermedia exchange' (pp. 43–44). Her description of a 'dominant medium', emphasising the more passive scenographic role of an auxiliary medium which merely 'decorates the scene with aesthetically pleasing images' (p. 44) in service of the live event, resonates with Greg Giesekam's definition of live/filmic multimedia performance in *Staging the Screen* (2007), in which the video acts merely as another of the 'apparatuses' of the stage (p. 8). For Giesekam, intermediality can be distinguished from multimediality as the former manifests itself 'where neither the live material nor the recorded material would make much sense without the other, and where often the interaction between the media substantially modifies how the respective media conventionally function and invites reflection upon their nature and methods' (p. 8).

However, it is no surprise to discover that multimedia has not been permanently relegated to merely define certain 'dominant' media interactions, as can be evidenced by Rosemary Klich and Edward Scheer's interpretation of the term in their 2012 publication *Multimedia Performance*, in which they note a 'haemorrhaging of nomenclatures', citing amongst others 'Cyber theatre', 'postorganic theatre', 'intermedial theatre' and 'new media performance' (p. 11), and, by destabilised the authority of such terminology, confidently reclaim and reframe multimedia in terms of, amongst others concepts, *interactivity* and *integration*,[31] stating it to be 'an intermedial and interdisciplinary formation in culture' (p. 8). This alternative view of multimedia is persuasive, for if we accept the earlier nuanced interpretation of theatre as a hypermedium, it would be churlish, if not naïve, to think that any medium within its bounds remains passive or merely decorative apparatus, as our perception of any theatricalised element may render it significant and transformative, no matter what the 'dominant' medium may seem to be. However, for clarity's sake, whilst acknowledging the diversity of views, I propose that 'intermediality' as a term is still fit for purpose in encompassing this latter articulation of multimedia.

It may be wise at this point to be cognisant of Andy Lavender's observation: 'We are less concerned with immutable ontological categories, and more interested in nuances, degrees, shifting combinations, and the play of unlike elements that together form something particular and effectual' (2014, p. 503) Certainly, the terminology is less relevant than the substance of media interaction, however we delimit it, and the potential it offers practitioners. A consensus in recent years, as highlighted earlier in the chapter, has undoubtedly centred on the interrelationship of *modes* within and between media, their 'intermultimodality', to use Ellestrōm's awkward term (one that will be returned to shortly). *Mapping Intermediality in Performance* (2010) highlighted these interrelationships and convergences of media in the context of the new media hybrids establishing themselves in the twenty-first century. This acknowledgement of media convergence was tempered in this text by a concurrent recognition of media distinctiveness (not to be confused with essentialism), with Robin Nelson, in the introductory chapter, referring to this as the 'both/and' paradigm, by which we can value the unique modal 'signature' of any medium whilst also acknowledging the multitude of modal and transmedial interactions. More recently, for Andy Lavender,[32] the germane term to express these conjunctions of media is 'hybridity', 'not literally, as some sort of mutant spawn of technologies of presentation, but as an *effect of becoming*, enabled by blended processes and forms' (2016, p. 64).

In the twenty-first century, media are now converging at both a *pre-semiotic* and a *representational* level. Through the blending of modes and cross-modal representation, they are *becoming* 'conceptually fused', making fleeting or durable transformations in their appearance and our perception of them. We possess the intricate capacity to distinguish different *technical* and *qualified* media (there would be consensus, perhaps not unanimity, on what constitutes a television set or a film e.g.), yet simultaneously we, for the most part, accede to the suffusion of these media across borders and the inherent transformations this creates in media we are accustomed to, and often hold affection for, because of their traditions and conventions.

ASPECTS OF THEATRICAL INTERMEDIALITY

What I offer in this section is a proposition of three notable aspects of intermedial theatre – **convergence, contrast** and **transformation** – that are particularly pertinent in the light of our specific analysis of media, modalities and modes. Mindful of the numerous previous texts on intermediality, and with the luxury of knowing that the rest of the book looks at many other specifics on the subject, these aspects are focused on *mediation* and *representation*, using Ellestrom's vocabulary of *modalities, qualifying aspects* and *transformation* (2010, 2014), in order to distinguish the multimodal dialogues which may be exposed or hidden within the theatrical experience. The aim here is not to delimit precisely how things are at present or prescribe a way of practising intermediality. It cannot, by any egotistical measure, be deemed comprehensive, as the chapters that follow, let alone texts not yet conceived, are all part of a gradual calibration of intermediality, but it does seek to bring a degree of clarity and practicality to the complexity, which may be overwhelming. The aspects outlined below may occur individually but also in tandem, and there are undoubtedly permeable and multiple relationships between each category. Let us first address the aforementioned complexity head on then, as Ellestrom himself identifies theatre as a particularly complicated medium

> consisting of different kinds of material interfaces, appealing to both the eye and the ear, being both profoundly spatial and temporal, producing meaning by way of all kinds of signs and, certainly, being circumscribed by way of historical and cultural conventions and aesthetic standards. Theatre may thus be said to be a qualified medium that is very much multimodal and also, in a way, very much intermedial since it combines and integrates a range of basic and qualified media. (2010, p. 29)

In this context, we may say that all theatre is intermedial, manifesting itself in relations between all manner of *basic, technical* and *qualified media*, and then more specifically through precise *modal* compounds. Our hotel room, as already intimated, is perceived through its relationships between multiple media, the *basic* amber light shining through the window in conjunction with the impassive *technical* medium of the television set and the *qualified media product* of the Western genre film emitting the *basic* pulses of sound and light from its screen. The forlorn human *materiality* of the character in sharp contrast to the inert *materiality* of the bed, the *spatial* claustrophobia of the room magnified in the *static* panoramas of the picture hanging on the wall. Whilst this book pays particular attention to contemporary developments in intermediality, it must be acknowledged that this innate complexity of modal and medial hybridity within theatre has existed for millennia, indicating its enduring receptiveness to experimentation.

Elleström refers to intermediality as 'intermodal relations in media' or 'media intermultimodality' (2010, p. 37). He is immediately aware of their slightly unwieldy linguistic quality and, in what Andy Lavender refers to as a 'nicely self-deprecating aside' (2014, p. 500), reflects that 'I do not expect these terrible terms to win general praise but I think there is a point in seeing intermediality as a complex set of relations between media that are always more or less multimodal.' (2010, p. 37) In stating that all theatre is intermedial, we are at risk of nullifying the significance or particularity of its practice, but if we invoke the 'both/and' concept from earlier, then it is possible to recognise, celebrate and harness *both* distinction *and* hybridity.

The 'crossing of borders between media', to cite Rajewsky, is both an overt and covert practice. Intermediality at times seeks to loudly declare its activity whilst on other occasions subtlety or indeed stealth is the favoured means. Sometimes, media are required to coalesce into a seamless event, but in certain contexts the disparity between them is purposely exposed. Often the intention is simply an unrepentant pursuit of entertainment and spectacle, whereas some theatre makers seek a more radical and politicised agenda through intermediality. The three concepts of *convergence, contrast* and *transformation* seek to elucidate some of the key processes within such practices. You will note that some liberties are taken with the practitioner examples, which stray slightly beyond the loose theatrical boundaries of the text, but I hope they creatively serve the purpose of exemplification and reveal the breadth of intermedial practice that has developed over the decades and is now at large today.

Convergence

Theatre is no stranger to appropriating a plethora of complementary *basic, technical and qualified* media alongside specific modes that may putatively be referred to as drama – the creation of role or dramatic narrative and dialogue, for example. With the dawn of the 'electric age', as McLuhan referred to it, at the end of the nineteenth and early twentieth centuries, this fascination with the convergence of 'electric' and corporeal forms advanced apace as the emergent twentieth-century film industry, with pioneers such as Georges Méliès in Paris, was quick to capitalise on the interplay between these media, interweaving film with live action in a theatrical setting as early as 1905. In that year Méliès made a film entitled the *Pills of the Devil*, a Faustian legend in which at one notable point the character on screen was seen to fall towards hell before finally tumbling on to the theatre stage, accompanied by pyrotechnics (Giesekam, 2007). In more recent times, the baton for experimenting with live/filmic convergence has been seized by notable artists including the internationally renowned Canadian theatre maker Robert Lepage, who has made his reputation with technically sophisticated productions from *Seven Streams of the River Ota* (1994 onwards) through to *Playing Cards* (2012), as well as in his work with Cirque du Soleil. His compunction for combining media within theatre was reflected upon in a 1997 interview, in which he stated, 'I've never really been interested in theatre as such. In my adolescence, I was more interested in theatricality' (Dundjerović, 2007, p. 2). He goes on to say that his generation of theatre makers were influenced more by 'rock shows, dance shows and performance art' (p. 2) than theatre per se. Sasha Dundjerović, writing specifically about Lepage, coined the term *'techno en scène'* (2007) to define his sophisticated technological scenography allied to a narrative structure.

Lepage is by no means alone in his aspiration to find synergy in diverse media, as evidenced in West End spectaculars, the integrated screens alongside the live show at large music festivals or the hermetic performance environments created within Disney or Warner Brothers theme parks. The ambition that connects these examples is the creation of a unified performance or presentation, wherein the modes of diverse media are harmonised by the *qualifying aspects* of specific umbrella uber-media, such as musical, rock concert or theme park, so that our perception of the event draws upon conventions that seek coherence between the assorted elements. Our own desire for concordance in these instances is aided by the producers' capacity to reconcile the modes of one media with another. For example, in a stage musical such as *Frozen* or *Wicked,* the *spatio-temporal* and *material* difference of a figure or a landscape on a screen is often given signification as 'magical', thereby reinforcing a sense of fictional coherence with the live action and obfuscating the different mediating processes of live acting and film. Likewise, any potential contrast between the *operationally qualifying* conventions of film and stage acting are frequently blurred by the *transmedial* use of screen acting techniques onstage alongside the film sequences, a technique often used in the genre that Petr Woycicki (2014) refers to as 'post-cinematic theatre', as seen in the work of Kneehigh Theatre, notably their production of *Brief Encounter* (2008), or imitating the dog, who have appropriated their onstage techniques in productions such as *Tales from the Bar of Lost Souls* (2010), from film styles such as noir and French new wave.

These last examples of British contemporary practice in fact lead us into a more nuanced mode of convergence as, whilst they seek to unify the stage experience, there is an element of celebrating and bringing some understated attention to the synergy. In an imitating the dog performance, for example, the theatre audience is often presented with opening and closing credits on screen, which may be recognised as novel and unconventional in that context. Andrew Quick, the artistic director of the company, also once acknowledged in a personal conversation that some of the most exciting moments of a performance were when the actors made minor mistakes onstage, reminding the audience that they were live and not merely embedded and automaton-like in the filmic aesthetic (2011). This delicacy or fragility in convergence is also exemplified, for me, by the current innovations in text/filmic intermediality, as seen in the work of Davy and Kristin McGuire and also Amar Kanwar. In considering this form of intermediality, it may be helpful to foreground the specific *basic, technical* and *qualified* media relationships at play in their practice:

Basic	Technical	Qualified
Written text	Book	Literature
Moving image	Projector and projection surface (paper)	Film

UK artists Davy and Kristin McGuire have built a reputation for creating pop-up theatre books that use miniature projection mapping on to the paper scenography that appears at each turn of the page. They first created a work entitled *The Icebook* in 2011 and went on to develop a theatre book version of *Macbeth* in collaboration with the Royal Shakespeare Company. Amar Kanwar created his own film/text hybrid for a project entitled *The Sovereign Forest + Other Stories* (2013), which explored environmental and political issues in India. I recall seeing this work at the Yorkshire Sculpture Park in the United Kingdom, part of it housed in one of their large underground galleries, with three tables supporting large books containing handmade paper pages. One of the books, entitled *The Prediction*, included sheets partly collaged with newspaper articles pertaining to the assassination of an Indian trade union leader, layered on to which were overhead projections of footage from the event, changing as the pages turned. The poignancy of the work was undoubtedly in the content, but also in the ephemeral intermediality, the sophisticated yet fragile interplay between the components. Our expectations of the two *qualified* media, literature and film, are confirmed by the weighty substance of the book and the quality of the projection, but then simultaneously confounded by the unexpected union of certain *basic* and *technical* media, moving image illuminating paper and also page as projection surface, with all the *pre-semiotic* modal elements converging within the same space, overlaid one upon the other. In addition to this, we are presented with the opportunity to blend *spatio-temporal* conventions, turning the pages as we wish, unshackling the *fixed sequentiality* of film via the *partially/non-fixed sequentiality* inherent in our autonomy over the book (Figure 1.1).

To return to our amended notion of hypermedium, the materiality of film and literature were intact, but they created a hybridised signification born out of an augmented text with a fluid blend of *icons* and *symbols* from cinema and newsprint, the definable spatiality and tactile sensoriality of the handmade pages 'complicated' by the virtual dimensions of film. In this beguiling engagement, the viewer constructs their own narrative, an *interaction* (to cite Klich and Sheer) of *intermultimodalities*. As a final thought for this section, you may wish to revisit the hotel room in your minds' eye, and the profusion of *basic, technical* and *qualified* media coalescing as a *representation* of a

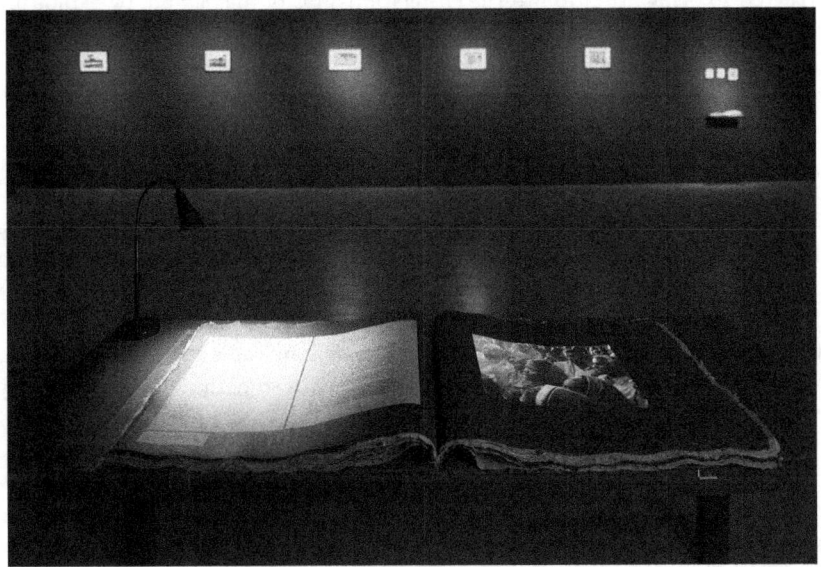

Figure 1.1   Amar Kanwar, *The Sovereign Forest + Other Stories* (2013). Photographer: Jonty Wilde.

coherent, unified fiction. Multiple media have, for a long time, converged in the live event of theatre.

Contrast

One of the most conspicuous manifestations of theatrical intermediality is in the form of overt media hybridity, the collision and contrast of diverse media, 'theatricalised' within the hypermedium of theatre. Citing a number of theorists, Claudia Georgi notes how 'theatre thus does not necessarily figure as a generally transparent receptacle for other media, but it may instead expose the workings of its own mediation as well as those of the media incorporated.' (2014, p. 48) This form of intermediality has many purposes: it may be designed to find wit and comedy, to seek delight and celebration in the discrepancies, as may be witnessed in the practice of the UK company Forkbeard Fantasy, who often in its early work in the 1980s collided spoof lecture with marionettes, inflatable dummies and cyborgs as well as films integrated into the live event or screened post-show (Giesekam, 2007, pp. 176–177). On other occasions, it may be constructed to bring attention to the co-relationships of media and, by exploiting their diverse *modes* and the *qualifying aspects* that we expect from each one, focus our critical attention on to the 'message' of each medium. The potential for this latter technique was seized upon in the early twentieth century by political theatre makers appropriating film on to the stage, as Michael Ingham highlights: 'Brecht and Piscator in Weimar-era Germany, were part of this *Zeitgeist* of mixed-media experimentation in the early decades of the twentieth century' (2017, p. 52). Erwin Piscator developed a dialectical relationship between the illusion of the stage and the realism of the filmic image, a method that Giesekam referred to as 'dynamic montage' (2007, p. 42). In reference to one specific production by Piscator, entitled *Tidal Wave* (1926), a piece inspired by the October revolution in Russia 1905, Giesekam identifies how the director 'used film to ground the more far-fetched aspects of the play in something more politically relevant. . . . a scene of a capitalist selling off his shares was followed by a clip of panic selling on the New York Stock Exchange, drawing an analogy between the fictional action and recent experience' (p. 42). Ingham identifies how 'the practice resurfaced in the postwar decades, starting with avant-garde theatre groups and directors of the 1960s and 1970s – like the 1920s, a more revolutionary period in which innovation flourished – and increased markedly with the advent and development of digital technology in theatre' (2017, p. 52). He refers to this development as the 'cinefying' of theatre and identifies significant recent practitioners in this field, including Robert Wilson and The Wooster Group.[33]

In terms of creating this overt 'awareness' of mediation,[34] the various media may occupy the same theatrical space but retain their modal structures and qualifying aspects more tenaciously than in convergent forms. Let us return to our hotel room, disassemble it and refashion it in this form of intermedial contrast. We are still seeking to explore the isolation and destabilising effects of separation and family breakdown but now uncouple ourselves from the correspondences between media, created in the presentation of the room with objects and body in conventional relation to each other. I will not expose my lack of directorial or conceptual flair by proposing an overly complicated strategy, so simply imagine the key components on wheels, slowly separated from each other by well-choreographed stagehands, stretching and then snapping their dramatic fibres (the components, not the stagehands!) until they come to rest some distance apart from one another. A character on a bed now sits oddly estranged from a window frame and curtains, and the amber light no longer shines through its' pane. We see now the origins of the light in the *technical* medium of a lantern, with its beam detached and redirected into the void of the auditorium. The door and the fire exit sign stand aloof, far away upstage, as the television set blinks into the wings. A projector on a trolley is manoeuvred on to stage, from which the picture of the horse and rider, having disappeared in its original material form, now reappears as a projected looped film, frame and all, on what remains of the wallpapered flats, the horse galloping briefly left to right until it 'hits' the limits of the frame, and then repeating and repeating.

Whilst we may alight upon multiple aspects of this media collage, there are a few concepts to prioritise. Immediately we are struck by the artifice of it all, the technical construction that cemented the original fiction together. The basic and technical media are now isolated and stand in sharp relief to one another – light, image, sound, text, body and projection – whilst the presence of the stagehands underscores the mediating mechanics of theatre. The spatio-temporal illusion of the picture is now exposed, as the rider can never escape to the virtual 'story-space' (to cite Chiao-I Tseng) of our imagination. Perversely, the transformation of the horse and rider image into a projected film serves to accentuate the *fixed* temporality of horse and rider, trapped in time, perhaps echoing the predicament of the character on the bed. The technical modes of production – projector, lantern, television set and so on – are revealed as such, to a point where the usually unconscious connection between pre-semiotic modalities and what they represent is ruptured. We are challenged to construct or reconstruct this image, to notice its composition, its form as well as its content. It is impossible to make bold statements here, as what has been created is purely imaginary and has never been tested upon an audience, but it may be proposed that even such a simple, disassembled scene enables us to construct an emotional response. The disconnections between media and modalities demand that we reconfigure how we view the *qualified* medium of theatre, as we notice the fragility and wilful naivety (on our part) on which it is based. Within the precarity and uncertainty of this, our own theatrical experience, we perhaps find empathy for the vulnerable character on the bed. The dislocation of media, in this instance, becomes a catalyst for meaning; the overt process of mediation directly impacts upon the representation.

Transformation

I am writing this section of the chapter as the sci-fi television persona *Dr Who*[35] transforms from a man (Peter Capaldi) into a woman (Jodie Whittaker), with the subsequent social media storm that this creates across the globe. It is an apt metaphor at this point, as media and their content have a similar capacity to regenerate in other guises or indeed to thrive within other media 'bodies'. Linking to the two previous sections, sometimes these shifts are consciously created in order for the contrast to be noticed, whilst elsewhere there are more subcutaneous transformations, in which media converge and absorb one another. Both these processes, and all variants in between, destabilise and reconfigure modalities and conventions, creating an infinite stream of media hybrids.

If we simplify the activities of convergence and contrast for a moment, then the materiality of the media is relatively straightforward to identify, as the technical media required to materialise the qualified media appear, more often than not, in their original and recognisable forms; musical theatre performers still appear live onstage for example, and, as in our last evocation of contrast, a television continues to project television 'product' consisting of small-scale moving images and sound, no matter where you place it. These technical media and what they produce are then, by their conspicuousness, more readily referenced against their cultural contexts and conventions so that we can interpret them accordingly as qualified media and therefore recognise their content as significant. However, as has already been alluded to in examples such as Amar Kanwar or the transmediative acting style of Kneehigh and imitating the dog, media and their 'products' are often, to switch to a geological metaphor, molten: exploding or oozing from one state to another, shifting and re-forming. Elleström refers to these processes as *media transformation* (2014), identifying *transmediation* and *media representation* as its two key manifestations. Whilst these transformative qualities of intermediality manifest themselves in the two categories of convergence and contrast that I have already proposed, they are particularly significant in contemporary practice and widely adopted within devising methodologies; hence the intention to consider them discreetly. Elleström's definition of *transmediation* reads: 'The concept of transmediation involves two ideas. Transmediation is not only *re*-mediation – *repeated* mediation – but also *trans*-mediation: repeated mediation of equivalent sensory configurations by another technical medium' (2014, p. 14). *Media representation*, on the other hand, 'involves the notion of one medium representing another medium. Media representation is at hand whenever a medium presents another medium to the mind' (2014, p. 15). In *Media Transformation: The Transfer of Media Characteristics Among Media* (2014), he identifies a wide variety of intermedial and intramedial transfers applicable across many artistic and non-artistic forms, but for the purposes of this text, I draw upon selective examples pertinent to theatre.

To ground this theory back on to a stage, consider the following scenario within our imagined theatre. The action onstage has continued, the actor is railing against the world, we feel there is something familiar in their words, an echo of something we've heard before. Their monologue continues with its tale of remorse and regret of all the things they should have done, but now it's too late. There is a recollection on our part . , , this is a book, or rather the adaptation of a book, about the stage. A memory of something read a while ago, now re-presented as a play. Elleström identifies this as a type of *intermedial remediation*, wherein there is intermedial relation between 'two different media products belonging to different qualified media' (2014, p. 89); in this case the product of a novel within the qualified medium of literature transforming into the product of a play within the qualified medium of theatre. I begin with this example as it is a relatively simple category to delineate and also because this strategy is now a ubiquitous practice within both commercial and more experimental theatre. The transmediation of *Harry Potter* from book to film, to stage, to theme park and so on is a well-documented contemporary phenomenon, but transferring literature to the stage is a well-trodden path, including the Royal Shakespeare Company's famous eight-and-a-half-hour staging of Charles Dickens's *The Life and Adventures of Nicholas Nickelby*, adapted by David Edgar back in 1980, through to the National Theatre's acclaimed adaptation of Mark Haddon's best-selling novel, *The Curious Incident of the Dog in the Night-Time* (2012 onwards), which utilised a range of modern technologies to suggest the complex thought processes and experiences of the central autistic character. Other companies, perhaps like Robert Lepage more influenced by contemporary media, go in search of televisual and filmic source texts, including Kneehigh (in collaboration with West Yorkshire Playhouse), who, as already noted, created a theatre version of the film *Brief Encounter* in 2008 and went on to stage the 1960s TV classic *Steptoe and Son* in 2012. Often in these remediative productions, actors face the inherent challenge of adopting filmic and televisual styles of performance within the live theatrical environment as a means of evoking the original *qualified* medium. It may be acknowledged that the staging of any existing play, let alone a television or film script, is a form of *remediation*, as a written text is transferred into a three-dimensional form, with all the incumbent shifts in *modalities* and *qualifying aspects* that this creates. However, beyond these more overt practices, *media transformations* often become a great deal more elusive, yet no less potent, for practitioners.

Such subtleties are to be found in Ellestöm's categories of intermedial *media representation*: 'whenever a medium presents another medium to the mind'. Theatre makers are adept at this strategy, exploring the potential of live performance to be evoked through the most inventive and often challenging of modes. In the past decade or so, performance makers have, for example, explored the potential of absenting what would normally be expected as the primary *technical* medium within a specific *qualified* medium and substituting it for another medium, often in the form of verbal explanation, as a means of evincing what would seem to be the 'original', yet absent, medium. In 2005, the choreographer Sally Doughty created a live work entitled *A Dance for Radio*, in which she 'suggested' a whole dance piece, seemingly involving multiple dancers and choreographic sequences, partly through her own solo physical movement in space, but significantly through the spoken word as she represented a 'memory' of dance through voice and text. Forced Entertainment experimented with a similar technique in *Spectacular* (2008), in which a performer, dressed as a skeleton on a bare stage, seeks to explain to the audience what type of 'spectacular' they will be witnessing, if the event had materialised as planned. He explains, in detail, the stage set and performances that should have been there, whilst being metaphorically and literally 'upstaged' by a female performer repeatedly enacting a death scene devoid of any context. This rumination on death and absence is also, as with Doughty's piece, an exploration in intermediality, seeking to interrogate the fundamental physical and visual elements of dance and theatre by consciously absenting, through transformation, these principle modi operandi. This intention is identifiable in Tim Etchells' (artistic director of Forced Entertainment) programme notes for *Spectacular*, in which he reflected upon how the performance investigates the potential of language and words to evoke actual events, as he noted: 'What's spoken in performance after all hovers, gains tangibility, and with the imaginative participation of an audience begins to appear' (2008).

The absence of light and the embrace of darkness has also been exploited as a means of conjuring one medium through another, and several theatre companies and festivals have explored this emphasis on the absence of the 'pure' medium of light.[36] In 2003, the UK-based company Sound and Fury created a piece entitled *The Watery Part of the World*, entirely staged in the dark in order to conjure the brooding unseen depths of the ocean. In 2012, the Odyssey Theatre in Los Angeles ran a performance festival entitled *Dark and More Dark*, comprising work entirely experienced in blackout,[37] whilst more recently in 2017, Benjamin Vandewalle and Yoann Durant created *Hear* for the Utrecht Spring festival in the Netherlands, a piece in which the performers moved and vocalised throughout the space in the light, but the audience, of which I was one, were blindfolded at all times. Whilst the specific merits of such work may be debated, the significance to alight upon here is the interest in and potential for *media representation*. The initial material transfer from light to dark subsequently creates new forms of mediation, arguably akin to a radio broadcast, but with the additional intensity of heightened sensorial awareness triggered by the absence of visual data. This immediately impacts on the sensorial realm, accentuating the significance of auditory *sense-data* and our memory, to conjure virtual images and sensations from the darkness. Counter-intuitively, the experience may become intensely visual in our mind's eye and even trigger physiological responses through the persuasive power of our imagination. We may even perceive changes in temperature or a sense of displacement of our body in space as our usual proprioceptive capacities are dislodged by the blackness. Lyn Gardner, who reviewed *The Watery Part of the World* for *The Guardian*, actually noted that it was 'as if you are experiencing the whole thing through your skin' (2003). Significantly, this type of theatrical transformation is predicated upon our expectations of the qualified medium of theatre, with all its conventional visual aesthetics. Theatre makers are aware that we have a complex, enculturated understanding of how theatre is habitually represented, so even when the expected *pre-semiotic* elements shift or disappear, we are able to map a perceived visual experience around ourselves. Our sense of a physical stage and stage action is arguably heightened by its sensorial absence as we 'bring it to mind' via other means.

IN AMONGST AND BEYOND

Not that long ago, I was fortunate enough to be standing in MoMA (Museum of Modern Art) in New York, staring at the 'combines' made by Robert Rauschenberg for the collaborative piece entitled *Minutiae* (1954 onwards). It was a reminder that in amongst all these aspects of *convergence*, *contrast* and *transformation*, there are, of course, a profusion of variants and combinations. *Minutiae* was a collaboration between Rauschenberg, a conceptual visual artist, the composer John Cage and the choreographer Merce Cunningham. Rauschenberg's contribution was a set of free-standing coloured panels, which became known as 'combines', alongside which the dancers created improvised 'chance' choreography in response to Cage's score, created independently of both other elements. Watching the 1970s footage of the performance, revisited in that period by the Merce Cunningham Dance Company, there are moments of convergence where, by 'chance', the choreography in-amongst 'combine' and score appear to find synergy, whilst at others the object appears in contrast, incongruous to the performance. There are also moments, if you watch long enough, where the combine 'brings to mind' another performer, with its suggestion of human *materiality* in its scale and protruding wooden legs, the interplay of colours, lines and circles on the panels, to the point where it seems to transcend its *static* temporality and engage with the dancers around it. A more recent example of such combinations can be found in Stan's Cafe Theatre Company's production entitled *A Translation of Shadows* from 2015. In this piece, blending live and filmic elements, the actor Craig Stephens performs the role of a Japanese Benshi[38] who comments on the film sequences projected behind him, which seem to portray an idyllic story of young love. There are elements of *media representation* here as the Benshi's role moves beyond mere commentary, in its poetic evocation of images that are not present on screen and that bring to mind, through text, a broader cinematic vision. At times the scenography is designed to seamlessly *converge* as image and spoken text syncronise and appear to respond to each other. This synergy is magnified as it emerges that the male Benshi is infatuated with the female lead of the film and seeks to manipulate the cinematic narrative and thwart the on-screen couple (Figure 1.2).

But then the symbiosis of virtual space and live space begins to fragment as the filmic characters 'rebel' against the Benshi's influence, reaching a climactic moment where a live female performer, in the guise of an aged version of the female lead, launches herself on to the stage to berate the Benshi for his actions. The shackles of the film's *fixed* temporality are broken, exposing the *contrast* between the illusion of film-space/time, which may capture and control an idyllic and youthful image, against the realities of the 'live', with all its encumbrances of conflict and decay. These are but two examples of what lies *in-amongst* and self-evidently there are many other practitioners and performances that experiment concurrently with the categorisations created here or indeed muddy the waters between them all. Thankfully, theatre – and performance in a wider context – are no respecters of boundaries. In the following chapter, Andy Lavender carries this point a stage further to propose that in our modern plurimedial world 'boundary crossing has become so commonplace that the boundary is less noticeable than the journey', reminding us in this text to concentrate

Figure 1.2 Stan's Cafe, *A Translation of Shadows* (2015). Photographer: Graeme Braidwood.

as much on the experience and affect of intermediality as much as, if not more than, an analysis of what it is, propitious as that may be.

The permutations of media and modalities are undoubtedly endless, particularly in the expanding realm of 21st-century performance, articulated in the chapters that follow, which dismantles divisions and creates new hybrids with such rapidity. Bateman et al. address this challenge when stating that 'as more experimental performances continuously attempt to blur the boundaries between audience and performer, it will become increasingly necessary to draw in richer multimodal frameworks to support their analysis' (2017, p. 260). This also returns us to the pertinence of *inter-multimodality* as a phrase for encapsulating these interchanges. Andy Lavender reflects: 'Perhaps Elleström's "terrible" term deserves a longer lease of life, for, contrary to its appearance, media intermultimodality turns out to be rather trim' (2014, p. 518). As he goes on to note, it captures both the 'aesthetic contagion' of certain types of intermediality (resonant of convergence and contrast) as well as the transformational hybrids built upon 'the incorporation of media within one another' (p. 518). For the sake of linguistic elegance, whilst we may respectfully register the applicability of 'inter-multimodality', I would rather propose the simple equivalence of 'intermediality' as a word to capture the fluid dynamics of media and modal interactions as described in this book. You are, of course, at liberty to use either term as you read on.

Before we bring this chapter to a close, it should be acknowledged that the theatrical experimentations that foment such hybridity bring risk. The perils of transmediating from novel or TV to film and the derision this can induce (note the reviews of *The Great Gatsby* [2013] or *Dad's Army* [2016] e.g.) remind us that disrupting the conventions and expectations of 'products' within one qualified medium through the modes of another can lead to trouble. We can often, as audience, be surprisingly stubborn and selective in our expectations despite our reliable capacity to accept many forms of media transformation. From a theatre maker's viewpoint, the observations on practice that follow, whilst celebrating the potential, are also testament to some of the anxieties and predicaments of intermedial creativity. It is impossible to know if a certain new hybrid or transformation will be productive unless experimentation is undertaken in a rehearsal studio or, more perilously, in front of or in conjunction with an audience. What is certain is that this book can only attempt, in its reflection on what exists, to merely speculate on what is to come. It is to our great fortune that theatre and its predilection for intermediality will always propel us beyond what we currently conceive of.

Practical ideas

Experimenting with modalities

Whilst this chapter has emphasised the inter-multimodality of theatre, there is creative potential in experimenting with specific modalities in order to test the boundaries of each parameter within a medium. Try the following with whatever devising idea or text you have to hand:

- Space – attempt to stage the 'text' in the largest possible space available to you (the whole auditorium), a field (use mobile phones to communicate perhaps) or just the full width of the room, and then compare this to rehearsing it in the smallest possible space: under a table, a narrow corridor, behind a curtain. Consider what the differences are and how intimacy and 'emotional distance' may work with or in contrast to the physical proximity.
- Time – extend the idea, through pause, movement and so on, into an elongated time span, and then contract it down to a full-paced dash through the material. What effect does this have?

- **Sensorial** – explore the potential excess of specific sense-data and also their exclusion. Try a text within which all actors are in 'touch' contact with each other (and perhaps the audience), or rehearse it in darkness to see what new sensations are revealed. Try staging a written text (perhaps just the sense of its fictional location) through olfactory/smell modes and shifts in temperature using fans, heaters, ice cubes and the like.
- **Semiotics** – explore how everyday objects can acquire a layer of theatrical significance when onstage. Gather a range of everyday objects (spoons, leaves, books, chairs etc.) Place these in equal 'piles' either side of the stage. An actor at each side takes it in turns to bring an object and place it onstage, followed by the other actor and so on. Objects can be placed in contact or at distance from any other object. Think of it like a conversation – how does each object speak to what has come before? Note: This is not the same as Object Theatre, as there is no expectation to animate the objects, but simply to let them 'be' onstage and see what resonates/what is signified. The performers can experiment with time and space (slowing down an entrance, placing an object in a certain way on top of another etc.).

Convergence

Experiment with converging the technical medium/media of one qualified medium with those of another, as in the work of Amar Kanwar.

- Try projecting a short film text, without the sound, on to human bodies (torsos, backs, shoulder blade – either clothed in a white T-shirt or on to skin) and add the spoken text from the film via the 'live' actors, who are being projected on to or others who might be available. A monologue or duologue with a slow paced text works well for this.
- Try performing a radio drama where the recorded text is lip-synced by actors who perform the actions of the work live. Think of the body as a technical medium in these instances.
- Consider how the convergence informs or disrupts the various media and the 'message'.

Contrast

Try a version of the 'disassembling' activity described in the chapter. Create a basic set, lighting rig (use stands if possible) and soundscape (moveable sound system if available) for a text you are familiar with, including actors onstage. It may be advisable to choose a dramatic, naturalistic text to start with. Now perform its disassembly – stagehand 'performers' move as many things as possible (including people) to disconnected spaces so that each technical medium is dislocated from its original place and signification. Ask an audience to watch the original dramatic piece and this new disconnected version in which each medium and its technical function is more overt. What is the effect?

Transformation

Experiment with two key elements of Elleström's transformation:

Repeated mediation: Take a notable object text or image from one medium (famous painting, play, TV programme, board game etc.) and remediate it into another medium. Try turning games such as *Kerplunk* or *Connect 4* into a performance installation, or a TV quiz show into performance poetry using the text verbatim. On a very subtle basis, what occurs when a written text such as a play becomes a radio drama? Try passing each remediation on to a new group for them to remediate again.

Media representation: Experiment with how 'a medium presents another medium to the mind'. Try using the technique from Forced Entertainment's *Spectacular* (2008), by 'explaining' (but not overtly showing) a dramatic text which may or may not exist. Try it with something well known, such as *Hamlet*, or with an event that happened in real life and is being reimagined for stage. This can be converged with modal experimentation as well – retelling a vast dramatic epic in a cupboard, in the dark, with scent, taste sensations and so forth.

2 Twenty-First-Century Intermediality

Andy Lavender

A JOURNEY: FROM INTERMEDIALITY TO MULTIMODALITY

Where better to start, in thinking about intermediality in the twenty-first century and its journey towards multimodality, than the year 2000. I also begin with a personal reflection that in its own small way touches on the history of intermediality as a concept and how it has changed over the course of a generation as the millennium approaches its third decade.

In September 2000, I travelled to Lyon, France, to participate for the first time in the annual conference of the International Federation of Theatre Research. I was attending the meetings of the Intermediality in Theatre and Performance working group, convened at the time by Freda Chapple from Sheffield in the United Kingdom, and Chiel Kattenbelt from Utrecht, Holland. I couldn't have wished for a more engaging introduction to the life of a working group. The work was very collegial and full of exploration, and we felt that we were gnawing away at several significant changes to contemporary performance, as theatre found itself more commonly inhabited by other media. The group has engaged for nearly twenty years with the shifting provenance of the term 'intermediality' – which refers both to relations *between* media and innovations to do with adaptations and combinations of media. It did so in the first decade of the twenty-first century by way of the publication of two volumes: *Intermediality in Theatre and Performance* (2006) and *Mapping Intermediality in Performance* (2010). Web 2.0 was only establishing itself in the first two or three years of the new millennium, so the group was doing its work amidst far-reaching changes to cultural production as digital interactivity accelerated. This speed of change was reflected in the differing perspectives of the respective volumes. One of the key interests of the first book was with the 'inter' in 'intermediality'. As the editors said in their introduction, 'Our thesis is that the intermedial is a space where the boundaries soften – and we are in-between and within a mixing of spaces, media and realities. Thus, intermediality becomes a process of transformation of thoughts and processes where something different is formed through performance' (Chapple and Kattenbelt, 2006, p. 12). That 'something different' is to do with the consequences of meetings of media, creating new expressions that drew upon the qualities of the media in play. The notion of a 'gap' having effect here was in part derived from Lev Manovich's account of digitisation in *The Language of New Media* (2001), itself published just after the turn of the millennium. As Chapple and Kattenbelt suggest:

> Crucially, the process of digitisation turns old media from continuous linear data into discrete data units. What is important about this is that each unit must be separate from other units – actually as well as conceptually – there must be a gap in-between the units even if that gap is not perceptible to the human eye. (2006, p. 17)

This outline of a kind of endless recombination of digital data units was conceptually extended to the idea of media in conjunction, but nonetheless with a sense of their separateness.

By the time of the second book, the group had become more interested in the concrete *combination* of media within an extended performance scene (as opposed to a predominantly theatre-oriented scene). The explicit move here is to see intermediality as inherently plural. As Robin Nelson suggests in his introductory essay, in preference to

> various conceptions of the 'in-between', we have come to think that the compound 'both-and' better characterises contemporary performance culture. . . . This very aspect of digital culture – where devices, events and activities are formed out of relationships, necessary interdependencies and mutually co-relating entities – provides a structuring principle that helps to explain the paradigmatic character of the digital. (2010, p. 17)

Nelson turns to Lars Elleström's conception of modalities in order to unpack this further with regard to digital culture, observing that 'the capacity of digital technologies multi-modally to integrate sound, visuals, words and temporal dynamics . . . have, perhaps radically, extended the multimodality of theatre' (Nelson, 2010, p. 14). Networks, interconnections, flow, fusion, merging, hybridity, routinely complicated multiplicity – these are the terms of our time and help to explain the development of intermediality in contemporary cultural production. Hence an expansion of interest into 'multimodality' as a key characteristic of this increasingly intermedial environment.

In his essay of 2010 entitled 'The Modalities of Media: A Model for Understanding Intermedial Relations', Elleström describes four modalities that apply to diverse media: the material (which defines the physical features of the medium, such as the screen of images that conveys TV programmes, or the sound waves that carry radio broadcasts or music); the sensorial (to do with 'sense-data' that help us to perceive the 'interface of the medium through the sense faculties' [p. 17]); the spatiotemporal (which address specific organisations and perceptions of time and space); and the semiotic (which is to do with meaning-making by way of diverse sorts of thinking and interpretation). Each of the modalities can be analysed by way of various modes that operate within it. This account has already taken us far beyond earlier distinctions between separate media, and Elleström's project here, in part, is to present a set of complex calibrations that aim to describe how 'the many possible intermedial relations within and between media' operate (2010, p. 37).[1,2]

The challenge offered by this analysis is fairly considerable: a precise account of the medial event that you're describing will require a bespoke set of coordinates across the various modes and modalities in play. This is possible if we look carefully at each artefact in question, but the complex and plural nature of much contemporary performance makes this a daunting procedure. In a subsequent monograph, Elleström examines 'transfers of media characteristics' between different media, as a key feature of intermediality (2014, p. 5). This more fluid exchange operates in and through the modalities, which provide a 'transmedial foundation' to the operations of representation and transmediation (2014, p. 38).

This suggestion of a 'transmedial foundation' is helpful, and connects with thinking in other disciplines. The notion of modalities is understood slightly differently in the field of linguistics and discourse analysis. Some basic points of principle help to give us this separate perspective on intermediality in performance. The first is that, as Gunther Kress says, concepts of mode and modality are significant 'wherever meaning is *the* issue' (2014, p. 60). This is a suggestive orientation, as it points us towards a discussion concerned with how things *matter* to people, and how, in terms of performance, such *mattering* is arranged. What also seems quickly obvious, however, is that modes – as distinct from media – appear to be rather proliferate. Depending on where you look, they include 'written language, sound, gesture, visual design' (Djonov and Zhao, 2014, p. 1); 'speech, gestures, prosody, facial expressions, head nods or full-body movements' (Fernandes, 2014 p. 1); all fitting with Kress's observation that '*Mode* is a socially shaped and culturally given resource for making meaning', where modes are integral to representation and communication (2014, p. 60). Sigrid Norris suggests that 'Multimodal (inter)action analysis . . . integrates . . .

objects in the material world (i.e. computers, cell phones, toys or pieces of furniture) and the environment itself (i.e. layout of a room, a city or a park)' (2013, p. 276). This opens all sorts of things (literally) to multimodal analysis, not least when they are seen, as Norris suggests, as semiotic resources – which brings us back to the centrality of meaning-making in modal transactions, and indeed in cultural production.

Modal analysis is inherently interdisciplinary. It entails consideration of space, time, social context and interaction. It is concerned with materialities (of devices, settings, objects, bodies); and affordances, both in terms of what modes permit and what they produce. Carey Jewitt provides a straightforward orientation: 'The basic assumption that runs through multimodality is that meanings are made, distributed, received, interpreted and remade in interpretation through many representational and communicative modes – not just through language – whether as speech or as writing' (2014, p. 15). Or, we might add, whether through sound, image, performance or visual design. Jewitt suggests that 'within social semiotics, a mode, its organizing principles and resources, is understood as an outcome of the cultural shaping of a material' (2014, p. 22). This brings us to consider the deliberate acts of creation in presenting material for an audience (of whatever kind); along with the conventions that derive from particular kinds of cultural production; and the intensities of engagement of spectators, consumers, participants.

What next, then, for intermediality? As Jürgen Müller suggests, 'It was clear from the outset [of intermediality studies] that media are to be understood as processes in which continuing cross-effects between various concepts occur, and that these are not to be confused with any simple addition or juxtaposition' (2010, p. 18). If media mixity is now a norm of cultural production, we become interested not so much in the 'what?' and the 'how?' of media interrelations (questions to do with form, function and technological adaptation), as the 'so what?' and 'to what end?' In which case, we are interested in intermediality's *affects*, the *actions* it performs or permits, and its *affordances* – for pleasure, participation, empowerment. In this expanded sense, intermediality becomes a vehicle for a different set of plural interrelations: those found in the meaning-makings and cultural exchanges of individuals in a decidedly pluralising and multiplying environment for cultural production. If intermediality used to be interested in boundaries and beyond – the things that happened when one medium intersected with another, or when one found oneself 'in between' media – we now inhabit a cultural scene that is much more routinely mixed, where boundary crossing has become so commonplace that the boundary is less noticeable than the journey, and the move from one entity to another less pertinent than the *feeling* of being amid transition.

In order to explore this further, I examine four productions that were presented in two different festivals in 2017. The first is the Fast Forward Festival in Athens, Greece; the second, the Theater der Welt festival, which in this particular year took place in Hamburg, Germany. In their 2017 iterations, both festivals engaged with themes of migration, transit, border crossing, and geographical and cultural dislocation, in response to the distressing and politically unresolved nature of the refugee crisis that resulted from the Syrian conflict, along with large-scale economic migration from a wider array of countries. In her introduction to the 4th Fast Forward Festival, Artistic director Katia Arfara writes:

> The 4th FFF is articulated around 'heterotopias of crisis', which is say around forbidden, invisible and marginalised places where, according to Foucault, spaces and times that could not normally coexist are intertwined. The common thread running through the heterotopias of the 4th FFF is the traumatic experience of forced displacement and the loss both of 'home' and of a sense of belonging. Using various forms of artistic expression, the Festival sets out to create a notional 'shared space' on the borderline between fiction and reality – a space of otherness which can dissect the hegemonic mechanisms of entrenchment and global strategies of precariousness while simultaneously testing the limits and the potential of art's social function.[3]

In a not dissimilar vein, the website for the festival in Hamburg indicates that:

> Theater der Welt 2017 takes the harbour as an inspiration and as a venue. The harbour is a gigantic marketplace for international trade, it's the site of arrivals and departures and also a place loaded with poetic significance: a place for welcomes and farewells, for wanderlust and home sickness, for awakenings and the joy of discovery, for births and deaths.[4]

Here again, themes of movement, migration, arrival and departure. The selected works in both festivals mobilise various experiments with theatre form, performance modes and spectator engagement. For my present purposes, they provide a rather handy conjunction of topic and tactic, where the massive challenges of migration and movement find a response in the energetic refigurings of art forms and representational modes. They provide some insight into what is happening to intermediality, where boundaries are crossed, dissolved and new combinations formed. This is a matter not only of media form and interaction, but cultural transaction and meaning-making. In Athens and Hamburg, a troubled Europe engages with experiences that are both immediately at hand

and arrive from further afield, and does so in ways that are notably intermedial and multimodal.

PIRAEUS HETEROTOPIA

Piraeus Heterotopia is a walking tour through parts of Piraeus, the port of Athens, with its busy waterfront and varyingly distressed apartment blocks and side streets. Conceived by Japanese director Akira Takayama, it started life as *Tokyo Heterotopia* (2013), in which audience members travelled to locations in Tokyo within the itinerary of a radio tour, tuning into specified frequencies to hear readings of texts drawn from research into aspects of the city.[5] The concept, working out from Foucault's notion of heterotopias as 'other' spaces that are nonetheless locatable and perceivable, was transposed to Piraeus. The Greek version of the work features seven short prose pieces by writers based anywhere but Piraeus, who were sent details of the location and asked to create a response. Already, then, there is something palimspestic about this project. A site-specific piece is refunctioned for another site, and writing is layered on, from a distance, whilst also expressing an immediate response to the place in which you find yourself.

You begin by downloading an app onto your phone. In my case (starting at Omonoia Square in Athens) I took the metro to Piraeus, the last stop on the M1 line. On the forecourt of the metro station, I accessed my first podcast, 'At Piraeus Station' by the Japanese poet Keijiro Suga, which I listened to through headphones, leaning against a ticket booth. 'I am a stranger and I am stranger than you are,' a female voice says. This, I am told, is Shima, a 21-year-old Japanese woman whose name means 'island'. She introduces several themes that are central not only to this piece but to the festival as a whole – indeed, to my topic here: themes concerning the movement of people, and of representation, across borders and boundaries, and various expressions of difference and arrival.

Piraeus is 'this port city filled with forgotten memories. . . . This is the port where everything is gathered from the whole known world.' The narrator tells us that this is said by Thucydides, an old man with a dog named Artemis. We might catch these allusions to the ancient Greek historian and the Greek goddess, and if so, the classical world infuses the present. Thucydides 'speaks English with an indeterminable transferable accent' – he is one of many. The text is gnomic and also evidently resonates with the sociopolitical context of displacement that has been felt so acutely in Athens, where at a peak of the crisis in 2015, according to the International Organization for Migration, 6,000 refugees a day arrived in Greece.⁶ There is a peculiar effect of separation from the city, listening to this reading through headphones while the life of a metro station provides an ambient bustle around you.

Piraeus is 'this unknown and unknowable port city where everything flows'. We too are about to flow. The app includes a map of the walking tour you will take, with its seven points. When you are in very close proximity with a specific point, your phone pings to let you know that you can access the respective podcast. In the open, without any text in front of you, with the multiple distraction of street traders, pedestrians, traffic, this utterance through the headphones is experienced not so much as a precise articulation – as if you were reading and concentrating on a novel – than as a set of evocative reference points and a stream of speech, coming in and out of focus.

Piraeus Heterotopia is specifically of and about Piraeus, but thinkable anywhere. It is paired with a video installation entitled *Piraeus Heterochronia*, directed by Hikaru Fujii.⁷ The work, evoking 'other' times but also a time of otherness, is a video installation shown on a large monitor next to a café within a small pedestrian mall. It features four dialogues in which successive pairs of residents of Piraeus interview each other, each observed by a fixed camera. An older man observes that 'Grandfather Mercouri goes to the USA to find work.' So many of these narratives – here and elsewhere in the festival – are to do with people moving to save, look after, protect, house their families, and simply to find work. Grandpa returned with money and bought five houses in Drapetsona, a suburb of Athens. 'Aside from the poverty of that time, we experienced everything in common,' the man observes. 'There was no distinction between the communities.'

As well as being a receiving port for migrants from abroad, Piraeus was subject to internal migration from the poorer rural parts of Greece. A retired dockworker tells how he was sent by his father to find work in 1968, even though his brother was already working at the port and could only find employment typically for one day out of five. The alternatives were worse. He became a temporary worker, then a probation worker, then a permanent worker – each involving a different identity number, which he remembers as if each were a pet name – until his retirement in 2005. Piraeus subsequently became a stopping-off point for refugees from Syria. One of the interviewees left Homs. He pauses in his interview when he hears bells. They remind him that the church bells of Piraeus, providing a familiar and regular soundscape, are part of the texture of this new place, whilst evoking memories of home. It is a moment touching in its specificity and its suggestion of how a place is made of more than its concrete structures and can be evoked in memory by strong associative triggers.

One of the prose contributions in *Piraeus Heterotopia* is by the Lebanese performance artist Rabih Mroué, who muses upon the relationship between forgetting and remembering. You can't forget something, the speaker says, unless it can be remembered. If you didn't know it in the first place, then there is no forgetting or remembering to be done. The playful conceit, and its troubling inference to processes that efface memory, and histories that cannot be forgotten however much one might try, lands differently amid the apartment blocks, the disused railway, the dilapidated wooden walkway of a port that is itself marked by change. The *Piraeus Heterotopia/Heterochronia* pairing presents a place in relation to layered and changing times: a history of a civic space, the histories of people who arrive and sometimes find that this becomes their home, and a present of uncertain movements of people. What does this have to do with intermediality? The media in play are variously video and sound files accessed remotely through an app on your phone, the texts of writers, the speaking of performers. These are wrapped into modes of encounter: the walk, the acoustic concentration, the increased alertness to other sonic elements that you must either block out or allow to infiltrate your consciousness; the mode of noticing, as you pause to listen and take in aspects of your surroundings that are either referenced directly or impinge upon your gaze. There is also the tracery of other modes of expression: a mode of yearning (for home, for security, for loved ones) and a mode of adventure (whether out of ambition or desperation). All this comes together in a diffused set of intermedial evocations. Media and mediation are bound up with your own personal interfacing and meditation.

EVROS WALK WATER

Conceived and directed by Daniel Wetzel and presented by Berlin-based company Rimini Protokoll, *Evros Walk Water* is a piece for twenty-four spectators at a time.[8] It starts with everyone watching a black-and-white video recording of John Cage's performance *Water Walk* (1960), comprising his intervention with and playing of a set of objects and items, such as a pressure cooker valve (to release a jet of steam), radio set and (at one point) a glass of beer, from which he takes a slurp. The apparent randomness of the piece, and on the other hand its imposition of a structure upon the seemingly random elements, provides a basis for what follows. The spectators are invited into a space that becomes part playground, part concert stage. There are twenty-four numbered stations: twelve in a rectangle set on a platform and the rest inside this perimeter. Each of the stations has a pair of headphones. The ones around the perimeter also have a music stand on which is typically a side of laminated A4 paper with a translation or explanation of the segment you will hear. The stations in the centre of the space are more varied. One is beside a rubber dinghy, the centrepiece of the entire installation. Another has you sitting at a zither-like musical instrument. At another you stand next to a toy gun. And so on.

The piece as a whole is geared around the testimonies of eight boys, refugees from Afghanistan, Iraq and Syria. The boys came across the Aegean by boat from Turkey, following the erection of a barbed wire fence by the Greek government to halt the flow of migrants across the border at the River Evros.[9] After arriving unaccompanied in Athens, all lived for a period in 2015 in a house in the area of Exarcheia, Athens, run by the Society for the Care of Minors. Wetzel, one of the co-directors of Rimini Protokoll, interviewed them there, and developed the piece on the basis of this engagement over a couple of months.

A time counter on a monitor stands at one of the sides, regulating the proceedings. Each segment takes place across a three-minute span, at the end of which we are instructed by the boy who speaks in that particular segment to move to a specific numbered station. There is a conceit that we will together make a concert at the end of the piece. Meanwhile, we hear the boys' testimonies, stories of families separated, the hardships of travel, and life in this new gathering of those seeking refuge. En route, we also perform various tasks according to the boys' instructions through the headphones, such as blowing up a paper bag and bursting it on cue; lifting a vase of flowers into the dinghy and watering it with a watering can; winding up and throwing a toy fish into the water, or striking the strings of the zither with a wooden stick. Some of the tasks intersect, as when the spectators at stations 8, 9 and 11 (each following the diverse prompts through their respective headphones) come together and put their arms on each other's shoulders as the voices describe the boys' gathering and parting.

How do we think of this piece in terms of intermediality? And who is performing it?

The boys' testimony is at the centre of the piece. This is conveyed by way of the sound files, arranged variously to play across the twenty-four sets of headphones. Initially each spectator listens to a different piece, and towards the end it becomes clear that the testimonies converge and we all hear the same thing – which cues us to click our fingers or clap in sync, for example. The concert provides a motif and something of an organising principle. We are the performers of a new piece of sound art that takes place (for us) afresh, as a kind of parallel experience to our focus on the boys' stories. Nothing is spontaneous, and everything takes place on cue as a task performed by the obedient spectator. Wetzel reports that the technical set-up requires a master computer and five slave computers to trigger all the audio files synchronously across the twenty-four channels.

This master/slave model is not inappropriate for the piece as a whole. Wetzel is the Cageian conjuror, marshalling the mix of playful, nonsensical and meaningful items and references, whilst the spectators have a functional role in their realisation. This is some kind of a metaphor, perhaps, for the situation of the boys themselves, pitched into a chaotic and unknowable journey, part-improvising as they follow a score established by others. And it expresses my current theme of intermedial conglomeration.

Here is a piece that depends upon sound recording and files; the scenic design that arranges objects and people in space; the theatrical paradigm of durational, live encounter (the piece lasts for around 45 minutes); snatches of narratives of the boy's stories; and the quasi-impromptu rendition of a concert, however fleeting and surreal. This is the condition of contemporary intermediality. We cannot say that it consists of stable relations between distinct media. Nor that it will always feature the same media in interrelation. We are sometimes participants, sometimes observers. There is extensive production – here, not least, by way of a fearsome amount of sound editing and rendering – but this goes hand in hand with a sense of serendipity and opportunism. The modalities of the piece concern its playfulness, compassion, careful surreality and invitation to form a group comprised of atomised individuals, all of which is conveyed through the blending of testimony, instruction and participant-performance. *Evros Walk Water* attempts a kind of reconciliation of art, (Cageian) art history and history. Its turn to embed the social in the aesthetic and the mediated with the experienced is characteristic of contemporary intermedial engagements.

DON'T FOLLOW THE WIND

The title *Don't Follow the Wind* comes from an anecdote concerning one of the survivors of the Fukushima Daiichi nuclear disaster in Japan in 2011. He was wheeling his family's snatched possessions away from his house, and realised that he was travelling in the same direction as the wind, which carried with it the radioactive fallout of the accident. He turned and went in the opposite direction so as to escape further contamination. Developed by the Tokyo-based artists' collective Chim↑Pom and curated by Kenji Kubota, Eva and Franco Mattes and Jason Waite, *Don't Follow the Wind* revisits the disaster.[10] Originally presented at the Watarium Museum of Contemporary Art in Tokyo in 2015, it is firmly focused on a time and a place: Fukushima, about 160 miles northeast of Tokyo, in the aftermath of the earthquake and consequent tsunami of 11 March 2011 that caused the nuclear meltdowns at the Fukushima Daiichi

Nuclear Power Plant. Fukushima was itself a seismic interruption to the march of late postmodernism, an insistence of both the brutal insurgence of nature over and against the technological future-present, and the fallibility of the technological.

Don't Follow the Wind plays out over parts of the four-star Classical Acropol Hotel, near Omonoia Square in Athens. The square is something of a contested space. At one point during the refugee crisis, it was a gathering ground for refugees. It lies on a dividing line between well-to-do and impoverished Athens. The hotel is already replete with cultural tension, then, as a scene of luxury overlooking a site of economic disprivilege. And it suffered its own downfall. It was closed in the same year as the disaster at Fukushima, meaning that the contents of the installation, evoking one site of abandonment, takes place amid the specific signs of another. The piece is installed in the bar near the entrance, a downstairs foyer, the first-floor restaurant, and a set of rooms on the third floor. A patina of dust covers much of this space, providing an unpurchasable effect, secured not by sprinkling some theatrical prop, but through the deep agency of time passing, which also evokes a sense of time standing still. What emerges is a sense of neglect, abandonment, forced flight and affective distress in the face of these disused and unusable sites.

Don't Follow the Wind is multimodal: part exhibition, part installation, featuring within its different rooms an array of artworks and documentary-inflected arrangements. In the downstairs foyer, I don a motorcycle helmet that has been adapted to house a small VR player. The compilation video shows testimonies from residents of Fukushima. One moves through an overgrown outdoor space with a pram. Another, a former employee of the power plant, speaks by way of a voiceover on a video of the nuclear power plant taken from a ship on the sea. There is a video showing an art installation project at the site, with different spaces containing work by different artists – arrangements of found objects, using and framing the detritus of disaster. Three of the artists stand amid their exhibits, wearing protective white overalls and masks. Another segment details Ai Weiwei's installation at the disaster site. Entitled *A Ray of Hope*, Weiwei arranged for a light to come on twice a day in one of the abandoned apartments so that it is the only one illuminated, periodically, in the block – a ghostly evocation of its former lived inhabitation. Inside a motorcycle helmet in a hotel in Athens, then, there is video, voiceover, the record of a visual art exhibition and of a memorial that uses the medium of electric light. The diverse intermediality of these elements is superseded by their play across geographical locations, temporal frames and the connected modes of memory and witness.

On the first floor, the first things you come across are the plates left on a blue tarpaulin, the memorialised residue of a picnic of Greek and Japanese food shared by the artists and installers arranging the exhibition. Work, art and memory fuse even here, in this metatheatrical exhibit of a daily activity – having lunch – that becomes an emblem of the topic of remembering. Everything leaves its trace, is a medium for witness and memory. Intermedia fold into the work's project of memorialising in a way that presents a decidedly vivid encounter. In *Remediation*, Jay Bolter and Richard Grusin describe processes of *immediacy* that efface the appearance of the artwork by giving the spectator an apparently direct access to its matter; and processes of *hypermediacy*, through which you see the medial arrangement that presents the artwork for your engagement (1999, pp. 33–34). *Don't Follow the Wind* oscillates between the two. It uses the concrete reference points of a relatively near past to create effects of presence where the exhibited nature of the work is emphasised. A large-scale photo of the picnic on the floor appears on the wall at the other end of the room.

A notepad bearing the Classical Hotels brand logo, and the slogan 'Classical means forever' lies on a table covered with the ubiquitous sheen of dust. How ironic this appears, and in Athens of all places, better even than Florence as the civic location of a past that people agree must not be effaced. The banal corporate notepad has become an artefact. On the one hand, it's like a Duchamp ready-made, appearing in full possession of its original function and now repurposed as exhibit. The artistry lies in its disposition and the ironies that are thereby propelled.

We are familiar now – in immersive theatre and performance, twenty-first-century installations, site-specific promenade pieces – with these disused and distressed buildings. They lend themselves to the trope and motif of impermanence as part of a contemporary fascination with constant change. The building, too, is a medium, and it is also multimodal, expressing temporality, spatiality, particular kinds of inhabitation and a specific negotiation of the generic (four-star hotel trimmings) and the specific (only here, in Athens, could the Classical Acropol disport itself in this way). The exhibition is palimpsestic through and through, laying the Japanese reference on the Greek building and layering its histories and geographical parallels in each particular space. It does so in a space that might be infected by the motifs that it houses, as if Athens too (Greece, Europe) gets remembered in a particular way, or perhaps (I think of Rabih Mroué's lines in *Piraeus Heterotopia*) exhibits a kind of forgetting that gets momentarily unforgotten. On the third floor, you wander along a hotel corridor that gives onto some rooms that are open. In one there are life-sized photographs of Japanese people in a different hotel room, one that almost exactly invokes the 'I' of the present room – layered onto it, as if one functional hotel space is much like another, and as if one people's experience might then be thought similar to another's.

A number of rooms are displayed in their now redundant readiness for guests – except that this is also an unreadiness given how dirty they've become with the dust of the city over time. This is dust as scenic device, a sprinkling of affect where you are invited to imagine a lived presence that has also been notably absence for a good while. Other rooms feature beds stood on their ends, like undressed witnesses to their own decommissioning. The final room, at the end of one of the corridors, contains a video loop playing on a monitor. It starts with a Japanese man in overalls sitting on the step into a shed. The superimposed text says, 'Can you please try to laugh?' 'Yes,' says the man. What follows is a sequence of fast-cut clips of the man, a series of staccato utterances that I presume are edited from his speaking – 'heh, uh, ha, ha' – as if laughter is only possible here by way of this effort of post-production. In the preceding room, the soundtrack plays from a speaker under the bed, a disembodied voice in an abandoned room, not laughing, not saying anything coherent, but simply marking a presence that is also emptied by history, nature and the passing of time.

Let's ask our current question again: what media are connected here, and how does this relate to performance? The spectator is witness to an exhibition that itself pays witness to two different sorts of abandonment – one, the enforced quarantine of the region in Japan following the nuclear leak; the other, the closure of a once-grand hotel in the face of Greece's economic crisis and civic downturn. The exhibition installs objects, artworks, films and soundtracks; arranges found elements – beds, glasses, cocktail menus – of the hotel; and, beyond this, simply reveals the spaces as they currently exist. How do we enumerate this? Video installation in Fukushima; videos shot in Fukushima; videos of installations; documentary-style voiceovers describing what we are seeing; commemorative artworks such as the cloths bearing text that are draped over armchairs; models and adapted objects (such as the motorcycle helmet) that house VR playback hardware; photographs. What's missing in the roster of theatrical presentation are live performers, except that the live presence is that of the spectator within the encounter. This intermedial work requires witness and spectatorship, but its combinations of medial elements cannot be codified very neatly, nor are their modalities the same from one space to the next. The modes of installation and exhibition contain everything, but they operate through a more complex interrelation of media that spill beyond conventional frames and containing parameters (screens, stages, spaces) and reach into civic space and cultural production more broadly. This reaching beyond – into the live experience of witnesses, the functional life of a city, the designated spaces of work and inhabitation that are also spaces of artistic consumption – is what makes this a definitively contemporary kind of intermediality. It has moved beyond the schematic relations of one medium with another, or the supplanting of one by another, or even the multifarious relation of diverse media in a digital domain. It is more rampant in its combinations, more pluralised, eclectic and bespoke. It is also in some way more connected with its environment, both that which it commemorates (the site of the disaster) and that which it reanimates (the disused Greek hotel in a country struggling with the tension between economic struggle and continental consumerism).

One of the features these works have in common is that you move through them rather than that they simply play out before you. This applies even in *Evros Walk Water*, located in a studio, where you transit between the numbered stations arranged within the space. *Piraeus Heterotopia* involves a walking tour through parts of the town, while *Don't Follow the Wind* is contained within a single building but nonetheless requires that you move to and through various rooms across different floors. The primacy of movement as a principle of encounter considerably expands the medial frame of reference. Is the city a medium, or the hotel? Yes, in some respects, for meaning accrues precisely (and also imprecisely, serendipitously) because of an organised engagement with the civic, social and interior spaces through which you pass. In themselves these become akin to stages, augmented by your own inhabitation of them. As you move through the city, you inevitably encounter the conveyance of action and activity that is the city's functioning. In the hotel, the medium of communication (aside from screens and artefacts such as objects within an installation) is the building itself, operating as a kind of container full of signification. Place (rather than simply space) mediates its own specific set of textures, defining rhythms, associations and relationships. We find ourselves *within* mediation, in the process encountering other kinds of intermedia (VR videoscapes within an installation, e.g.) that are layered as part of this larger mise en scène. Intermediality is not the most noticeable feature of this artistic arrangement, but rather its substrate, underpinning a more diverse gathering of multimodal elements (promenade, witness, happening, video, sound file, text, utterance, gallery-style exhibition). Intermediality has become *conventional*, in the sense that Raymond Williams describes:

> A convention is an established relationship, or ground of a relationship, through which a specific shared practice – the making of actual works – can be realized. It is the local or general indicator, both of the situations and occasions of art, and of the means of an art (Williams, 1987, p. 185).

As Williams suggests, conventions are 'historically variable' (1987, p. 185). In his ensuing discussion, he focuses in part on dramatic performance, which he notes 'is a convention instituted in specific periods within specific cultures, rather than any kind of "natural" behaviour' (1987, p. 186). The implicit notion that dramatic performance may cease to be an unremarkable norm is borne out in the twenty-first century by the incursion of the post-dramatic, and indeed by the kinds of artworks that I have been discussing in this chapter. Whilst these are at the more innovatory end of the performance field, they nonetheless mark a growing interest in site-specific, immersive, reality-based and schematic production. They also suggest that intermediality – once a zone of exploratory interrelations between media – has come closer to expressing a cultural norm in which aesthetic arrangements, technologies of mediation, the use of diverse media and spectators' interactions are becoming routinely mixed to the point where a synthetic plural engagement, experienced as a single field of meaning and mediation, replaces the sense of being in the face of *specifically different* media and signifying elements. Twenty-first-century intermediality, then, provides a supportive cultural resource-cum-apparatus for a series of more extended multimodal operations. One final example will help to round out this reflection.

SANCTUARY

Brett Bailey's *Sanctuary*, produced by his South African–based company, Third World Bunfight, was presented at both the Fast Forward Festival and the Theater der Welt 2017 festival in Hamburg, where it was installed in a large industrial space in the former train station at the Oberhafen (Hamburg's harbour area).[11] In developing the piece, Bailey visited refugee camps in France, Greece, Italy and Germany, and along with dramaturg Eyad Houssami interviewed around sixty prospective performers from refugee and activist communities. Out of this process Bailey developed eight scenes, each of which was inhabited by a different performer playing a fictional character. The result was a performance installation that functioned by way of a set of smaller installations, with audience members following a designated route in order to move from one 'station' to the next. The piece was overlaid, perhaps rather nebulously, with a reference to the labyrinth of the mythological minotaur, by way of a red thread tracing a route through the space and connecting the various stations.

The arrangement overall evokes a holding compound, rather more a place of incarceration than the retreat suggested by 'Sanctuary', created by wire mesh fences and industrial lights. Each station has a printed scene title, making this a gallery-like collection of pieces. In the second, 'Red Carpet', a man in a small booth-like shelter holds a baby swaddled in a red blanket, behind a plastic curtain with 'Police' printed across the middle. They are surrounded by shoes, plastic bottles, passport photos – the detritus of refugee transit. On a sheet of brown packaging cardboard there is a statement: 'My father too held me in his arms in such a place . . . Mahmoud, 36, dress shop owner.' There is a peculiar meld of actuality and fabrication. Even if (in these fictionalised scenarios) this isn't actually Mahmoud who was once a dress shop owner, the stillness and concentrated simplicity of the arrangement makes it easy to assume that the figure in front of us *stands in* for an actually displaced person whilst also perhaps *being himself* one of the displaced. There are reality effects in the nature of the casting, the fact that Bailey has drawn performers from the refugee community, and the quasi-naturalistic arrangements within these spaces of exhibition. Partway through our encounter, the man turns and looks at me – an action that performs the reversal of a gaze (for a moment, he observes me observing him) – and flirts with a boundary, as this look out of the installation is both a performance and the refutation of acting. This oscillation is characteristic of the piece (and indeed a swathe of reality-trend performances more broadly). It evokes an actual sociopolitical scenario whilst framing it for consideration in a moment of immediate engagement.

In 'Black Friday', a shop window frames a woman in a white dress, sitting in a wheelchair, twigs coming out of her sleeves, facing front. There are handbags alongside a 'Sale' sign, a mannequin and high-heel shoes. A text appears on a monitor. The character before us is a 23-year-old make-up artist. She was sold to a 60-year-old man from Raqqa, who tied her hands and feet with cable, raped her and eventually sold her on. A map shows the red thread running from Iraq to Athens. In 'Natural Resources' a cutout of the Minotaur holds the thread. A black woman sits on a chair in front of a mirror, wrapped in a towel, which she then drapes over a TV monitor that shows a plume of fire (perhaps from an oil field). The red thread is tied around her ankle. The installation has a small beach of sand on one side, on which are some white bones, and a miniature desert on the other, with boats crossing from the desert to the shore. There is a pile of euro notes next to the Minotaur. After this station, we sit in a waiting pen on benches facing each other, divided by a wire fence. There is a guard watching from one end, behind another fence. A sign says 'Five Freedoms'. The list includes 'Freedom from hunger and thirst', 'Freedom from discomfort', 'Freedom to express normal behaviour'. There is a snatch of classical piano and an odd fluttering sound. This is all arranged under a fluorescent light.

Scene 6, entitled 'Collateral Damage', features 'Tony, 31, Fixer, Translator, Photographer'. In capital letters on a piece of cardboard a sign says: 'I see you not seeing me'. The performer is sitting cross-legged amid black bin liners, a blanket over his lap, wearing a beanie hat. The red thread runs past a toy dog and through the cardboard signs of a hitchhiker, which read 'Wien', 'Paris'. Scene 7, 'Europa', shows a living room. There is a cardboard cutout of a TV showing the *Front National* leader Marine Le Pen (the installation was created and presented either side of the French presidential election, 23 April–7 May 2017, in which Le Pen was one of the candidates). An elderly woman knits a red blanket. There is a cardboard cutout of a dog lying on the floor, a goldfish bowl, a rug, a copy of the newspaper *Nice-Matin*. The set includes a sofa, net curtains and a standard lamp. A card on the floor says 'Penelope, 74. Retired receptionist'. On a fence in the passageway before the exit, there are faces and details of the performers.

I hope by this bare description to convey something of the aesthetic and political strategies of this piece. It accumulates some obvious signifiers of migration by way of objects (personal items, safety jackets and so forth), spaces (the holding pen, the shelter) and people. The latter assume a calmly insistent presence. They hardly perform any actions but instead offer themselves up for observation as exhibits. Their passivity echoes the lack of agency of the refugee when they are subject to the jurisdiction of others. Nonetheless, we are invited to see these scenarios as if through the eyes of their inhabitants. The scenic spaces – living room, shopfront, park, street – place this subjective experience in recognisable interior and exterior locations, bringing the refugee crisis more overtly into a Western European horizon. The embedding of TV monitors and video screens within a number of stations allows for a mix of geographical references through images of maps, actuality-style footage of events or instances (a firework display, e.g., or the oil-field flame) and textual information about the characters. *Sanctuary* presents an ironic and open-ended response to migration as both cultural crisis and individual experience.

LANDING POINTS

In an essay of 2010 considering intermediality as a phenomenon, Irina Rajewsky (2010) discusses media as they are conventionally perceived to be distinct from each other, arguing that identifying borders and separations allows for a subtler analysis of the operations of media at and across medial boundaries. This makes sense in relation to an earlier phase of intermedial production, but the very formation of the contemporary performances that I have discussed above appears to efface boundaries and separations, and ask now for a different kind of analysis. We are interested here less in determining media types and interrelations, and more in the way in which 'the cultural shaping of a material' (Jewitt, 2014, p. 22) is performed. This shaping incorporates diverse media without any necessary blueprint for their interrelation except that they will coexist within a single schematic. It adopts several modes simultaneously: text, utterance, sound, visual design, the disposition and actions of performers, and the choices, observations and reactions of spectators.

In *Multimodal Discourse*, Gunther Kress and Theo Van Leeuwen pursue a focus on *practices* of representation and communication rather than on 'fixed, stable entities' (2001, p. 4). This opens out into a sociocultural understanding of the 'multimodal resources' of a piece (2001, p. 4), which are set in play as part of a wider relation between a communication event and its audience or participants – in our instances above, we might say between the organisation of the performance and the spectator's interaction with it. As Kress and Van Leeuwen suggest:

> Modes are semiotic resources which allow the simultaneous realisation of discourses and types of (inter)action. Designs then use these resources, combining semiotic modes, and selecting from the options which they make available according to the interests of a particular communication situation.

> Modes can be realised in more than one production **medium**. . . . It follows that media become modes once their principles of semiosis begin to be conceived in more abstract ways (as 'grammars' of some kind). This in turn will make it possible to realise them in a range of media. They lose their tie to a specific form of material realisation. (Kress and Van Leeuwen, 2001, pp. 21–22; bolding in original)

I suggest that this is happening increasingly with contemporary performances and related artistic and cultural works. Intermedial processes and combinations provide a necessary facilitation. In the instances I have discussed above, intermediality as a paradigm is entirely suitable to the themes that are confronted. Boundaries are crossed, new spaces inhabited. Intermediality provides an artistic strategy – but one that must be understood within a wider frame of 'cultural shaping' where meanings are negotiated and forms of engagement transacted. In personal and political terms, there may still be tense interactions and often drastic separations – but this travel across places also marks a kind of necessary incorporation, where bodies, messages and meanings are mixed anew in a more widely multimodal ensemble. For many people, it seems, and also for intermediality, there is no turning back.

Practical ideas

- Look at a piece of performance that you find interesting. Think about the different media that may be in use here – and think about whether it makes sense also to consider *modes* that might be in use. These might include different sorts of writing, video and movement; different modes of engagement and interaction of spectators; and different modes of presentation through (e.g.) video, exhibition, live performance and written text.
- Think about whether a particular artistic arrangement is especially well suited to the material that it addresses. Does it help to provide different perspectives, for example by using different modes and media? What kinds of meaning emerge, and is this helped by the form of the work?
- Does it help to think about performance as *cultural production*, drawing on a wider set of techniques, technologies and approaches that we see in contemporary culture? Think of a work that you like, and see whether it can be set alongside other (and possibly quite different) works that use similar techniques. Are these in any way 'new'? Can we get a better understanding by looking at events and performances as products of their wider culture in some way?

3 The Performer in Intermedial Theatre

Joanne Scott and Bruce Barton

You are a performer in a live event. You perform for an audience, though perhaps they are not in the same physical space as you. You perform with others, who might also be present in different forms and modes. You perform through other elements; your skill and craft is formed at an intersection with mediatised things – images, sounds, apps and digital processes, in the form of binary code, algorithms, automated and generative happenings. Sometimes, this means you have to hit a mark onstage to fit into an image that has been timed to appear there; sometimes, you are an onstage technician, activating the technology as well as performing those activations for a present audience. You might need to perform to a camera onstage and to an audience at the same time or communicate with your audience through online messaging or dance with a virtual partner. Sometimes you feel engulfed by the visual or sonic power of your mediatised 'scene partners'. At other points, the smallest shift of your presence can reconfigure how the audience experiences the intermedial event you are part of creating.

INTRODUCTION

This chapter works from the premise that there is a particular set of skills and approaches, actions, relationships and feelings associated with being a performer in an intermedial event. It sets out to examine what it means to be an intermedial performer, who intermedial performers are and what they do, what relationships they form with media in live performance events and what principles for making and performing might emerge from considering the role of the performer in a range of intermedial works. It also outlines how you might put such skills and principles into practice in your work, performing in intermedial environments.

There are two authors of this chapter, Jo and Bruce, who enact a dialogue around the points above. Jo firstly outlines some aspects of being an intermedial performer, including the thorny issues of presence and status, before moving on to a more active consideration and analysis of actions, interactions and relationships between elements in these types of performances. In addition and as an active discourse with this writing, Bruce's thoughts are threaded through the chapter. He intersects with, possibly counters and certainly finds different perspectives on Jo's ideas, which allows a dialogue about the performer in intermedial theatre to develop as the chapter continues. Through this discourse, we are signalling very clearly to you that there is no singular reading of this topic – we both have opinions which are based on our experiences as makers and audiences, as researchers and practitioners. Equally, intermedial performance is a wide and various field; as such, there are many ways in which you can counter or develop some of the thoughts presented here, and please feel free to do this. Our intention in the chapter is to open up a space of discourse – an active discussion about the performer in intermedial theatre. We start this discussion here and now, and we hope it continues in your studios, classrooms and performing spaces in the future.

Jo's Approach

In order to further these discussions, within this chapter I draw on my experiences as an intermedial performer, as well as those of Anna Wilson, performer with imitating the dog and Niki Woods, associate artist with Blast Theory and long-term performer and collaborator in its live events. In combination with these 'insider accounts' (Nelson, 2013, p. 89) of intermedial performing, there is also some consideration of the different roles the performer plays in a range of intermedial events that I have experienced as an audience member or participant, along with the effects, feelings and meanings this creates.

Bruce's Approach

I approach our topic from a more narrowly focused set of considerations than Jo, albeit one that is arguably of central importance: that is, the potential for/of/in *intimacy* in intermedial contexts. Throughout the chapter, I take my lead from Jo in her identification of dominant issues, themes and dynamics, and propose key sites where the essay will linger a bit, employing questions related to intimacy as something of a magnifying glass – that is, as a means to expand upon and peer deeper into fundamental points of consideration.

As we both note, discussions of intermedial performance have historically demonstrated a preoccupation with the tensions between 'live' and 'mediated' experience, and the possibility of intimacy between performers and audience members is regularly cited as a distinguishing feature between these two states. But both Jo and I challenge this oversimplified opposition, and I, in particular, concern myself with how intimacy is transformed within intermedial performance contexts into a thoroughly contemporary and highly productive dynamic between performers, between performers and audience members, and between all participants and the new media forms they employ, engage with and are shaped by.

As a performance creation artist and scholar, I bring the perspective of a director, designer and dramaturg to bear on the status and experience of the intermedial performer. Thus, by extension, I formulate an understanding of these dynamics primarily from the position of *reception*. At times in my contribution, this reception is understood as the one *anticipated* by the participating artists; at other times, it is the reception *intended* or planned for by the work's creators; at still others, it is the (sometimes surprising) reception that has been *observed* or *perceived* by artists (including myself) in actual performance contexts.

FRAMING THE DISCUSSION (JO)

You will note from the introduction that I am deliberately using the word 'discourse', both in my discussion of the performer's actions within the intermedial environment and in framing this writing. In this way, I am seeing all the elements in an intermedial performance as constantly in dialogue and at play in generating the event. I am also interested in thinking of performance with and through Derrida's reading of discourse as 'a system of differences' (1978, p. 354) – in intermedial contexts these 'differences' exist as a layered, shifting site within which an active conversation between media takes place. Following Experience Bryon's (2014) lead, this puts the focus not on the performance event as a product, but on a 'middle field' of performing (p. 35). In this active field, the intermedial performer's actions are part of a range of complex 'doings' or activities, which include the 'throw of a light, the cough of an audience member, the extension of a leg, the swell of the orchestra, the projection of an image, or the reach of one character to another in the effort to convince' (p. 194). In intermedial work, we could add to this the internal digital processing of an application, the algorithm through which movement, in certain interactive pieces, can be made to generate sound or image and various other technological 'doings'.

This approach prompts you to see intermedial events not as static elements, cues and directions, or as the outcome of a set of actions, but rather as a set of dynamic and interconnected processes which are always happening and making and affecting and bumping up against one another. This then leads analysis and making to focus usefully on the particularities of those intersections – how combined 'doings' create effects, feelings and meanings – and the specific relationships that are formed between performers and their technological partners in the act of performing. This is what Bryon refers to as the '*way* of *doing* in process' (2014, p. 61), placing emphasis on the how of making (process – performing) rather than the what of that which is made (product – performance). This also prompts you to address what is specific and significant to you as a performer in intermedial theatre, *in the process of performing*; what makes your role and actions different to other modes of performance-making, and the skills, approaches and understandings that you need to be an effective intermedial performer and maker.

FRAMING THE DISCUSSION (BRUCE)

In many ways, Intermedial performance serves as a litmus test for the evolving nature of performance in general, providing heightened examples of many of the dominant trends in contemporary creative process and critical analysis. Jo's proposal – following Bryon – that we shift the emphasis to 'the how of making (process – performing), rather than the what of that which is made (product – performance),' describes a productive, even necessary shift of perspective when thinking about almost all aspects of post-dramatic performance. Similarly, Jo's suggestion that we approach an intermedial performance event as an 'active field' of '"complex doings" or activities' parallels emergent interpretations of both cultural dynamics and human cognition. For instance, the understanding of cultural forces known as *performativity*, as shaped through the writings of authors such as Judith Butler and Jacques Derrida, proposes that the formation of both individual subjectivity and collective ideologies is 'a question of *doing* rather than *being*' (Gade and Jerslev, 2005). At the same time, the assertion within multiple understandings of human embodiment that 'sensory and motor processes, perception and action, are fundamentally inseparable in lived cognition' (Varela, Thompson and Rosch, 1991) similarly reinforces this shift from a preoccupation with firm categorisation and final products to an effort to map and navigate fluid and mutable networks of interacting responses and proposals.

Few aspects of contemporary life – and, by extension, contemporary performance – are evolving as rapidly as our relationship with technology. Training as a performer in this context, therefore, is not about attaining 'mastery' or a comprehensive set of stable attributes, but rather involves developing heightened awareness and a skills-based responsiveness to a rapidly evolving set of dynamics. 'What we perceive,' Alva Noë (Noe 2006: 1) has observed, 'is determined by *what we do* (or what we know how to do); it is determined by what we are *ready* to do.' In a sense, then, becoming a successful performer in intermedial contexts is a heightened process of learning to perceive through action. The implications of this shift for the possibility and experience of intimacy is nothing short of profound – a topic I return to later in the section on the status of the performer in Intermedial performance environment.

WHO IS AN INTERMEDIAL PERFORMER? (JO'S PERSPECTIVE)

Every performer who is part of a developing live event is engaging in an intermedial act. In any performance, the actor, bearing the signs of costume while being lit by the activation of the technician and choice of the lighting designer in an environment created by a scenographer, and performing according to their training, interpretation of the text and that of the director, is always already intermedial. Performers mix their physical actions, skills and approaches to the act of performing with visual, sonic and material elements, in a range of forms which, in their shifting and evolving state, constitute the live performance event. The effect and affect of the piece emerge from those elements in combination as they move and intersect through the performance.

However, this volume specifically addresses intermediality in the wake of the digital revolution, paying attention to performance practices which are enabled, activated and formed through interactions between performers and machinic or digital processes as part of a live and developing event. As such, in this chapter the focus is not on the intermedial environment described above, which is active in all performance events, but on that which is technologically enabled – mobilised through the workings of various different media in discourse in the context of the performance. As explored below, this leads to a range of technical, functional and expressive skills which you, as the performer, may need to learn. It also generates different experiences and affects for those spectating, experiencing or actively participating in the work.

THE STATUS OF THE PERFORMER IN INTERMEDIAL PERFORMANCE ENVIRONMENTS (JO'S PERSPECTIVE)

The ways in which performing with and through technological interfaces and representations affects your status, power and agency as a performer is a topic that has been considered by a number of theorists. For instance, Philip

Auslander famously cited actor Roberts Blossom's perspective that in 'mixed media performances' the actors appear, in comparison with filmed images, as 'fifty-watt bulbs waiting to be screwed into their source' (2008, p. 41), indicating the dominance and draw of the screen in this context. Auslander himself goes on to claim that from his perspective, in intermedial dance works, where digital materials are employed in relation to live dancers, 'we . . . experience such work as a fusion . . .taking place within a digital environment . . . the cultural dominant'. His conclusion is that 'Dance + Virtual = Virtual' (p. 42).

The very notion of intermediality, which addresses the mixing, threading together and combination of various media in the context of an event, rather than seeing them in competition, runs counter to this conclusion, suggesting that the experience created is a lot more complex than the 'arithmetic' above suggests. However, what Auslander's fairly bald statement does indicate, which is probably worth considering here, is some ongoing anxiety about the positioning and status of the performer in the intermedial event. This is perhaps an understandable concern, particularly when we align the 'intermedial turn' with post-dramatic modes of making and presentation. In these contexts, the performer often manifests as an element – a set of actions, behaviours and intentions – which functions alongside other elements to generate 'a (meaningful) texture' (Lavender, 2006, p. 63), or what Lehmann terms 'chora-graphy' – 'a space and speech/discourse without telos, hierarchy and causality, without fixable meaning and unity' (2006, p. 146). This is in contrast to viewing theatre and performance as 'the anthropocentric art-form *par excellence*' (Lavery and Finburgh, 2015, p. 4), where the human condition, experience and –crucially – body sit at the heart of the performance event as the locus and central signifier, with all other elements arranging themselves in a unified way to *serve* this central performance.

Rather, in a lot of intermedial and post-dramatic work, the performing body and actions are part of a deliberately multiple set of happenings, not all of which centre our attention on the performer. As Robin Nelson states, 'The performer today is just one of many signifiers in a complex, multi-layered event' (2010, p. 23). Equally, with the growth of motion capture and motion sensor technologies, this can be taken further, in that the performing body can function primarily to trigger and manipulate the mediatised elements in play – a tool to generate another parallel set of technological events. From my conversations with dancers, I am aware that being 'suited up' for motion capture and asked to move in this or that way, to modulate the sound just so, or create that particular visual effect, can be frustrating. Being a performer in this type of environment *feels* different, and your capacities, agencies and sense of meaningful creative work can be affected by the relationships formed between your actions and those of the media, particularly when the feeling is that one is in service of another.

My experiences of being an activating performer-technician in intermedial events are also ambivalent. In the live works that I create, I manipulate sound and image, object and text, in real time to generate shifting intermedial spaces. I am in control of these intermedial combinations, and through the interfaces I have chosen, the media are responsive to my actions. However, this is not always how it *feels*. Rather, there is often within these intermedial events a sense of being prompted, called and triggered, as an element in the event, by those digital processes and their products. This means that a shifting vocal soundscape I have created might pull me towards certain image choices or lead some improvised text creation. I have articulated this as a feeling of 'precarity' (Scott, 2016) – a precariousness or instability – that is induced by being part of a set of contingent, responsive, controlling, activating and dependent actions with and through technologies in a live space (Figure 3.1).

It also resonates with key writing in the area, namely from Susan Kozel, who has written extensively about her experience of performing as part of the seminal telematic work by Paul Sermon, *Telematic Dreaming* (1992). Here, Kozel evocatively outlines that:

> The experience of performing with layers of technology such as projectors, digital imagery, prerecorded and live film sequences, interactive sensors and telematic links is one of seeing yourself and others multiplied and spread across degrees of materiality ... All states of being and interaction swirl and encroach in a fluid play of degrees of materiality (2007, p. 125).

The feeling of being multiplied, spread, dispersed and scattered across a live performance space or event is a common one for intermedial performers because of the capacity of the technological doings to reiterate, loop, stream, modulate and play with the body's actions, presence and parameters. As such, there is a strong sense of the post-human in play in such work, where 'there are no essential differences or absolute demarcations between bodily existence and computer simulation', and the performer manifests as 'an amalgam, a collection of heterogeneous components, a material-informational entity whose boundaries undergo continuous construction and reconstruction' (Hayles, 1999, p. 3). I find this theoretical perspective helpful, as an intermedial performer, in productively positioning my activity and actions in relation to a network of happenings or 'doings', which, in combination, generate the event. It also emancipates you, as the performer, from feeling that your physical presence in the space is the 'alpha and omega' of the performance and points to agency being formed at an intersection with all elements of the larger event. In relation to this, Karen Barad describes 'agency' as 'not something that someone or something has ... Agency

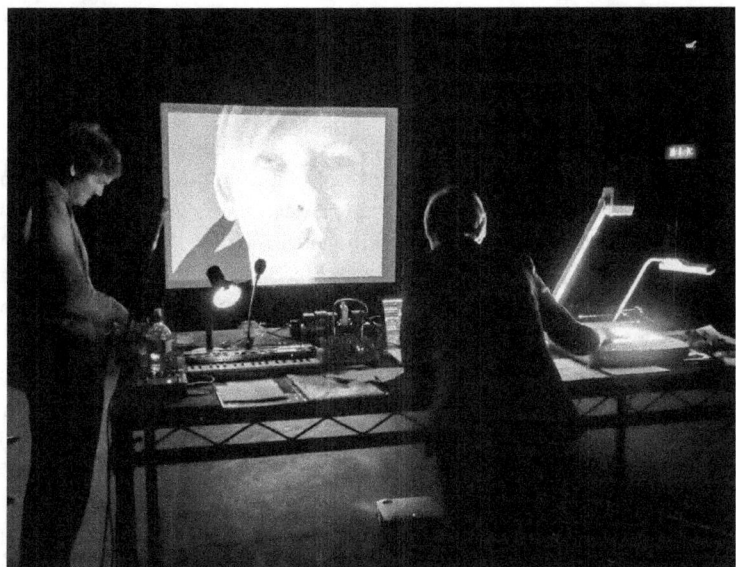

Figure 3.1   Intermedial spaces being constructed live, as part of *re-cite* by Jo Scott (2012). Photographer: Matt Taylor.

is "doing" or "being" . . . It is the enactment of iterative changes to particular practices' (2007, p. 178). Drawing on this theoretical framework, as an intermedial performer, it is not about whether you *have* status, power or agency in the context of the event as a whole; it is how, through your intersections with the other elements in play, you might *enact* agential action and 'iterative change' in the event.

Of course, this may be helpful in a theoretical sense, but does it really help when you feel that your role and status are diminished by the dominant 'doings' of the screened image or Internet connection? Perhaps, as an intermedial performer, if you do feel like this, you might reflect that this is no worse or better than the actor whose creative impulses and interpretations are dominated and undermined by a dictatorial director, or the dancer who feels that their body is simply the fleshy material through which the choreographer's vision emerges. There are many conditions associated with the act of making live events as a performer which can affect your feeling of status and agency. In this case and in relation to all acts of performing, as Barad points to above and as Bryon also advocates in her writing, you should focus on the power and agency that exists in the 'way of doing' of your performing – whatever that might be – and not 'passively transfer' (2014, p. 61) a prior meaning, situated in the '*prescribed*'

(p. 193) text or programming of a digital device, but *make* meaning in the moment of performing, through agential actions in collaboration *with* these elements.

So, what do intermedial performers themselves think of their status in these relationships between body and media, between biological and technological processes, between their acts as performers and how those intersect with the operation of the media? Such 'insider insights' can help you as you grapple with this topic and the practicalities of working with technological processes. Anna Wilson, for instance, performer in a number of intermedial works with imitating the dog, discusses the dominance of media in the creation and presentation of some of this work, while also indicating the different modes of agency and satisfaction that emerge in these contexts. Anna reflects firstly on her experience of making and performing in *Hotel Methuselah* (2011), a 'contemporary ghost story' where a prerecorded film plays and the live performers mirror the actions of their screened selves, with the combination 'viewed through a six metre letterbox-shaped gap, like cinema widescreen, which only reveals the performers' bodies from knee to neck' (imitating the dog, n.d.). In relation to this experience, Anna comments that 'you have to take the back seat as a performer' and 'relinquish yourself', also remarking that in a piece where the film's timing and framing leads the live action, 'there's no space at all for playing the moment – you really are a kind of servant to the projection – to the technology – and the more you can completely sync up, the more effective it is'. Rather than seeing this as a negative aspect of her performing experience, Anna reflects on the 'satisfaction' she gains through syncing effectively, 'getting that level of detail' (Wilson, 2017) and, in doing so, contributing to the sometimes breathtaking visual effects created through the tightly framed live action in combination with prerecorded filmed images. Anna's comments on her experience as an intermedial performer in this piece reflect the anxieties outlined in the discussions above about the diminution of the status of the live performer, who 'serves' the media in the intermedial relationships established. However, it also indicates how Anna's sense of 'agential action' and satisfaction as a performer emerges in the precise intersections she generates with the screened images and the powerful moments of performance this creates that would not be possible without her detailed choreographic and technical work.

In the case of Niki Woods and her work with Blast Theory, Niki disagrees that the performer's status is necessarily diminished in intermedial work, and instead points to 'working with or through technology to allow for an exchange, an experience, an event, a discussion' to happen. For example, in *Ulrike and Eamon Compliant* (2009), audience-participants were led individually on a journey through a city, through precise triggering of calls to a phone. Niki's role, as an 'invisible performer' in this piece, was to watch for the appearance of the participants from a café, where she was seated, and trigger the calls associated with that part of the journey. In this role, she reflects on working with her technological interface to respond carefully and sensitively to the participant in the real space of the city:

> They've been told 'We'll call you back – beeeep' . . . Okay, when do I call them back? I can't take too long, of course, because there's going to be another one coming round – there is a steady stream – but they're tying their shoelace or they've taken another call on their phone, they're texting or they're having a drink or they've just sat down – so I'm just reading what they're doing because I can see them, but they can't see me' (Woods, 2017).

Though 'invisible' as a performer in space, Niki is nevertheless responsible for using her technological interface to actively shape the experience of audience-participants through the triggering of the phone call that will move them to the next stage of the piece. The relationship is close up, intimate even, as she watches them, reads their behaviour in the moment and judges when to trigger, but she is hidden. Anna too, in *Hotel Methuselah*, is partially hidden as a performer, as only certain sections of her body are revealed in the live space. In both cases, though, it is the intersection of the live action of the performer with the technological capacity of the image or device which is crucial – the timing, precision and 'iterative changes' to the experience that it generates. Both performers, in their sensitive, detailed 'doings', are crucial to the composite effects and feelings generated in each moment, and both gain satisfaction from this aspect of their work as intermedial performers. Having said that, it is certainly the case, as indicated through these examples, that the positioning of both Anna and Niki within the events they describe – how their bodies, actions and presence are either revealed, modulated or hidden by the technology with which they are performing – does shift how their *presence* as performers is experienced by an audience or participant, and this aspect is discussed further below.

THE STATUS OF THE PERFORMER IN INTERMEDIAL PERFORMANCE ENVIRONMENTS (BRUCE'S PERSPECTIVE)

Jo's nuanced description of the 'precarity' often experienced by intermedial performers identifies one of the defining features of intermedial contexts – and, by extension, one of the most significant challenges to the fostering of intimacy. Intimacy is, of course, a complex idea and experience, one that has been studied extensively within a wide range of disciplines including psychology, sociology, philosophy and performance studies. Although the specific definitions of intimacy vary across these fields, many refer to a common subset of baseline criteria that are necessary for the establishment of intimacy. Throughout the past decade, I have drawn on the evolving research of the psychologist Karen J. Prager, who has proposed the following 'necessary and sufficient conditions' of intimacy: 'self-revealing behavior, positive involvement with the other, and shared understandings' (1995, p. 45). Effectively, for intimacy to be achieved (i) participants must be prepared to expose aspects of their behavior and personality that they normally keep private; (ii) they must enter into the exchange with full and positive attention for the other – and the confidence that the other participants bring the same intentions to the meeting; and (iii) the exchange must produce a sense of shared understanding or knowledge of the other.

The other primary contribution from Prager that has been instrumental in my understanding of the potential of intimacy in performance is her distinction between an intimate *relationship* and an intimate *interaction*. Intimate relationships are long-term arrangements based on familiarity, predictability and stability that, ironically, may rarely demonstrate explicitly intimate behavior. By contrast, intimate *interactions* occur 'within a clearly designated space-and-time framework' and may occur between strangers precisely *'because* of the unlikelihood of a further relationship and the attendant opportunities for betrayal' (Prager, 1995, p. 19).

I have written at greater length about the implications of these ideas for performance creators and audiences working in intermedial contexts (Barton, 2009); for our purposes in this article, the primary takeaway relates directly to Jo's description of the powerful 'precarity' of intermedial performance. This condition, although arguably present in almost all performance contexts to some degree, is particularly pronounced in mediatised performance, and on one level it profoundly complicates the traditionally understood criteria for intimacy that involve a full, positive and mutual engagement by both or all participants. However, this same media-fostered condition is also precisely the experience that, in a sense, levels the playing field for performers and audience members alike. This shared 'precariousness or instability,' which so accurately reflects contemporary societies' relationship with technology generally, forcefully foregrounds a common condition of twenty-first-century existence and becomes the context and catalyst for potentially powerful intimate interactions between performers, between performers and audience members, and between all participants and the semi-autonomous technologies they collectively engage.

PERFORMING PRESENCE IN INTERMEDIAL SPACES (JO'S PERSPECTIVE)

Cormac Power, in his study of theories of presence in the theatre, claims that 'in the most general sense, we could define presence as being the simultaneity between consciousness and an object of attention' (2008, p. 3), and goes on to say that 'theatre can be seen not so much as "having" or containing presence, but as an art that plays with its possibilities' (p. 8). There has also been some notable writing around the distinctions between the 'live presence' of the performer and those of any mediatised elements in the event. Hans-Thies Lehmann, for instance, talks extensively about the division he sees between 'theatre-bodies' and images of those bodies, created through technological means, which are 'nothing but representation', lacking the 'aliveness of life' (2006, pp. 167–171). Erika Fischer-Lichte also talks of a 'dichotomy . . . between live performance constituted by the bodily co-presence of actors and spectators and the autopoietic feedback loop and mediatized performances which sever the co-existence of production and reception' (2008, p. 68). Though it is not entirely clear that Fischer-Lichte's 'mediatized performance' equates with the intermedial practices discussed in this volume, it is certainly true that a division between two modes of presence is highlighted in both cases, specifically in relation to how communication and feedback happens between the performer and the audience.

Intermedial perspectives, though, by their nature, are more interested in how elements combine to create particular effects and meanings and how presence is constructed through these combinations. In line with Power's study, your focus as the intermedial practitioner and performer is not 'Do I have presence?', but 'How is presence constructed, played with and reconfigured through my actions in combination with other elements?' In this sense, depending on the intermedial combinations created, intermedial performers may have very different experiences of how their presence is 'in play' in the work and how the technological devices with which they perform are part of this.

This is evident in the experiences of intermedial performers. As indicated by Niki in her work with Blast Theory, far from viewing a technological interface or apparatus as a barrier to connecting with an audience, she experiences the opposite effect:

> What I love about devices is that experience – how we can participate, the different levels of participation that are activated – and that can be the performer through the technology, the audience-participant through the technology, the witness who doesn't really participate but who observes through the technology (Woods, 2017).

In this type of intermedial work, the performer's presence and present engagement with the audience-participant is enabled but also significantly modulated and shifted through the technology employed. As a performing presence, Niki is constructed through the technological interface in question, which can afford and indeed prompt 'intimate *interactions*' such as those outlined by Bruce above, even when she as a performer is physically distant from or invisible to the participant.

The notion of constructing performing presence is not specific to this type of intermedial performance. Auslander, writing twenty years ago about postmodern shifts in performing, states that 'what we refer to as the actor's self is not a grounding presence that precedes the performance, but an effect of the play of *differance*[1] that constitutes theatrical discourse' (Auslander, 1997, p. 36). More recently, Tim Etchells also reflects on the fact that in performance 'being present is always a kind of construction. Perhaps we could think of presence as something that happens when one attempts to do something, and whilst attempting to do that thing you become/visible; visible in "not quite succeeding" in doing it, visible through the cracks or the gaps' (in Giannachi, Kaye and Shanks, 2012, pp. 184–185). Such perspectives have resonance with the ways in which Niki's presence as a performer is constructed, shifted and made anew through the technological interface, the actions of the participants and the choices she makes as to her interactions with them in each moment.

It is in the 'doing' of intermediality that meaning happens, the event is created and presence is made and unmade. This is something I have also interrogated and tried to think through in relation to my presence as an intermedial performer (Scott, 2016, pp. 61–69). I consider that my presence in intermedial performances is not just mobile and multiple, but actively constructed through intermedial engagements and actions; my actions intersect with the intermedial space and environment to generate composite, distributed and diverse modes of presence, not all of which are tied to my physical body. In the performances I make, 'presence exists as a mobile, composite entity which intersects with the apparent oppositions between the various forms and modalities present, pushing these presences together in the live moment of constructing intermediality' (p. 74).

Anna Wilson provides a further perspective on the question of presence, arising from her work with imitating the dog. As already discussed, Anna was very much aware of *Hotel Methuselah* emerging through the precise alignment of performing actions with prerecorded screened images. In other imitating the dog pieces, where there was more 'play' possible in the live performance, this shifted her role and relationship with the media, in turn changing how presence was constructed. In *The Zero Hour* (2013), for instance, a piece that worked through the performers being live filmed against a range of screened backgrounds to create different environments, Anna describes that 'there was far more space to change . . . to play the moment and react' (Wilson, 2017). She also outlines an increased feeling of responsibility, in comparison to *Hotel Methuselah*, because her choices in each moment as a performer were more open, and these choices were a more visible and present part of the intermedial mix experienced by the audience. What Anna describes, then, is how the changing configuration of technology, performer and audience shifts the sense of the performer's role and responsibility within the event, which in turn reconfigures the 'presencing'[2] (Garner, 1994, p. 43) that emerges between your 'doings' and the technological events that are happening simultaneously.

This is also very clear to see in other intermedial work. One of my favourite go-to examples of this type of collaboratively constructed and composite 'presencing' comes in the combinations of animation and live performance found in the work of 1927. In their recent piece, *Golem* (2015), I witnessed, as is customary in their practice, beautifully timed and constructed intersections or conversations between the live score, the performer and prerecorded animation, creating composite and pleasing modes of intermedial presence. At one point, a character places his hand under some animated water falling from a tap. The animation bounces off the hand, creating an illusion that the hand is indeed stopping that water in its tracks. In this moment, the physical presence of the performer is in an intrinsic and causal relationship with the presence of the animation – there is an illusion created that is very clearly an illusion, but which also manifests as real in the clearest sense of 'seeing and believing'. The performer's presencing – how they appear, feel and manifest to me – is utterly entwined in and activated through that crucial interaction with the projection and equally, the presencing of the projected image shifts simultaneously. This is interesting to relate to Barad's notion of agency, discussed above, and 'agential action'. This performer, like Anna in *Hotel Methuselah*, has to hit a mark at a designated time and their hand must be positioned 'just so' for that effect to be created – they are absolutely subject to the demands of the prerecorded media which has been formulated in advance. However, they are not without agency or status – in combination with the presence and action of the projection a new, invigorated, distinct and engaging set of presences happens in that moment *because* of their actions.

Though a very different mode of intermedial practice, this also relates to the 'presencing' of the performer in Blast Theory's *I'd Hide You* (2012). In this context, when I logged on to the online platform as a remote player, I was confronted with a familiar mapping aesthetic and figures, represented by different-coloured dots, moving through the figuratively represented streets of

Manchester. On clicking on a coloured dot, I was 'onboard' with the runner in real space, experiencing what they were filming live with their video camera. I suppose you could say their presence was 'distributed' across the real space of the city, the map of the interface and the images of the movement/sound of the voice I can hear. However, my distinct memory of that performer's presence was that it was shifting and moving, fading and reappearing, asserting and effacing itself, according to the workings of the machinic processes – lags, glitches, as well as smooth operation – and my interactions with the performer through those processes. The only moment of crystallised and clear presence was when the runner, to whom I was communicating various instructions via text, spoke back to me. I heard their voice speak my name, and a real rush of excitement resulted from that – their presence rushed to the fore of the event and shifted my experience of it completely.

As part of our conversation, Niki Woods discussed the numerous considerations associated with performing in this event, which included carefully framing shots and 'setting the scene' for participants; technical challenges, such as running with the camera; and wider concerns to do with being in public space. She describes simultaneously 'thinking about framing, thinking about levels, thinking about proximity, thinking about privacy – what you do film, what you don't film – safety mechanisms for you as the performer' (Woods, 2017). The set up for *I'd Hide You* may appear simple, but in actuality the multiple demands on the performer's attention are bewildering.

She also has a distinct memory of an encounter with a player on the first night of *I'd Hide You*, when she was depicting a space for those onboard with her, at 'the back of a restaurant', filming the air vent and 'describing all these smells of spices coming out . . . and then I looked down at the phone . . . where I would see all the texts coming in from you guys playing and one of them was like "What the? Shut up! Get on with it! Get me some catches, man!" and I was devastated' (2017). Niki reflects that this particular encounter felt very 'exposing' for her as a performer because of the intersection of the live-feed camera and the real-time interventions of the unknown and faceless participants. However, 'after that moment of panic and 'oh no – I've failed!', my response was 'X – if this is too slow and meditative for you, you can always cut across to Abi, who's yellow, or James, pretty much saying, "Off you go – don't let me keep you!"' (Woods, 2017) This readjustment in the wake of a challenging encounter – rolling with the punches and 'learning through doing' – is typical of a set of skills, aptitudes and a sense of resilience that Niki describes, in relation to her work with Blast Theory. In this work, a set of technological interfaces intersect with an emergent set of events and 'doings' on the part of the participants, requiring a sensitivity and ability to 'read' and respond, accommodate and shape the experience of these participants, without, as is evident above, compromising the event itself.

In concluding my thoughts in this section, I do not propose that we should entirely debunk the concerns expressed by theorists and practitioners alike about what can be perceived to be unbalanced relationships between the performer and the mediatised elements with which they are performing in intermedial work, or indeed what happens to human presence when it is enacted with and through a range of machinic, automated and generative processes. However, I do want to move past these concerns towards a more active and practical consideration of what you make in those intermedial moments and how; what it takes for an intermedial performer to operate effectively in such spaces and how you might employ these particular skills and approaches in your making and performing. Equally, in light of the examples above, I propose that your focus as an intermedial performer is not whether your presence is diminished or undermined by your technological scene partners, but how presence is constructed through your actions and interactions with these elements.

PERFORMING PRESENCE IN INTERMEDIAL SPACES (BRUCE'S PERSPECTIVE)

Jo's explanations and examples effectively articulate the ways in which the basic criteria for intimacy – specifically, intimate *interactions* – are complicated within intermedial contexts. One of the key conditions of intimacy is 'self-revealing behaviour,' a dynamic that has never been more prevalent – indeed, insistent and unavoidable – than in today's surveillance-heavy, thoroughly social-mediatised landscape. However, the ability to gauge and assess precisely *who* is involved in most mediatised exchanges, let alone be confident of their positive intentions, is virtually impossible (pun intended). As such, what I referenced earlier as an intimate relationship – an extended exchange, developed over time and based on familiarity and predictability – more accurately describes the experience of many patrons at more traditional theatrical performances, which regularly rely on firmly established conventions for both performers and audience members. By contrast, the constantly shifting conditions of intermedial performance that rely on, in Jo's words, an 'emergent set of events and "doings" on the part of the participants,' can produce situations of spatial and temporal dislocation, undetected and unilateral observation and anonymous critique or manipulation. Conversely, however, the same conditions can facilitate a pronounced 'strangers on a train' environment in which instances of abrupt and intense interactivity potentially render its participants suddenly, unexpectedly and intimately co-present.

Gabriella Giannachi and Nick Kaye, in their extended discussion of performing 'between the live and the simulated,' (2011) offer a number of definitions of the term 'presence', many of which undergo subtle but significant adjustments in intermedial contexts. The state of 'being before, in front of' and 'in the immediate vicinity' of another is fundamentally altered in today's pervasive realms of Facebook, Twitter, and Instagram. To be present is to be accessible to another 'now; immediately, instantly, at once'– a common expectation we have of one another and service we regularly provide, however little the editors of the Oxford English Dictionary anticipated such applications of the term. Even more usefully, according to the Shorter Oxford dictionary, to be present involves 'senses relating to place' and is understood as 'being in the place considered or mentioned . . . existing in the thing, class or case mentioned or under consideration'. An important piece of the puzzle here is that for the intermedial performer, 'place' refers to the virtual space of mediatisation itself, as much (or more) than to the material and physical spaces of performance and reception. Further, being present requires 'having presence of mind, collected, self-possessed . . . prompt to perceive or act, ready, quick' – precisely the characteristics of the intermedial performer that Jo has effectively described in the preceding sections. As one particularly well-known Elizabethan playwright once proposed, 'the readiness is all' (*Hamlet*, 5.2.10), as the emergent, transitional nature of intermedial performance renders up temporary yet experientially charged opportunities for intimate exchange.

A primary consideration in the potential for intimacy in intermedial contexts, one Jo has noted several times, relates to issues of *attention*. Traditionally interpreted as a conscious or intuitive choice – to 'pay attention (or not) to something' – attention may be more accurately understood as a necessary implicit tactic to compensate for human beings' limited capacity to handle vast amounts of stimulus available from the sense organs and memory stores. We can only process so much information – far less than is constantly available to our senses – and increasingly it is the intermedial space itself to which we are attending and with which we experience, in a sense, a virtual intimacy. As an intermedial performer, the technologies drawn upon are not merely tools and do not merely facilitate a surrogate experience for physical co-presence. Rather, the potential for intimacy in intermedial performance is transformed by and reliant upon preexisting relationships with a range of new media applications – with which we share precisely the combination of self-exposure, positive attention and gratification traditionally associated with interpersonal intimacy. In a sense, when intermedial intimacy occurs, it does so not *despite* its mediated nature, but *because* of it.

INTERMEDIAL ACTIONS AND INTERACTIONS (JO'S PERSPECTIVE)

In this section, I provide a list of some of the primary actions/interactions I have engaged in, and witnessed performers in intermedial environments doing, that are specific to those types of performances, as well as what these actions demand of the performer and relevant practice examples. Following on from this, I consider some of the relationships between the performer and mediatised elements that are formed through these interactions, offering my thoughts as to what types of experiences these are disposed to create and the choices we can make, as intermedial performers, as to how we position ourselves within events of this nature. These final sections act as direct prompts for the 'Practical Ideas' section, which concludes the chapter.

Intermedial Action 1: Dovetailing/aligning your actions with prerecorded media

- Moving/positioning yourself in a choreographed and predetermined way to **intersect** and **align** with prerecorded images or video footage
- Timing your responses to **dovetail** with a set of prerecorded sounds, to create the sense of a 'live' conversation in performance

What does it demand of the performer?

- A focus on timing, precision of action and a heightened and sustained awareness of the physical dimensions of the performance space, the functioning and appearance of the image in the space and in relation to your body, as well as the angles and positioning of each, which allows the intermedial moment to 'click' for the audience
- Rigorous preparation in order to form and rehearse the precise choreography of body and image, or live and recorded sound, that works in each moment, and an understanding of how both move in relation to each other
- An ability to combine this precise temporal choreography with a performance style that is open enough to include an audience in the work; in the case of 1927, the performers often 'share' these moments with the audience through a complicit glance or movement in their direction

Practice Examples

- Imitating the dog's *Hotel Methuselah* – Here, the live performers sync their actions with prerecorded versions of themselves to generate a hybrid live-screened experience.
- 1927's performance work, particularly *The Animals and Children Took to the Street* (2011) and *Golem* (2015) – The performers again sync their actions with a set of prerecorded animated images, to create composite intermedial moments of performance. The live score that the group often uses helps with this feat of timing.
- Bo Burnham's stand-up comedy practice – This offers examples of choreographed live and recorded sound conversations used to comic effect.

Intermedial Action 2: Activation of technology within an event

- **Activating** onstage media live to mix elements such as sound, image and text, revealing this process of construction to the audience
- **Activating** cameras, apps and devices as part of the performance, including filming others' performance work and triggering phone calls or text messages

What does it demand of the performer?

- Technological know-how in terms of the capacities of the technology – how to zoom a camera smoothly; which buttons, sliders and mechanisms have particular effects
- The ability to read and respond to the developing event as you make and activate
- The ability to shift effectively between different 'modes' of performing, where in one moment you may be directly performing a role for an audience, and the next you may be moving objects and cameras for someone else's performance moment
- Poise, precision and the ability to efface some elements of your performance so that you can effectively technically facilitate without drawing attention to your actions, if doing so would not be appropriate
- The ability to 'read' a situation carefully and sensitively to ensure that the technological activation of key elements maintains the experience for the participant, rather than breaking it
- A familiarity with the technological interface and its affordances, as well as an understanding of the 'processes' and timings involved in the experience and how the activation of the elements you are responsible for links forward to the next moment

Practice Examples

- Complicité and Simon McBurney's *The Encounter* (2016).
- Live media practices, such as live coding[3] and live audiovisual performance[4]
- Katie Mitchell's intermedial pieces, such as *Attempts on Her Life* (2007), *Waves* (2006) and *Some Trace of Her* (2008), where performers work with cameras and props onstage to construct intermedial moments, switching between performing and technical facilitation of others' performance
- Blast Theory, *Ulrike and Eamon Compliant* (2009), where, as described above, the different stages of the experience are activated through the triggering of phone calls by 'invisible' performers

Intermedial Action 3: Doubling, dividing and being multiple

- **Doubling** – creating **'dual-purpose'** performance actions, for example those that happen onstage for a present audience, but also to a camera filming live
- **Multiplying** – working with technologies to create multiple versions of the self, for example through live-feed images, vocal looping, avatars and other technologised versions of the self
- **Dividing** – offering attention to a number of aspects of the experience as it unfolds, including technological processes and activations, as well as the user, audience or participant, and the path/script/direction of the event itself

What does it demand of the performer?

- The ability to manage multiple and diverse demands on your attention
- The aptitude to manage and respond to a number of versions of yourself that are simultaneously in play, for example live-feed image, online text, live body in real space
- A focus on a mode of performance that suits and responds to the demands of both stage and screen performance – detailed nuances of facial expression or gesture in combination with offering the performance to a live audience

Practice Examples

- **Doubling** – The Katie Mitchell pieces referenced in the example above involve performing in a live space while simultaneously being filmed, often in close up, with this projected simultaneously.
- **Multiplying** – Imitating the dog's *Hotel Methuselah* (2011) plays with multiplying the stage image so that live performance syncs with prerecorded performance, creating multiple iterations of space and time onstage.

- **Dividing** – In Blast Theory's *Can You See Me Now* (2001) and *I'd Hide You* (2012), the performers are required to divide their attention between an online engagement with participants and the real space of the city through which they move.

Intermedial Action 4: Responsiveness/interactivity

- **Responding to/interacting with** other performers/participants through mediatised modes
- Responding to the possibilities of the technology in a live situation

What does it demand of the performer?

- A sensitivity to the experience of the other performer/participant and how this is modulated, shifted and enabled through the particular technological interface in play
- An understanding of effective modes of communication that are suited to particular connections or interfaces
- An openness to the live and developing possibilities of a participatory event that is enacted through technological interfaces

Practice Examples

- Blast Theory, *I'd Hide You* – This piece, as described above, is predicated on the performers being responsive, open and sensitive to the actions and responses of the participants, but also to the affordances of the technologies in the creation of the event and experience for those participants

Intermedial Action 5: Triggering/generating media elements in the space of the event

- Using movement to automatically **trigger/generate** a visual/sonic element in a mediatised space (through motion tracking/gestural technologies)

What does it demand of the performer?

- An understanding of the relationships between action and effect (causality)
- An ability to modulate and shape movement in order to create particular effects
- A creative engagement with the capacity of the technologies in combination with human movement/modulation and, in some cases, the openness to explore the capacities of that relationship in real time

Practice Examples

- Performance work that plays with the capacities of gestural technologies – Imogen Heap, for example, has developed a 'data glove' that uses 'motion data-capture systems' and 'user interfaces' (Heap, n.d.) to generate and manipulate sound in real time, according to the movement of the arm, hand and fingers. This can also be seen in the work of Franziska Baumann, who uses a 'SensorGlove' to loop, modulate and manipulate her singing voice in real time (Baumann, 2017).
- Troika Ranch has worked extensively with motion-tracking technologies in combination with the Isadora software developed by co-founder Mark Coniglio. In *16 [R]evolutions* (2006), for instance, a series of sonic and visual elements were programmed to be activated and modulated through the movement of live dancers.

The categories of actions the intermedial performer might engage in, indicated above, point to a range of relationships and conversations that happen between the performer's actions, those of the technological representation or interface, and the audience or participant experiencing the event. As a performer, your actions may be linking together diverse elements of an experience or indeed disrupting these. You may be framing an experience for an audience through the technology available to you – triggering a text message or focusing a live-feed camera. You may also be choreographing and 'fitting' your action to a set of prerecorded media and following the lead of that fixed set of events in your movement through a live performance.

Whatever the particular labour in which you are engaged as part of an intermedial event, it is important to move beyond an exclusive consideration of *your* work in order to focus on the relationships you form with the other elements of the event and specifically the types of experience they are disposed to generate for an audience or participant. In the final section, the analysis aims to address these questions through considering three recurrent combinations of elements in intermedial practice, before formulating some prompts for your making as an intermedial performer.

PERFORMER-MEDIA RELATIONSHIPS: INTERMEDIALITY IN ACTION

Example 1: Predetermined and prerecorded sets of visual media in combination with the actions of the live performer

This first example addresses live works where a prerecorded set of visual media is activated as part of the performance and the primary role of the performer – as articulated above – is to align, dovetail and intersect with these prerecorded images through a precisely choreographed set of actions. As a performer, the precision of your acts and attention to detail are crucial in forming these intersections effectively, but what mode of experience does this create for an audience? In my experience of watching such work, there is a complicit delight in witnessing the joining up of the separate elements of body and image into very particular combinations. The use of the performer's body to 'complete' an existing picture – a strategy often used by 1927, as described above – creates a frisson of pleasure for the audience. This is not because we are convinced that the two actually fuse and see the results as a coherent whole, but exactly because of the intermedial conversation or discourse between the performer's actions and the prerecorded images that is ongoing through that moment.

This is distinct from *Hotel Methuselah*, for instance, where the performer's actions still need to align with prerecorded media, but where they do not 'complete' the images established, but mirror them. This creates a more fractured, disjunctive set of combinations which play with our sense of space, time and perspective, in this case effectively mirroring the temporal play present within the plot of the piece itself. Lacking the immediate satisfaction of the types of combinations 1927 create, these intermedial forms open up meanings, states and possibilities, emphasising multiplicity and doubling rather than precise alignment to create a single stage picture.

In both cases, the audience experiences a present and, I would argue, pleasurable duality of experience, in that when such combinations 'click', there is an absorption in the effect of the combination while also a delight in its present construction, and particularly the live performer's actions as bringing together the experience in the perception of the viewer.

Example 2: Preprogrammed apps, devices and frameworks in combination with an active participant and responsive performer

A contrasting combination of technology, performer and audience is that which is present within a lot of Blast Theory work and where applications, devices and platforms are programmed in advance to create a live environment within which both performers and audience-participants meet. The operations of the media, though programmed in advance, are deliberately open to the actions and responses of both participants and performers. As Niki Woods describes above, this allows the performer to mould the experience of the audience-participant to shift the encounter that happens between them and to use the technological interface – whether that is a device that triggers phone calls, a camera filming live or an application that allows text messaging to be sent and received – as the point of connection.

As an audience-participant in such work, you discover the capacity of the interface through doing – moving your avatar around in virtual-real space or trying out the capacity of the text message app to communicate. The experience that is created is necessarily layered and active – you can shift your position within the event, but the technologies have specific parameters aligned with the objective of the game. Equally, the performers, as described above 'presence' and mean different things to you, according to that position and how you intersect with their particular journey and experience in real space. This type of intermedial work is much more about a playful, open and exploratory set of relationships between the technology, performer and audience. Unlike the preset media and choreographed relationships above, there can be no shaped and predetermined moments or set pieces, and as a performer, rather, you have to be alive to the possibilities that may emerge through the confluence of elements in a particular instant. The audience-participant's relationship with the technology is as a player or 'user', enabling a close-up engagement with the performer that can feel exposing, as Niki describes. Equally, as Niki also comments, there is a need to accommodate the possibilities of the range of responses you may get in a single night to work within a piece like *I'd Hide You*, as well as working with a given interface to maximise its potential to shape the experience of the participant.

Example 3: Devices with the capacity to record, playback and mix live in combination with a present 'performer-technician'

The final synthesis is that of media present within a performance space, in combination with a present 'performer-technician' whose role is to activate that media to generate the event. This aligns with my intermedial practice as well as elements of work created by Katie Mitchell, Complicite and in live audiovisual pieces (see examples above). I argue that this work is disposed to create a different experience to the examples described above, specifically because of the role played by the performer, which is not just to use or perform with the media device or representation, but specifically to activate that media as part of the experience. In these contexts, and as an audience, we watch people not just make performance, but make the performance happen through live technical activation that may include tapping on a computer, adjusting the zoom on a camera, positioning props, filming live or mixing sound.

The construction of the intermedial space, rather than the results of that construction, or live play with a predetermined set of technological parameters becomes the focus, and there is a duality in play in terms of how we experience the performer's work. Similarly to both of the two examples above, the performer's presence emerges through their interactions with the present media in intermedial combinations. Also, like the examples above, the role of the performer is shifted because of the presence of the media in the space. However, in contrast to both examples above, the performer's role is not to perform with or indeed through the technology, but rather to activate that technology as a mode of performing. This requires a different skill set and also often results in different modes of presence on the part of the performer, where there may be a more focused, inward attention rather than a playing out of the performance to the audience. An audience may feel less attached to the action because of this – a little excluded, operating as an onlooker, searching for meaning and presence in the actions of the performer.

CONCLUSION

Each of these examples of intermedial combinations and the effects and affects generated indicate the shape of the experience that emerges from the positioning of the performer in relation to the technology and the audience or participant who witnesses or engages in it. As an intermedial performer, you may see yourself in many different manifestations and roles – as interlocutor, as mirror or double, as activator or technician, as a precise tool, an element in the mix, a voice in the conversation or a catalyst for action. You may feel very differently about your technological scene partners, whether that is a projected image, networked device, sound mixer or generative programme. Is this a partner, a window, a spur to action, an overpowering force, a tool, material to manipulate, or a mirror to your actions? Finally and crucially, what do you create together as an experience that is viewed, entered into or participated in by an audience member?

We are now, or certainly we should be, past the point where anxieties and debates centre on the performer in an intermedial environment as either diminished or undermined; on whether the screen or network is the dominant force in an experience, rather than the moving body. Intermediality, as a set of theoretical perspectives and practices, focuses our attention on the ways in which all elements of the event combine – how the 'doings' associated with each meet in the live performance moment and what that meeting generates as an experience.

As such, your focus as an intermedial performer must be on considering with care how specifically you want to be part of the events you create – what role you wish to play, the skills and actions associated with that and the experience that will emerge from those actions and interactions with technology.

This chapter began with an assertion that being a performer in an intermedial environment is different than performing without technology as a tool and partner in your process, and this difference is undoubtedly a very real and present part of your world as a performer in the twenty-first century. The skills outlined above – which are required to work effectively with and through technology in the events described – of responsiveness, flexibility, precision, patience, sensitivity, openness, relinquishing of the self, managing multiple demands concurrently, learning the capacity of a device through doing, managing an intimate encounter sensitively with a participant, and a range of technical know-how – are not necessarily part of current actor and performer training. In this case, then, how do you prepare for being part of this type of performance-making? It is my hope that there may well be some future work that can facilitate that specific training, whether through writing or practice. In the meantime, the practical ideas section below gives you some routes into the different modes of intermedial events outlined above and how you might start to practically explore performing in these contexts.

Practical ideas

Idea 1: Pictorial configurations

Take a series of still pictures. These could be images of people, 'still life' configurations of objects, or locations. Work with a collaborator, who can project these images in a workshop or performance space and experiment with how you can position yourself within the projection to create interesting and diverse effects. This may involve working to 'complete' the picture in some way, that is, as part of a group photo, but you can also play with more abstract effects of combining live body and image. Capture images of the intermedial configurations, and discuss the differing effects created and how these could be used.

Development: Work with moving images to discover a choreography of movement on the part of the live performer that can be aligned and timed with the projected image. Think about mirroring, disrupting, dovetailing with, completing and doubling the images through your positioning and actions.

Idea 2: Live feed, live filming

You will need a video camera with a connection to a projector for this practical activity – a long connecting lead between the projector and camera can help, as it allows the camera to be moved freely around the stage area. Working with another performer and a collaborator to act as an 'outside eye', devise a series of 'vignettes' that each individual can perform in turn – these could be short movement pieces, monologues or a sequence of actions. While one performer repeats their vignette, the other experiments with filming them live – zooming, panning, focusing and so forth – to create diverse images of the live stage action, which are simultaneously projected. The 'outside eye' documents, comments on and helps to shape the positioning of the camera and the choice of how to film each to create a range of effects. Also look at cross-cutting between the vignettes, so each performer is prompted to move fluidly between technical facilitation of another's performance work and performing their piece. Finally, pay attention to the positioning of the camera and image in the space, and think about how these elements can be part of the intermedial mix created.

Idea 3: Technological interactions

Choose a technological application that allows for real-time communication between a performer and participant, for example Snapchat, Whatsapp, Twitter, Facebook Direct Messenger. Devise a game that can happen in a real space – a park, series of rooms, area of a campus – and involves the participant or participants moving through that space. Think about:

- The aim of the game, for example to find other participants, hide, reach a particular location, find something (treasure hunt)
- The rules of the game, for example participants can only move when they receive a message
- The functioning of the technological application as part of the game
- The parameters of the game (physical and virtual)
- How you will find out if it works (user testing)

Experiment with how an 'invisible' performer can use the technological application to communicate and interact with the participants as part of the game, that is, giving instructions, sending visual/textual clues and so on, and consider how they perform through the interface and how this performance is part of the experience created.

Development: Turn the roles around so the game involves the participant activating the technological application, using the performers as 'avatars', as part of their game play. How does this change the performer's role and required actions? Which technological application suits this activity best?

Idea 4: Being Multiple

This activity prompts you as a performer to experiment with the condition of being made multiple through technological means and the implications of this for your performing practice. Firstly, identify a piece of performance work you know well – a monologue you have rehearsed or a set of movements/actions with which you are familiar. Work with two collaborators – one in the space with you and one who is witnessing your performance work through a webcam which is broadcasting the images to a remote location through Skype, Facetime or equivalent. Firstly, perform the piece entirely for your physically co-present audience. Next, experiment with how you can perform the same material 'to camera' for your remote audience member. Now work with how you can combine, juxtapose and play with these two modes so that they coexist or are both present in how you perform.

Development: Working with other collaborators, take an extended piece of text delivered by a character in a play or performance you know well, and distribute the performance of this text across different performers and technological applications: that is, one performer offers movements related to the character's feelings; another types the words of the text into a word document that is projected; another creates sound using an onstage mike; and another films and picks out elements of the multiple modes of performance to be projected in a separate image, or picks YouTube videos to accompany the action (a vision mixer is useful here to shift between the live feed and the Internet content). How can you play with the multiple performance of this singular text? What happens when different elements of the experience are separated and mediatised in this way? How can you shift the emphasis and experience through reconfiguring the separate elements in space and time? How might you devise performance for this distributed company, and what different skills and aptitudes would you have to develop and refine for this type of performance?

4 Time in Intermedial Theatre

Joanne Scott

You sit in an auditorium. A button somewhere above and behind you is pressed. Computational processes are activated, and animated video images appear on the screen onstage. This hand-drawn, carefully edited and structured set of images is fixed in time, but when it meets the actions of the performers, something happens. The choreography of the live piano score, in relation to the positioning of the performers and the movement of the images, forms an engaging conversation in and of time. As the prerecorded animated rain falls on the performer's umbrella, and as the same performer enacts a live conversation with an animated character, you have a present and bubbling sense of temporality, actively constructed and playfully enacted, through the very particular and precise combinations of live performance and animated images – through intermedial exchange.

INTRODUCTION

In this chapter, I open up ideas about time in intermedial performance practices, pointing to some key features of intermediality and how you can use these to generate productive and powerful temporal encounters in performance. These features and the use of intermedial tools open up a mass of temporal possibilities for a performance maker. As you will see in this chapter, in some intermedial performances, the time and 'timing' of a live act can be crystallised through the precise alignment and combination of the diverse elements in play, sharpening our experience of the present moment. On the other hand, intermedial performances also have the potential to displace, re-present, multiply and reconfigure time through employing shifting combinations of elements – sound, image, body, network, technological device – all of which have their own ways of representing time and all of which *happen* differently in the live moment. Finally, intermedial pieces often reveal the construction and curation of time as a key element of performance-making, offering it up to the viewer as a distinct feature of what and how we experience when we watch a piece of performance. As an intermedial performance maker, you can take your audience out of time, as experienced in an everyday sense, while simultaneously unsettling how that time happens. With a range of technologies at your disposal, or even just with a camera filming live onstage, you can also actively *play* with time as a fundamental feature of performance. In short, when you make intermedial theatre and performance,[1] time is not just a key element to consider, as it is in all performance-making, but it is also a crucial tool in generating feeling states and meanings for an audience, which they experience through and because of the mixing of media in a live space.

Keeping in mind those feelings and meanings that you might want to emerge, this chapter prompts you to consider how you can curate time in an intermedial performance, with all the temporal tools available to you. Firstly and fundamentally, there is the time that passes as the piece is performed; then there may be the time it takes for prerecorded video footage to play and how that is positioned in the passing time of the piece. What about doubling up the present moment through a live feed or combining that with prerecorded footage and sound? This does not even start to address the time it takes to make this type of work and the precise temporal choreography it requires to make a piece like 1927's *The Animals and Children Took to the Street* (2011) (evoked in the chapter opening above), where prerecorded animation is played out in perfect sync with the actions of the live performers and a live musical score. How you can employ intermedial tools to generate distinct temporal experiences, as 1927 and other intermedial makers do, is what this chapter aims to reveal.

Time and Performance

Of course, and as referenced above, time is significant in any performance event. Live performance is a time-based art form – it takes time for it to happen, unlike let's say, a painting, sculpture or photograph. As such, when theorists have addressed time in performance, they have often focused on the 'here and now' (Elam, 2002, p. 91) of its happening, of the encounter between the performer and the audience in a given, shared space (Fischer-Lichte, 2008; Phelan, 1993). This present moment of engagement is crucial to most live performance – you *have* to be there. Simultaneously, though, a performance is always in the process of evoking, depicting and representing other times, the passage of time or shifts/fissures in time. Think about a dramatic piece, which aims to tell a particular story and, in doing so, may deliberately be structured according to movement between different time periods, perhaps mirroring the memory of the protagonist. A durational performance, on the other hand, may emphasise time as slow moving, excruciatingly extended and difficult to experience. As David Ian Rabey describes it, in theatre 't]me may be presented, communicated, contemplated and transformed – condensed, stretched, subverted, displaced, and transposed' (2016, p. 3). As this comment suggests, a performance does not just take time to happen; to some extent, it is always *about* time and the experience of it. It is an element you always have to consider, when making theatre and performance, as the experience of time is a crucial part of performing and spectating.

Indeed, you could go further than this – every single individual engagement of performance and spectatorship generates its own distinct experience of time; a temporal manifestation which only happens to and between the performer, spectator and what is presented and represented. This is the case because we all experience time differently and because each performance, even of the same material, will inevitably have temporal variations, however slight. When you perform, how time passes – how you experience it as part of the act of performing – is also subject to variation, depending on how long you have been performing a particular role, the level of temporal play allowed for in the piece and the responses of those with whom you perform. My experiences, for instance of being an intermedial improvising performer, generating mixes of sound, image, text and object 'on the fly', are intensely temporal – from the endless extension of a prospective two-hour set, to the ravishing and breathtaking speed of a flowing section of improvisation, to the elongation of a layered and repeated intermedial moment that I want to endure forever . . .

As Anne Ubersfeld states, in theatre and performance, 'time must be situated in relation to a here and now which is the here and now of performance and also the spectator's present time', but also acknowledges that 'It is only through the mediation of performance signs that performed time can become duration, a feeling of time on the part of the spectators' (1999, p. 135). This feeling of time, as indicated above, is also crucial to the act of performing – duration, or temporality – and this is what is of interest in this chapter and to you, as a practitioner. David Couzens states that 'the term "time" can be used to refer to universal time, clock time, or objective time. In contrast, "temporality" is time insofar as it manifests itself in human existence' (Couzens, 2009, p. xv). It is this 'manifestation' of time which is significant in practical terms when making intermedial theatre and performance – not how long a performance takes, when measured in 'clock' time, but what experience of time is created and made manifest, specifically through intermedial modes of performance-making. It is here also that your intervention as an intermedial practitioner can be crucial because the choices as to structure, sequencing, pacing, pauses, rhythm and the 'timing' of actions are complicated by a whole other set of considerations. In intermedial performances, typically a range of different times and timings happen simultaneously through a variety of technological means. This could be as simple as a prerecorded projected image playing out behind the live performance of an actor, or as complex as a set of generative programmes which allow various events to happen or be triggered through movement or sound. Understanding *how* time happens in these mixes is crucial for the intermedial performance maker.

Intermediality in Performance

Following on from this consideration of intermedial mixes and as a brief aside to the central topic of time, this chapter aligns with Mark Crossley's perspective, expressed in the first chapter of this volume, that in writing about intermediality 'there is a need . . . to consider what may actually be meant' by this term, but also that it is 'essential to avoid a mere thesaurus on media and intermediality', as this is not helpful in a set of writings that focus on your engagement with practical ways of making performance. This is a topic I have thought about a good deal in relation to my own intermedial practice, specifically the definitions and concepts that best explain and reveal the workings of intermediality in that context. Here, I came to rest upon the term 'discourse' as one that in relation to all the media in play within an intermedial performance event – including digital technologies, images, sounds, devices, computer programmes and algorithms, objects and, of course, performers – 'encompasses a range of diverse interrelations' between these elements. Such interrelations include 'fusion, intersection, fragmentation, completion, as well as disruption, displacement and disjuncture' (Scott, 2016, p. 54), depending on how the media are combined as part of the performance event. This term also speaks of the 'conversation' between elements, which is always in process, through an intermedial performance, reconfiguring the functioning of all media in the mix. Nothing is fixed and immutable here – even a piece of prerecorded media, which is operated on cue – as the discourse between this piece of footage or sound and the other active elements of the piece – will affect how we read, understand and experience its playback.

Time in Intermedial Performance

As such, and returning to the topic of this chapter, what is at stake is what changes in the manifestation and experience of time when a range of media (armed with their own particular temporal logics) are brought into conversation in performance. How does this encounter reconfigure how time is made and experienced by an audience? As referenced above, I believe that a performance engaged in the mixing of live acts with and through mediatised functions, devices and happenings can sharpen, unsettle and reconfigure our experience of the passage of time. My most present feelings of joy and satisfaction in watching and making live work have been formed at the intersection of a series of elements aligned in a moment, forcing me into a presentness and consideration of that moment that had not been possible prior to this alignment. Equally, I have been unsettled and unseated in my everyday temporality through pieces like Complicité/Simon McBurney's *The Encounter* (addressed in more detail later in the chapter), where the technological dance that happened before me, and within my head through the headphones I was given, brought me into a vertiginous relationship with a deep and elemental sense of time while also grounding my presence in the moment of performance. Intermedial relations allow you to play with time, certainly. They also prompt a consideration of time as curated, controlled and wrestled into submission by the performance makers, using the tools available to them. The fact that the intermedial maker's armoury includes a range of machinic and digital temporalities opens up the possibilities both for immersing an audience in a complex temporal experience and presenting to them a sharp and crisp moment of presence and the present through the particular alignment of these processes and biological/technological events.

In order to ground some of these fairly visceral experiences and hunches that I have about this type of performance-making, in this chapter I firstly consider how the technologies employed within intermedial spaces intersect with time as a fundamental property of performance and how this might affect how you work intermedially as a maker and performer. Some key ideas related to temporality in contemporary intermedial work are put in play; for instance, we consider the notion of digital temporality and how that intersects with the present moment and human presence in intermedial performance. We then move on to consider Elleström's 'modalities of media' (2010), which you will be familiar with from the first chapter. In this context, Elleström's fastidious deconstruction of the functioning of different types of media will help you to understand how time is represented in intermedial work, where these media are mixed – a crucial element when making and thinking about this area of performance practice. These ideas are developed and tested out through placing them in conversation with two intermedial performances I have experienced, where very particular experiences of time were generated, specifically because of the use of media and how they functioned in and in relation to the live act of performance – *The Encounter* by Complicité and Simon McBurney, which I experienced in the Theatre 1 at HOME, Manchester, in March 2016, and *Birdie* by Agrupación Señor Serrano, which I saw in Theatre 2, also at HOME in April 2017.

The Encounter is a solo performance, directed and performed by Simon McBurney, which tells the story of National Geographic photographer Loren McIntyre's 1969 'encounter' with the Mayoruna tribe when he becomes lost in the remote Javari Valley in the Amazon rainforest. With the use of various sound and image technologies, including onstage microphones with modifications applied, loop pedals, a phone, an MP3 player and a binaural head,[2] McBurney constructs the world of the story and its characters while also offering various commentaries on its main themes through recordings of interviews he has conducted in the process of making the work. Throughout nearly all the piece, audience members wear headphones through which they hear all aspects of the performance and which allow the sonic elements to manifest binaurally, making us feel like the sounds are happening in and around our heads.

Birdie is described by Agrupación Señor Serrano as 'a multimedia[3] performance with live video, objects, Hitchcock's "The Birds" revisited, scale models, 2000 mini animals, wars, smugglers, a massive migration and three performers handling this messy world' (Señor Serrano, n.d.). The piece addresses the current migration crisis through the lens of a single image, depicting migrants climbing over a razor wire fence in North Africa while golfers in the Spanish enclave of Melilla play a serene game on the pristine greens below. Working from this image, the performers in the piece use two live video feeds, prerecorded footage and a range of sound, all mixed live, to address and evoke themes of movement and immigration through the flight and perspective of migrating birds.

The two pieces that I have chosen to analyse in detail each have a very particular approach to the curation of intermedial time in performance. This is also true of the other intermedial performances, which are referenced in the opening sections, in order to ground the theoretical discussion. As such, I am not suggesting in the least that they 'stand for' or represent intermedial performance-making in its totality. Rather, they provide us with productive examples with which we can grapple; crucibles within which we can start to form features of temporality as made in these contexts. It is also through the process of considering these particular performances in relation to time that strands and threads of making intermedially emerge, informing the final practical ideas section of the chapter. However, before any of that, in this first section we interrogate time and technology in a little more detail, as such ideas are crucial in our understanding of how intermedially constructed temporality works in practice.

TIME AND TECHNOLOGY

Our contemporary world is fast and getting faster, due in no small part to technological developments. From the ability to travel from one continent to another in a matter of a few hours, to the lightening quick speed of the Google search you might habitually use to access information, things are quicker now ... or are they? In reality, this speeding up only applies to those who have access to the resources referenced and the economic capacity to use them. However, in the late or arguably, post-capitalist[4] world, many of us feel, rightly or wrongly, that time manifests differently; that our experience of the world can be giddyingly quick. Indeed, this perception has become so ingrained in recent years that it has resulted in cultural backlashes such as the 'slow movement' (Honoré, 2010), which is challenging the 'cult of speed' through 'making room for slowness'.

In terms of the role technological advancements play in this sense of a world moving fast, Timothy Barker talks of 'developments in the speed of technological processes, such as the horse and cart, the jet engine, the telephone, telegraph and new communications technology [that] have resulted in a "time-space compression," experientially shrinking the globe' (2012, p. 2). N. Katherine Hayles also addresses how technological advancement has fundamentally shifted our experience of time, arguing that 'film directors accept as common wisdom that the time it takes for an audience to absorb and process an image has decreased dramatically as jump cuts, flashing images, and increased paces of image projection have conditioned audiences to recognize and respond to images faster than was previously the case' (2012, p. 97). Hayles argues that, far from being a hindrance, this kind of 'hyper attention' or ability to take in, manage and process images and information quickly, 'makes young people better suited to live in the information-intensive environments that are becoming ever more pervasive' (p. 99).

Of course, this mode of attention has implications for the theatre, which, in its elongated and unedited consideration of a present moment, has a different relationship with time. As Rabey points out, theatre 'demands a designated duration of (various degrees of) sustained focused attention ... It does not permit the audience member to select briefer opportunities for attention, as we may when reading a novel or "working our way" (as the colloquial phrase goes) through a DVD box set' (2016, p. 18). Equally, in making theatre and performance, you are engaging in the passage of time as it happens, as opposed to the editing, reordering and compiling of moments of time that is the domain of the film-maker. In relation to this, Rabey comments:

> Time in theatre is not reversible, as is the running of a film (which when played in reverse mode, can make a throw appear a catch, or poured water flow upwards). Theatre actors may *simulate* performing an action 'in reverse' (for example, walking backwards off a stage after they have walked on to it), but they and their actions will be different on some muscular and molecular levels. (2016, p. 44)

In contemporary intermedial performance, both the reversing of the film footage and the very different 'reversing' of an actor are processes that may be simultaneously happening. Often a range of different elements, images and manifestations are present as part of the mise en scène, some of which will have been subject to the sort of technical temporal manipulation described above. As such, intermedial modes of live performance can be seen as an appropriate response to the condition of hyper-attention Hayles describes, a way of making live performance suitable for the hyper-quick digital age. However, this historical positioning does not work as neatly as that – technological applications in theatre are not new. and the notion of intermediality is also far from novel.[5] In addition, speeding up the action and multiplying the possible foci of attention in the live space, in order to mirror our hybrid world of 'second-screening',[6] pervasive computing and insistent interactivity, is not the only way in which live performance, and intermedial work in particular, responds to these conditions.

Indeed, the mixing of media in performance can be a way of highlighting and drawing attention to the singularity of the live moment – a moment of making, happening with and for the present audience – which makes the temporal experience of performance so different to fixed media works and forms. Intermedial performance, by its very nature, has the capacity to question the mores of the temporal technological world through positioning some of those functions, processes and devices in a performance space where they are laid bare and considered in a different, refreshed way. An example of this is in The Wooster Group and the Royal Shakespeare Company's (RSC) much maligned production of *Troilus and Cressida* (2012), where strange and unsettling moments of intermedial performance (created by the Wooster Group) intersected with a more classical treatment of the text on the part of the RSC actors. In the intermedial moments, technology was employed that was almost anachronistic in nature – small, boxy televisions, whose representation of Inuit, Native American and Midwestern American farmers' lives intersected in a quite bizarre manner with the actions of the performers as they spoke the Shakespearean text. Here, we were asked to examine the intersection between the televisual image and the live performance act at length – not shifting restlessly between a variety of sensory inputs, but reflecting on an elongated temporal exchange between the two. These sections felt anything but fast, and my attention to them some way from what Hayles describes as 'hyper'. They prompted a heightened consideration of the films playing out in the space of the performance, specifically because the performers, at moments, mirrored the action there. This strange intersection of divided and diverse worlds, of cultural markers in opposition and fundamentally in modes of temporality happening in unusual relationships, created an extremely uneasy feeling, which many of the audience present clearly found dull and difficult, leading some to describe this as 'a bizarrely disjointed spectacle' (Billington in Mancewicz, 2014, p. 66).[7]

This raises a few points that you may want to consider as an intermedial maker. Firstly, what effect does the choice of technology you employ have on how your audience or participants experience time? Secondly, how is the temporality of the piece affected by *how* you combine the live and mediatised elements? Thirdly, what relationships might you highlight between different types of temporality on the intermedial stage, and what types of meanings might this make? To help develop some understanding of what is at play here, when you place 'new'[8] technologies into active conversations with the actions of the live performer, following are some thoughts about digital temporalities in particular, as digital technology is a significant marker or our age, as well as one of the key tools employed by intermedial practitioners. As such, some understanding of how digital temporalities manifest and operate can be useful for you as you engage in the act of making intermedial work.

Digital Temporalities

Mark Hansen states that our contemporary experience of time 'has changed in the wake of the digital computational revolution' (2009, p. 295) because of the 'extensive work of temporalizing that is currently carried out by technical artefacts'. He goes on to say that we are in 'a new kind of temporal reality' in which 'human beings temporalize in conjunction with and on the basis of largely autonomous technical inscriptions of time by computational machines'

(p. 298). This is probably a fairly familiar notion. The ubiquity of computational processes in our daily lives, through mobile and wearable technology and the 'Internet of things',[9] is definitive and constitutive of contemporary temporality – the Facebook timeline, measurement of steps taken in a day on a Fitbit, temporally defined route planning on Google maps (45 mins to get to Piccadilly Station, 3 minutes slower if you take a different route), or the 0.58 seconds it takes to bring up 825,000 search results on Google. Our experience of time has become entwined with such processes, though Hansen also points out that these types of interactions with digital technology 'generate technical processes which remain dissociated from, and ungraspable by, the experiences they inform and make possible' (p. 310). As such, though we may be very familiar with the interfaces and interactions these experiences prompt, we are largely ignorant of the processes underlying them. If you asked me what my digital computer is actually doing and at what speed, as I type these words, I would probably look at you quite blankly,

Timothy Barker takes up Hansen's theme in his discussion of 'digital temporalities'. Barker claims that 'digital processes and relationships may produce new experiences of temporality and concepts of time' (2012, p. 6) and specifically that 'when we interact with digital technology, we interact across multiple temporal rhythms'. Barker goes on to argue that in networked digital interactions, 'the time of the user meshes with the time of the software, the non-sequential time of the database, the time of the network and the time of other users' (p. 14). This is a particularly interesting concept to put in play when considering time in intermedial work, which often employs, as an aesthetic strategy and function of its making, human interactions with digital technological applications and interfaces. According to Barker, this means that what we experience, either consciously or not, is the melding of different temporalities – different 'manifestations of time' – through the distinct biological and digital processes that intersect in the performance.

Mark Hansen also refers to this distinction, addressing the 'lived affective temporality of human experience and the "intensive" time of machine processing', particularly in terms of the speed of the latter in digital technologies, which renders the processing 'literally speaking, "beyond experience"' (2004, p. 235). For most of us, as referenced above, this processing sits underneath our interactions with technology and beneath our consciousness, only coming to the fore in moments of rupture or disjuncture – when you are confronted with a screen of indecipherable letters and numbers on the crashing of a computer programme for instance. If this is the case, then perhaps it is the same when making or experiencing performance, employing these processes: they are not part of our conscious temporal experience of the event. However, sometimes you will encounter intermedial performance work that deliberately plays with and reveals these distinctions, showing us clearly how our 'lived affective temporality' either differs from and/or is affected by machinic processing. Troika Ranch's 2009 piece *loopdiver* explored the concept of loops as a 'structure pervasive in culture since the popularization of the computer'. Within the performance itself, 'we see the performers in a constant struggle to adapt to an externally imposed machine rhythm' (Troika Ranch, n.d.) while the digital materials loop and repeat perfectly. This practical playing out of the distinct temporal processes, indicated by Hansen and Barker above, reveals the capacity of intermedial performance to disrupt our everyday understandings and experiences of digital and technological temporalities. Even when these temporal disparities are not highlighted as part of the content and form of the piece, time does manifest differently when machinic processing is part of how we directly experience it. This is true of any machine, digital or not, but temporality is particularly shifted because of the sheer speed of digital processing and how this intersects with our much slower and more elongated 'lived affective temporality'.

The vast majority of contemporary performances use digital technologies in one way or another, and as such, this speedy digital processing is always part of how they are made, but intermedial theatre and performance is distinct in its more active consideration and implementation of such technologies in the construction and conception of the work, weaving its processing with that of the performer. This is also for me what is exciting about watching an intermedial performance like *loopdiver* – seeing these distinct temporalities acknowledged, shared, manipulated and at play, so that our experience of the 'here and now' shifts actively in response.

TIME AS A MODALITY OF MEDIA

A different approach to the question of time and technology is adopted by Lars Elleström in his detailed consideration of the 'modalities of media'. Elleström concerns himself less with the speed of internal technological processing. Rather, his focus is on temporal representation in different forms of media and how this affects our experience of them. Through examining the various modalities identified, of which time is one, Elleström draws our attention to how different types of media – video images, sound, objects, a live performer – work to create a range of impacts upon us, offering a framework for understanding what is happening to our temporal experience in an intermedial context, where different representations of time are in an active conversation.

In his discussion of time as a modality of media, Elleström firstly focuses on the notion of 'sequentiality' as fixed or fluid, essentially paying attention to whether temporal progression in a particular medium is subject to some shift or whether it is 'fixed' in nature. He explains:

> Motion pictures and recorded music . . . have fixed sequentiality. Hypertexts and much music accompanying computer games can be said to have partially fixed sequentiality. Mobile sculptures, truly improvised music and a performance broadcast live on television have (at least potentially) non-fixed sequentiality. (2010, p. 19)

Elleström is focusing here on the extent to which a particular medium's sequentiality is 'fixed', meaning it will always play out its represented content in the same order and timing (a film for instance) or 'non-fixed', meaning that the order and timing is subject to change as it plays out (an improvised performance for instance). This is significant because we experience media with fixed sequentiality differently to those that are not fixed – the latter can change with and in time, as we experience it, whereas the former is 'fixed' in time.

According to Elleström's theories, in intermedial performance we have a range of different 'sequentialities' in play (as identified in Chapter 1), from recorded media which is 'fixed', to the 'partially fixed' nature of a rehearsed live performance, to the 'non-fixed' nature of any improvised work. Often, intermedial theatre and performance will deliberately play with the dissonances created by prompting these different temporal modes to meet in performance. For instance, in *The Encounter*, Simon McBurney deliberately activates layers of 'fixed' sound recordings, through his 'partially fixed' live performance actions, so that the fixed sound recording takes on a different temporal character – you could say that it is unfixed or temporally set loose through its live activation. Of course, it is not actually the case that the pre-recorded sound loses its quality of fixity – it still cannot play out in any other way than that imprinted when it was recorded. However, through McBurney's live activation and modulation of that sound, we do experience its temporality differently – it becomes live or, as I characterise it, 'lively' (Scott, 2016, p. 94) in its effect and representation of time now and time past, of a machinic process of recording and marking time and its live temporal manifestation in the now of performance. Here, time becomes a hybrid set of happenings, and temporality is generated, which is affectively reconfigured by the nature of these combinations – we *feel* the recordings differently because of their activation in the live space. As I argue below, McBurney, the intermedial performer and maker, is very much aware of how time is at play in this piece, and he deliberately directs our experience of it through manipulation not just of different eras and schemes of time, which are part of the story he tells, but also through how these are temporally represented through combinations of media as part of the live performance.

Elleström goes on to reference other aspects of time as it manifests and is represented through distinct media. He states that 'some media have corporeal interfaces that are simply not temporal. Yet, it is important to note that all media are obviously realized in time: all perception and interpretation of media and what they mediate are necessarily inscribed in time' (2010, p. 20). To expand on and exemplify the point here, he uses the example of a photograph as a 'corporeal interface' which is not temporal in nature, in contrast to a dance performance, where, if you close your eyes for a minute, unlike when looking at the photograph, you will miss a section of the piece as it unfolds in time (p. 21). Similarly to theatre, performance, live music, live and performance art, dance is a time-based art form, which takes time to happen and where the treatment, manifestation and representation of time, through the movement of the dancers, is fundamental to how we experience it. However, as Elleström acknowledges in the final section of the quote above, even a photograph, which does not appreciably progress and shift through time, unfolding as a dance performance does, is still 'realized in time' and therefore, through how it is positioned in the context of a live performance for instance, is subject to and part of our temporal experience of that moment.

Again, in intermedial work the employment of media that do not progress temporally in their 'corporeal form' can be a deliberate site of play and invention – I'm thinking specifically of live animation[10] here, where objects are made to move in time according to their manipulation by an animator and the live filming of this temporal manipulation. Here, there is a deliberate play with the temporal capacity of the video image, and the performance itself, to move and progress, which intersects with the fixed temporality of the object in play. Such techniques were a central part of *Birdie*, where the movement of the camera, filming live in the performance space, was used as way of animating and 'unfixing' a range of objects or 'corporeal interfaces', lending them a sense of movement and progression in time (see analysis below). A lot of this type of performance is hugely enjoyable to watch, exactly because we see, experience and appreciate the play with time that this represents, and we engage not just with the result of that play but also the temporal act of its creation; work like this always results in a frisson of pleasure on my part, as I am both delighted by the effect and happily complicit in its construction.

Time in Intermedial Theatre 103

A final point about time as a modality of media made by Elleström relates to what he calls virtual space and time: 'virtual space and virtual time can be said to be manifest in the perception and interpretation of a medium when what is taken to be the *represented* spatiotemporal state is not the same as the spatiotemporal state of the *representing* material modality' (2010, p. 21). This point relates to media where the material media object itself is temporal in a way which is different from what it represents. An example would be the televisions used by the Wooster Group in their performance of *Troilus and Cressida*, which in their material state – glass, plastic, aluminium and so on – do not shift in the time of the performance, whereas the images of the film clearly do. In some ways, through Elleström's modalities, a television set is always engaged in a representation of virtual time – there is a disconnect between the corporeal interface and what it represents. This is particularly interesting, without even considering the cultural connotations of the screens and how these have been insistently used in previous Wooster Group work, as this virtual time, 'fixed' in sequentiality, is set against the 'real time' of the actors' performance, with all of this existing *in* time and subject to our perception *of* time passing. This is only further complicated in this piece by the fact that the 'partially fixed' sequentiality of the live performers' actions is a deliberate imitation of the 'fixed' and 'virtual time' of the televisual images.

Within the first chapter, Elleström outlines a development in his thinking around virtual space and time, which adds another layer here. He specifically addresses what he feels was an omission in this initial analysis, namely 'virtual materialities and virtual sensory perceptions' and how we, as the receiver of the 'sense-data' of a medium, construct virtual space, time and materiality beyond what we see represented (see examples in Chapter 1). In this sense, the film footage employed by the Wooster Group, through its depiction of everyday life in remote regions, offers an expansive sense of space and time. This extends beyond the images shown and complicates further our reading of the actors' performance as they mimic actions originating from that spatio-temporal realm, dislocating and isolating them in the now of performance. This temporal disjuncture, interruption and complication, formed at the intersection of the actors' performance and the virtual expansion of the worlds depicted through the filmed images, is at the heart of what I found so mesmeric about the piece and, equally, what others clearly found so off-putting.

There is a deliberate complexity in the above description of what seems like a fairly simple temporal set-up. Elleström, through breaking down media into 'modalities' as he does, forces us to pay attention to the detail of how they function and intersect in live performance, and uncovers some of the ways in which media impact temporally upon the live act of performance. As such, they represent a useful set of prompts and starting points for you as a practitioner interested in the way that temporality can be in play in your intermedial performance-making. As Elleström suggests, when thinking about which media to employ and how, you might consider how time is enacted and represented through the medium, in what ways the material interface of the media we see intersects with the temporality of what it represents, while bearing in mind that which Ellesträm calls 'perceptual time' is always present in our experience of what we see (p. 36).

PERFORMING INTERMEDIAL TEMPORALITIES: *THE ENCOUNTER* AND *BIRDIE*

So far, we have considered broader notions of time and temporality in performance, some issues that relate specifically to digital temporalities and a set of tools, proposed by Ellesträm, to help us to read and understand how different types of media create distinct temporal representations and experiences. In this next section, I want to bring into play how a live performer in an intermedial piece might temporally intersect with the 'machinic temporalities' referenced above, and the effect and affect of this particular intersection, through consideration of the two pieces of intermedial performance introduced at the beginning of the chapter. As evidenced below, even prerecorded or fixed elements of media are 'unfixed' in the temporal space of live performance, creating a set of shifting hybrid temporalities, crucial to our experience of intermedial work. The witnessing and unpicking of what happens in such work is a way of allowing you into the ways in which you might adopt or adapt similar tools and approaches in your performance-making.

Complicité/Simon McBurney's *The Encounter*: Playing with Intermedial Temporalities

The Encounter (2016b) is a piece of intermedial theatre about time[11] – time is the primary subject matter, but also the manipulation of time is a key tool in the presentation of the source material, *Amazon Beaming* by Petru Popescu, which depicts traveller and photographer Loren McIntyre's 'encounter' with the Mayoruna tribe of the Amazon in 1969. The elemental 'deep time' of the universe is evoked by the chief of the tribe, named 'Barnacle' by McIntyre, and his exhortation that the Mayoruna must return to the 'beginning', rather than remaining anchored to the present moment through the trappings of material goods.

The term 'deep time' was coined by John McPhee in order to 'distinguish geological time from the scale of time that governs our everyday lives' (in Gee, 2001, p. 2). Henry Gee explains that 'McPhee meant the term to refer to the immense intervals, measured in millions of years . . . too long to be readily comprehensible to minds used to thinking in terms of days, weeks and years – decades, at most' (2001, p. 2). It is this deep and unfathomable sense of time that is evoked by Barnacle's words and actions, the tribe's burning of their material possessions and their dogged movement through the forest and away from their temporally bound existence in a world being eaten up by global companies prospecting for oil, towards a primeval, prehistory. It is also that sense of deep time which McBurney plays with throughout the piece, deliberately drawing it into the now by activating the layers of time present in the story through the use of onstage technologies.

A number of layers, or 'encounters', are bound in time but brought into the present through McBurney's intermedial practice. They include the moment of the encounter between McIntyre and the Mayoruna; the moment Popescu learned and wrote about that encounter; McBurney's own encounter with Popescu's text; recordings of encounters with experts who offer their thoughts on various emergent themes, including consciousness, time, fossil fuels, nature and ecology; as well as the poignant appearance of McBurney's daughter, Noma, as she interrupts him in his making, fixed in time as her five-year-old self. Finally and most presently, there is the now of our encounter with the performance of the story, which McBurney generates through mixes of live and prerecorded sound, using his phone, a speaker, microphones with various effects enabled and the ever-present binaural head. There are also external sound effects, activated by a technical team in response to the live performance and Foley sounds created live by McBurney and then looped. We, as the audience, encounter all of this through binaural sound, which we receive through individual headphones, allowing for a visceral sonic experience to take place between the stage action and the sound, happening seemingly in and around our heads.

An example of this is when 'the actor', as McBurney's persona is described when he is not playing Loren McIntyre or any other character, uses phone recordings of his previous encounter with Petru Popescu, describing his own 'encounter' with Loren McIntyre. This recording is activated live and the sound fed into the microphones of the binaural head. In this present moment, Popescu's meeting with McIntyre is layered with McBurney's meeting with Popescu, recorded and fixed in time and then played back, in such a way that the voice feels present not just in space but within our heads, similar to the 'old language' Barnacle uses when speaking to McIntyre, where the words manifest within him without being spoken. The intermedial manipulation of time here is both playful and vertiginous,[12] evoking a depth of meaning and sense of time which is made present because of the conditions of its activation, presentation and reception; because of the layers of time that are brought into the present and into the individual hearing space of each audience member.

This play with temporality reverberates through the contemporary digital technology of the smartphone, wireless speaker and binaural head into the 'deep time' and prehistory evoked by the story itself and the wilds of the Amazon forest, which feels simultaneously beyond what we can imagine while also viscerally present through the rustling of tape, the crushing of plastic and sloshing of water. There is intermedial magic created in the piece – a cast of characters brought to life through sound, another place placed here, but also, crucially, a sense of deliberate temporal disjuncture as these distinct moments, recordings and imprints are strung together.

An example of this intermedial 'unhinging' of time is an interplay between McBurney speaking live and a recording of his voice brought into conversation:

LIVE.	My voice over there is a recording; he doesn't exist.
RECORDING.	*What do you mean I don't exist?*
LIVE.	You're not real.
RECORDING.	*Well, of course I'm real.*
LIVE.	He's a recording from the past.
RECORDING.	*No. I'm in the present and you're in the future!*
LIVE.	No, you're in the past and I'm in the present.

(Complicité/McBurney, 2016a, p. 10)

McBurney then goes on to describe and recreate the place where the voice we hear was recorded:

> This was recorded six months ago in my flat.
> Over here is my desk. And here is a window . . .
> *Opens the window and the sound of the street comes rushing in.*
> *Closes the window.*
> That was the street outside my flat in London. And there's a sink here. I'll just go and wash my hands
> SFX: *water running.*

(p. 11)

In these moments, the present activation of prerecorded sound alerts our attention to the imprint of the recorded voice – the moment in time it represents – and how that rushes into the present when it is activated. In my experience, this is a recurrent feature of intermedial performance – to enliven the technologically recorded past and play with its existence in the present. Equally, the 'sound effect' of the street, often a supporting or subordinate element in theatre and performance practice, asserts its presence, offering a heightened awareness of how it functions to construct time and place for us. This playful revealing of technological temporal construction is another feature of contemporary intermedial performance, drawing us into a closer and more complicit relationship with the ways in which the materials and content are being manipulated.

Intermediality is crucial to the effects and meanings inherent in *The Encounter*. It is through the employment of cutting edge technology and simple Foley techniques in combination – positioning the live, modulated, shifting and prerecorded in carefully choreographed combinations – that our sense of time as active, present and at the forefront of the meaning of this work, is created. The capacity for the digital devices employed to store the data of the moments of the making of this piece and reveal the temporal progression of ideas that then are played out in front of us is primary to this experience. However, it is not just the capacity of the technologies to activate and shift moments of time past in the present that is in play here: it is the time and timing of the performer. This temporal construction is not just about the meaning and effect inherent in these elements being combined – it is about the act of combination and the time taken to perform these actions and to experience them. Our temporal encounter in the present with McBurney's time-stretching, bending, twisting piece makes it distinct as intermedial performance practice.

Agrupación Señor Serrano's *Birdie*: Exploring the Timeliness of 'Real Time'

A contrasting piece of intermedial performance, created in 2016 by Barcelona-based company Agrupación Señor Serrano and titled *Birdie*, involved one performer mixing video and sound, using onstage laptops, while the other two manipulated video cameras, filming live a set of static objects onstage, which included a surreal sweep of miniature plastic animals and buildings arrayed across a green baize flooring (more of which is discussed later) (Figure 4.1).

In combination, the performers' actions constructed a layered and shifting set of images, projected on a large back screen, as well as sonic environments and states, through the filming of the objects onstage, mixed with sound effects and music and interspersed with prerecorded footage, mainly from Hitchcock's *The Birds*. The piece addressed contemporary migration by asking us to consider

Figure 4.1 Miniature animals and buildings arranged on the green baize floor in Agrupación Señor Serrano's *Birdie* (2016). Photographer: Roger Costa.

a snapshot of our current times – a picture of migrants climbing a huge razor wire fence and hanging precariously on its top while, below them, golfers drove balls on the greens of a course in the Spanish enclave of Melilla, North Africa. The actual picture was taken by the migrant rights activist José Palazon in October 2014, and through the prism of this moment, ideas, narratives and temporal states related to movement, flight and migration emerge and are remixed through the live action of the performers precisely manipulating the video cameras' framing of objects onstage.

This 'real time' of the live footage captured by the onstage cameras is a continuous elongated present in the piece, always re-engaging our attention with the detail of the tiny objects on set that we could never see from the auditorium. The careful and precise timing of the cameras filming the set tells the story of the morning the picture was taken, recreates the picture itself through a mini box set onstage and finally, through sweeping across the plastic figures and objects, takes us from the primordial soup through the discovery of jewels and oil, from early settlements to refugee camps and finally to the present moment. The petrified plastic figures, fixed in time, come alive through the movement of the camera, so that we see suffering and progression in the most banal formulations of animal and environment. Through the scattering of icing sugar and spraying of water on these objects, in combination with the panning of the camera, we pass with ease through geological eras and eons of time.

Unlike *The Encounter*, where we are prompted to stand on the edge of a temporal precipice through the intermedial interactions and contemplate our miniscule existence in relation to 'deep time', in *Birdie* we pass over the endless flow of humanity and life, always moving but only grazing its surface, without lingering on any one era, but rather, through the camera's gaze, adopting an almost indifferent perspective of all that is below, represented through tiny, immobile plastic forms. As the company say in their notes about the migrant crisis that prompted the piece, 'We flee from the here and now and the rush of the news . . . and we started to think on a different approach, something less direct, less filled with anger, shame and fear, and more with humanity' (Señor Serrano, n.d.). Time and timing – specifically, time as constructed intermedially – is crucial to this more measured, expansive and critical response to the emotive and charged subject matter.

So how does the group achieve this? In what ways are intermedial approaches harnessed in order to manage our temporal experience? Firstly, there is the 'timing' of the movement of the camera, referenced above, combined with the poise, precision and focus of the performers as they film. This is analogous to McBurney's choreography of sound as he moves between devices, to create and loop live, and which we then experience as a totality of mixed sound through our individual headphones. In the case of *Birdie*, an unsettling duality is created through the simultaneous construction and presentation of the screened images, mirroring the juxtaposition of the plastic toys and their fate, the migrant up high on the fence and the golfer down below. The piece gently but precisely draws these elements together through the dual temporality of the passage of time on the stage, occupied by the performers interacting with technology, and the screened results of their actions.

Alongside the passage of time on Earth and the endless flow of migration and movement, there are also more challenging representations of time glitching and grinding against itself, through repeated clips from *The Birds*, which appear sometimes within and occasionally on top of the live images. Here, we are lifted into a different temporal state as images and sounds that are culturally familiar and arguably iconic – Tippi Hedren smoking in front of the climbing frame, the sound of the children's singing in the school as the birds gather on the frame behind her and the fleeing of Hedren and the children from the birds as they attack – replay in short, uncomfortable bursts, representing a captured, truncated and tortured sense of time which sits uneasily next to the flow of the live-feed camera across the stage.

110   *Intermedial Theatre*

In contrast, the passage of time is represented simply in another moment through the live filming of a newspaper's pages being turned and then changed, as photos are physically placed on the pages. In combination with a lively soundtrack, this activity succeeds both in giving the sense that a prerecorded montage might of the passage of time, while also prompting us to linger on the changes described, specifically because of the materiality of the human interaction with the objects. This combines with the technological capacity of the live feed to create an uneasy, sharpened sense of time as present and passing. These intermedial actions, calmly describing the progression of the migrant crisis and its representation in the news, do remove us somewhat from the immediate temporal lurches of those moments to hover above, birdlike; but conversely the actions of the performers, in bringing this reality into being in front of us, also construct a gentle and simultaneous interrogation of the events described.

The careless brutality of time passing is certainly brought to the fore in this mix. The birdlike floating over the suffering beneath us places us in a critical relationship with the crisis – we are removed, through the camera, the construction and the toys onstage, from the immediacy of actual events. In a similar way, the composition of the photograph of the migrants and the golf course is deconstructed through a video mix of live writing/drawing on the filmed image of the box set, pulling us away from the immediacy of the disparity between Melilla and the migrants, the golf course and the fence, and forcing us into a more banal consideration of perspective, foreground, background and other aesthetic aspects of the image's construction. However, there is also something about these intermedial combinations which actively points to the construction of the representations of the present crisis while positioning these events, as *The Encounter* also does, in the context of a much larger view of migration over vast expanses of time.

Time is both compressed and expanded through the elements in combination here. Through the precise positioning of the live-feed cameras in relation to the myriad of diverse objects present, moments are framed and captured, pulled from the melee into a distinct live formulation and distillation of the bewildering possibilities of the set in front of us. Equally, through the ceaseless movement of the camera through the space, we pass through time – the time that measures our existence on the planet. These intermedial actions bring the live moment into focus while using that technologically enabled now to represent the passage of time, from the beginning of life on earth to the present day (Figure 4.2).

In both pieces, there is thoughtful consideration of how the combination and construction of elements in each moment can create sets of complex and sometimes contradictory meanings and feelings. As referenced in the introduction,

Figure 4.2 A performer filming the tiny elements of Agrupación Señor Serrano's *Birdie* set live (2016), with the footage projected behind him. Performer: Àlex Serrano. Photographer: Pasqual Gorriz.

the pieces exemplify the capacity of intermedial work to bring us into a sharpened and strikingly constructed present while also layering, multiplying, leading and pulling us into other temporal states through evoking the expanse of time and its ceaseless movement. There is a playfulness with machinic temporality – the capturing and imprinting of time through technology – which is then released into and complicated through its playing out in the present. This ability to play and to loop, to replay and rewind, to record and form and layer and overlay, all through present actions in performance, makes time in intermedial performance a crucial tool for the maker – something which, as explored above, can prompt distinct and powerful experiences, meanings and feelings because of the ways in which intermedial actions intersect with the content they activate.

EMERGENT THOUGHTS AND IDEAS

At the end of this chapter, then, we are left with some threads, ideas and possibilities for you as an intermedial practitioner. Following, I sum up some of the thoughts that have emerged for me in considering this topic, before offering a set of practical ideas and prompts for making, designed to help you to explore the possibilities of intermedial temporalities in your performance-making.

Firstly, it is important to say that, despite its capacity to create multiple layers of space and time through live and recording technologies, intermediality in theatre and performance is not just about generating complexity. As the examples in this chapter prove, you can use combinations of media and the actions of a performer to create a sharp and defined singular experience of a present moment, or to play out an elongated relationship between elements over time, for your audience to experience and consider. Intermedial practices are also particularly well suited to playing with time – both being playful with different types of temporality generated through technological means and putting time into play through layers and combinations of these temporalities. Intermediality in theatre and performance can reveal and highlight the differing temporal processes of the machinic tools employed through their positioning in the rarefied performance now, but it can also use technological processes to draw our attention to that now – zooming us in on that moment so that it plays out in a distinct and sharp way, and we notice it more and feel it differently.

Equally, intermedial performance, through its different representations of time in combination, is able to address time thematically through this playful mix in the present – through a balancing act of the now and various other nows – which helps us to feel the present in a renewed and refreshed way. In my opinion, 'nowness' is particularly crucial to intermedial practice because it is the temporal progression and 'partially fixed' nature of the performance moment that reconfigures the other temporal 'logics' of the technologies employed; they are liberated and we feel their temporality differently because of their activation in the present moment.

This is somewhat different from Chiel Kattenbelt's 'hypermedium' theory, referenced by Mark Crossley in the first chapter, where the TV footage, projected image and recorded sound are housed within the medium of performance. According to this theoretical framework, the media are held within the 'host' hypermedium of the performance, which 'stages' their activity (Chapple and Kattenbelt, 2006, p. 20), without significantly shifting the nature of the media themselves, in contrast to the way in which a scanned image of a physical photograph is shifted in form and nature by its digitisation and presentation in the hypermedium of the Internet. In contrast, I am suggesting that performance is always in a process of undoing the temporalities of its media, specifically in the examples above and other intermedial pieces I have made and experienced, because of the intersection between the 'timing' of the performer's action and the temporality of the media with which they intersect. Intermedial activation in live performance wrestles the fixed media from their moorings and sets them loose, so we *feel* their happening differently and the temporality of the piece itself also shifts.

These conclusions represent theories and ideas that arise from this chapter and its attempts to understand how an intermedial performance piece can employ, represent and curate temporality within the clock time of its occurrence. Next, some of these emergent ideas shift form to become prompts for your making and the ways in which time can be productively at play in your intermedial performance work.

Practical ideas

Idea 1: Multiple voices

Make a number of separate voice recordings of people you know speaking, using a mobile device or voice recorder. Experiment with how you can interact in live performance with the playback of these fixed media recordings. Might you question them? Converse with them? Interrupt them? Overlap their voices?

Development: Think about a range of different modes of activation – that is, you activating the sounds live as part of the performance, using a smartphone or equivalent; someone else activating sounds from offstage; or a combination of these. Consider how the temporal multiplication and complication this represents might be brought to the fore of the piece and what meanings are at play in these interactions.

Idea 2: Playing with movement and time

Take a short piece of video footage of anything moving in space, for example a ball being thrown, a cat padding across a room, your feet walking forward on a path. Explore the playback of this footage in a studio space, using a free-standing or pico projector to project it in different ways within the space (e.g. large in scale and into the corner of a space, small in scale and onto another person's body or object such as a chair or table). Play with how you might physically mirror, intersect or form contrasts with its time and timing, as it plays back. You could also experiment with slowing down, speeding up or reversing the footage.

Make notes on the following and the effects of different combinations, focusing specifically on the temporal relationships that are created:

- **Scale** of image in relation to body
- **Positioning** of image and body – how they are composed in the stage picture: above, across, against, behind, beside, inside, opposite, over, through
- **Relationships** between body and image: fused together, one responding to another, in opposition, separated, moving, still

Idea 3: Playing with telematic present(s)

Work with Skype, Bambuser (www.bambuser.com), Facetime or another equivalent platform to establish a live connection with someone in another space. How can you make your two 'nows' connect? Play with passing an object from one space to another, mirroring each other's actions, having a conversation, playing tag or snap.

Development: Think about how the 'unity' of a particular scene might be distributed across these different spaces and how you might creatively work with some of the temporal difficulties, such as lag and loss of connection with your scene partner.

Idea 4: Bringing the past into the present

Think about how you might use image, text and sound to curate an intermedial sense of your past and memories as part of a live performance. Gather footage, sounds, words and objects related to memories from a particular time or of a particular moment or person. Experiment with how the intermedial mixes of text, image, sound and object can generate different effects and affects, and work towards creating a series of intermedial moments where you bring the elements together through your live performance actions.

Idea 5: Animating an archive

Gather a set of historical artefacts that exist in the public domain – documents, reports, texts, images, footage, first-hand accounts – and which document a particular historical event or moment. Think about how these elements could be 'activated' live within a performance so that they are 'animated' and mixed to create different effects and meanings. Consider live filming of static objects or documents, mixing this with prerecorded footage and live writing/drawing, using a video mixer such as Modul8.[13]

Development: Consider how this type of 'live animation' of an archive can be used, as documentary theatre often is, to relate a particular or politicised version of an event.

Idea 6: Looping time

Generate a loop of action, words or sounds that can be performed by one or two performers. Record the loop in various forms – as a video/sound recording, as a written description, as a social media post. Work with the performers to experiment with how the live loop of action might be mixed with or interrupted by its mediatised equivalents. Play with the pace and rhythm of the live loop and its recorded counterparts.

Idea 7: Extended intermedial encounters

Generate a variety of social media posts or communications by a fictional character, and experiment with the timing of releasing these posts to a group of friends or collaborators so that this character's experiences interrupt their daily routine at various points, demanding or prompting particular responses from them.

Development: Look at how a whole drama between sets of characters might play out temporally over different social media platforms

Idea 8: A month in the life

Video yourself every day for a month, for 1 minute at the same time every morning, wherever you are and whatever you are doing. Use the 30 'minutes' of footage as the basis for a devising process whereby you play with the sequence of actions, what they represent and how your live performance intersects with these fixed moments of your recent life.

Idea 9: Activating intermedial events

Play with a performed interaction between you and a set of fixed video images, so you develop a choreography whereby it appears that you are making the image shift; that is, when you touch the screen, the image changes colour. Rehearse this choreography carefully (a particular piece of music can help you do this) and present.

Development: Experiment with how the tightly choreographed temporal activations you have developed might break down or deconstruct as part of the performance. What feelings or meanings does this breakdown of intermedial relations create?

5 Technology and Intermedial Theatre

Rosemary Klich

In June last year, I was excited to participate in the Blast Theory and Hydrocracker production *Black Antler* in Chatham. This immersive event was to be in a 'secret location'; I was instructed on purchasing the ticket to make my way to Chatham, and told that I would receive a series of texts with instructions as to where to go and what to do once I arrived. It appeared that having a working mobile phone was going to be a crucial requirement for participation. The day of the show had been busy, protracted and generally hectic. I'd left home in Whitstable around 7 a.m. and had been involved at a research symposium in London. On finishing work, I realised that my phone battery was low, so I headed into the Westfield shopping centre, intending to use one of the mobile charging lockers, but – just my luck – every locker across the three floors of the centre was either occupied or broken. I was concerned because if I could not charge my mobile phone, then my means of access to the show would have disappeared. Would I be able to participate in the magic of that evening's performance? I hoped the train down to Chatham might be one with electrical sockets, but no, not that peculiar day. The malevolence of the technology gods must have been momentarily distracted, and I had just enough remaining power to receive the text from Blast Theory telling me where to meet. At this point my phone died, but on arrival at the meeting point, I managed to find other participants, explained my situation and tagged along with them. Luckily, participation in the show eventually entailed working in pairs, and we only needed one working mobile between us.

On the train home, as I reflected on the show that actually turned out to have little to do with mobile communication and a lot more to do with face-to-face role-play, I could not help but dwell on the fact that my evening's theatrical engagement had nearly been scuppered by the uselessness of my depleted mobile. Without electricity, my phone was nothing but a solid, static brick. I had never thought about my phone in this way, as an inadequate inanimate object, and I spent some time on the train, thinking about my relationship, not with the media, but with the machinery of the phone. What do you think of when you consider what your phone actually means to you? Do you perhaps think of the photos it has taken and stored, the voice memos you have recorded? Or Whatsapp, Facetime, Instagram, email, Messenger, Snapchat, Spotify and some variation of Candy Crush? Or do you think of the physical object that allows you to access these platforms, that relies on electrical charge, without which it is a very expensive and shiny paperweight? In its state of inanimation, my phone had become separated from me, disconnected from the assemblage through which I exist, no longer purposed to mediate – neither intermediary nor mediator (in the sense meant by Bruno Latour, 2007, p. 37). For me to interface with my phone, it must first interface with a power socket. Without electrical energy, the object itself gives and transmogrifies nothing: although software affords engagement, without keyboard, keys, buttons or plug-ins, the physical object affords very little.

Although it now seems obvious, I have rarely considered the materiality of this device as a physical interface with the affordances of sleekly hidden buttons and some kind of invisible interior components. I suspect I have been conditioned not to notice the hardware, but instead to be mesmerised by the self-proclaimed magic of the device. Indeed, Apple's advertising campaign for the iPhone 7 is that it is 'practically magic', and the word 'magic' reappears and is reinforced in many Apple advertisements. The iPad launch video in 2010 opened with Jony Ive, then senior vice president for design, suggesting that something becomes magical when it surpasses your ability to understand how it works. The 2012 iPad trailer opened with the suggestion that technology is at its best when it is transparent, when the user is no longer conscious of the device, but only of what they're doing with it, and the iPad is described as a 'magical pane of glass'. At the end of the 2013 iPhone 5s advertisement, Jony Ive reemphasises this idea, suggesting that technology is at its most empowering when it disappears.

The 2014 advertisement for the iPhone 6 does focus partly on the hardware specs, but perhaps this strategy proved less effective than the suggestion of sorcery, for the promise of 'magic' was back with the iPhone 7; the iPhone 7's 'practically magic' campaign was launched during U.S. coverage of the 2016 Emmy Awards. On the whole, Apple products have been consistently painted as little white boxes full of magic. The wireless Apple keyboard with rechargeable batteries is marketed as the 'Magic Keyboard' (released in 2015); the mouse is 'magic', as is the trackpad (all as advertised on the Apple Store website in February 2018), and at the launch of the iPhone 7 and 7 Plus, AirPods were introduced as 'magical headphones'. Apple staff members are called geniuses, implying that you have to be a genius to understand the workings of their products (and I suspect if you were to take a look inside your Apple product yourself, you would inevitably void your warranty).

Apple's advertising strategy would seem to have been inspired by one of sci-fi writer Arthur C. Clarke's 'three laws', which were intended to offer means of evaluating claims about scientific progress. Clarke's third law states, 'Any sufficiently advanced technology is indistinguishable from magic' (Clarke, 1973, p. 21). Magic is magic because it precipitates events that defy explanation; it obscures the mechanisms by which it is produced. 'Sufficiently advanced technology' similarly leaves its user mystified by the mechanics of its production, mesmerising the user with the content it produces whilst leaving the user mystified as to the processes of production. Clarke is not the only fiction writer to link magic and technology: C. S Lewis describes the relationship of 'serious magical endeavour' and 'serious scientific endeavour' as being like 'twins'. In his book *The Abolition of Man*, he links magic and 'applied science' (technology) as a result of their pursuit to dominate the natural world: 'For magic and applied science alike the problem is how to subdue reality to the wishes of men: the solution is a technique; and both, in the practice of this technique, are ready to do things hitherto regarded as disgusting and impious (1947, p. 88).' The notion of magic implies the 'supernatural': forces beyond scientific understanding. Technology for Lewis is, like magic, a means of exercising power over the natural order.

Magic suggests achievements gained by mysterious means, of hidden or complex machinations producing inexplicable effects beyond the understanding of mere mortals. Technology too is, in the eyes of Apple, at its best when its machinery is hidden, as Jony Ive, Apple's Chief Design Officer, stated at the 2010 launch of the ipad: 'when something exceeds your ability to understand how it works, it sort of becomes magical.' This trend towards invisible technology seems to align with a wider trope of immateriality; since the telegraph first transcended space and time, the possibility of overcoming the constraints of physical existence have occupied our imagination, epitomised in the cyberpunk fiction of the 1980s and its visions of uploadable consciousness and unconstrained cyberspace. It is also reflective of the push towards dematerialisation, a concept within economics and design that champions the use of fewer materials through efficiency, savings and reuse. Although dematerialisation is a crucial step towards improving sustainability and decreasing environmental impact, the claims of invisibility and magic made by companies such as Apple serve to obfuscate the technology and enforce distance between the user and the hardware. As I write this, the early advertising for the iPhone X has just been released, and though the term 'magic' has yet to be suggested, the advertising insists on the de-materialism of the phone: Jony Ive explains that the iPhone X is Apple's response to a ten-year mission to 'create an iPhone that is all display, a physical object that disappears into the experience' (in the 'Introducing iPhone X' video on the official Apple YouTube channel, posted September 2017).

Although William Gibson's visions of mind uploading and telepathic hologram projection may indeed come to bear, media materiality persists. As Mark Crossley explains in the introduction to this collection, 'Media *must* manifest themselves physically in some form, to bring to ground and capture our ephemeral or illusive creations.' Our digital technologies and information-processing machines –indeed information itself – require physical forms to house and transport them and enable human interaction. Despite the push towards dematerialisation and the lure of immateriality, media still require material instantiation. Lev Manovich asserts, 'Although the word "information" contains the word "form" inside it, in reality it is the other way around: in order to be useful to us, information always has to be wrapped up in some external form' (2008, p. 335). Indeed, as the 'Internet of things' continues to expand its territory, the material dimension of the digital has become more varied and pervasive as household objects become digitised and potentially mediatised.

This chapter explores the various ways in which theatre works both with and against this recognition of media materiality and the 'object-ness' of media technologies. The traditionally material world of theatre has long embraced technology-enabled mystery, staging media spectacles to wow and amaze. Christopher Baugh, in the introduction to his 2005 book *Theatre, Performance and Technology: The Development and Transformation of Scenography*, which provides a comprehensive history of stage technologies and scenic machinery, explains that stage technologies have frequently been used not just as means to an end but as 'ends in themselves':

> For example, the intense pleasure of the 'now you see it, now you don't' moment as a special effect takes place; the inexplicable transformation of one location to another in the baroque theatre; the flash of 'lightning' and accompanying sound effects when Mephistopheles appears as if by 'magic' on *Walpurgisnacht*, have all been reported as significant moments in the history of theatre and performance. (Baugh, 2005, p. 1)

Contemporary intermedial theatre continues to embrace the 'now you see it, now you don't moment' enabled by digital technologies. Sound and visual special effects create ever more realistic 'lightning', and with image projection technologies having moved dramatically beyond the eighteenth-century 'magic lantern', the contemporary stage is populated with animated and filmic imagery creating virtual scenery and augmenting reality.

The following sections explore the aesthetics of magic and materiality as manifest in various contemporary theatre productions. Although high-tech productions, such as the Royal Shakespear Company's (RSC) *The Tempest* at the Barbican in 2017, represent a 'mixed reality aesthetic', productions such as Daniel Kitson's *Analog.UE*, Simon McBurney's *The Encounter* and *Charleroi Danses: Kiss and Cry* eschew the 'magic' of digital media and stage the materiality of media technologies. It is suggested that the specific intermediality and affirmation of the material in such productions manifests a distinctly 'post-digital aesthetic' as articulated by theorists such as David Berry, Michael Dieter and Florian Cramer (Berry, 2015; Berry and Dieter, 2015; Cramer, 2015). It is argued that these productions represent a rejection of the fetishisation of the new that has been associated with digital culture, and in the following analyses various 'post-digital strategies' for performance practice are identified.

STAGING MEDIA MAGIC

The potential for intermedial theatre to stage the 'magic' of media technologies is epitomised in the RSC's production of *The Tempest* (2017), directed by Gregory Doran at the Barbican. With projected scenography, the production manifests a kind of augmented reality or virtual aesthetic; the technical achievements are thrilling and cleverly realise the magic enacted by the characters within Shakespeare's play. Characters appear in both live and animated form, with the seemingly three-dimensional projections displayed on hanging, concentric, circular, moving sheets of gauze that are at times almost invisible, so the imagery projected appears as if floating without material instantiation. Ariel, of course, is a magical, winged sprite, and in this production he is able to manifest and control a projected double of himself, conjuring an ephemeral avatar bathed in sparkling light that can fly and transform like the magical being of Shakespeare's pages.

In the memorable banquet scene, Ariel summons an enormous and terrifying spirit, a devil-like harpy with bat-like wings, spreading flames as it swoops across the stage. A literal 'now you see it, now you don't' moment amazes as the harpy appears to make the banquet magically vanish; before your eyes the food banquet table bursts into flames and completely disappears. As well as these mesmerising special effects, projection is used to completely transform the world of the stage. The play begins with a shipwreck; the stage is framed by the enormous wooden skeleton of the hull of the wrecked ship, and as the storm rages, reverberating sound and projection creates the illusion of the ship lurching and pitching as waves crash against it. As the ship floods and sinks into the depths, bodies of sailors float lifelessly in the middle of the stage, descending into the blackness. When Prospero reminds Arial of his imprisonment in a 'cloven pine', Arial's digital sprite appears, suspended mid-stage, encased within the tendrils of a tree, as images of reaching roots blend with the wooden husk of the ship to transform the stage into a lush forest prison. The masque scene, Prospero's play within a play, paints the stage awash with rainbows and starry lights, fields and flowers, and an opera-singing goddess hovers above the stage in an over 10-foot-high skirt that is vividly decorated with images of fruit and feathers.

More than a couple of reviews of the production have understandably used the phrase 'digital wizardry' to describe the onstage effects (see, e.g. Hemmings, 2017; Paulson, 2017; Runcy, 2016; Taylor, 2016). The spectacular visuals, whilst inevitably requiring a material surface for projection, still seem to appear out of the ether, as if by magic. As you watch, you quickly come to realise the connection between the movements of the actor Mark Quartley (Arial) and the movements of the projected hologram sprite, but it is not foregrounded and is easy to overlook. The show is the result of the RSC's two-year collaboration with information technology company Intel and The Imaginarium Production, which was co-founded by Andy Serkis and specialises in performance capture. The performer playing Ariel, Mark Quartley, wears a body suit laden with seventeen miniaturised wireless sensors that track his movement, triggering projected animation that he can manipulate in real time. The technology also involves real-time facial capture, with a camera recording Quartley's facial expressions and feeding them to a computer system which reproduces them on the harpy. The production also uses sophisticated projection mapping, employing optical motion-tracking cameras and software and twenty-seven projectors to project imagery as if wrapped around the actual material set. This technology is at its most impressive when the cameras track the performers' movements during a large, celebratory dancing scene and trigger small projections onto moving, handheld drums; each performer holds a drum on which is projected the face of an individual wolf, together creating the effect of forming a rabid pack.

The projection of the three-dimensional holograms, and particularly the facial tracking technology, is cutting-edge, which is in keeping with the Shakespearean historical context and the tradition of the Jacobean masque. The designer Brimsom Lewis explains, 'In Shakespeare's day, all the technology available in the seventeenth century would have been used to create a one-off, huge spectacle ... They'd use candles to focus and reflect light, use live animals and their own forms of automation. We're not grafting this stuff onto the play – it was asking us to find new and exciting ways to present it' (in Dawood, 2017). Jacobean court productions of the time used all effects available, including fireworks and thunder sheets to represent a storm, wind machines, trapdoors, aerial rigging and trickeries of candlelight. The RSC's production follows in a tradition of using the latest technology to produce huge spectacle, visual trickery and theatrical magic.

In order for this spectacular scenography to ensnare, fascinate and mesmerise, the technology remains hidden; the digital scenography hides the mechanics of its production and places the actor amidst an intangible but vivid environment that is unbound by the laws of material instantiation. Alongside other productions using motion capture, three-dimensional projection mapping, and computer generated animation, such as the National Theatre's production of *The Curious Incident of the Dog in the Night-Time* (2014) and other productions designed by the award-winning media company. fifty-nine productions such as The Young Vic's *The Life of Galileo* (2017) and The National Theatre's *Emil and the Detectives* (2014), Gregory Doran's *The Tempest* deploys an aesthetic of mixed (or even virtual) reality in which seemingly magical imagery appears alongside and even interacts with the physical performers and material stage world. The means of the magic, the computer hardware and software, the projection technologies and often even the surface of the projection, are largely unseen so as not to distract from the phantasmagoria.

MEDIA MATERIALITY

There is danger in accepting a perception of media as 'magical' and technology as best hidden. Software's obfuscation of the mechanics and materials of media may be understood as problematic for various reasons. Firstly, as media archaeology is revealing to us, the persistence of hardware implicates various economic, environmental and human costs. Representative of the 'material turn' within media studies, which focuses on the materials and technologies that enable media content rather than on the content itself, as well as championing an emerging branch of environmental and ecologically concerned media studies, Jussi Parikka, in his 2015 book, *A Geology of Media*, asserts, 'The design culture of the new hides the archaic materials of the planet' (2015a, p. 137). Parikka interrogates the alternative materialities of technical media culture and reminds us, 'Media work in and through bodies, or more widely, through materials and things' (2015a, p. 93).

Although hardware may be obscured by digital software and the interface, the digital remains bound to concrete, material form. As Parikka warns:

> It is of course true that we are often catered the idea of hardware as disappearing or perhaps always already immaterial – that the digital does not carry a weight but is the sum of its mathematical transactions in topological dimensions without a topography – but this is just blatantly wrong. . . . It is not immaterial – even if it disappears from before our eyes. (2015b, p. 215)

For all their appearance of magic, media technologies function through very tangible elements such as circuits, power supplies, storage and voltage differences (2015a, p. 57). Parikka is particularly concerned with the ways in which natural resources are mobilised in the production of media; to ignore the material basis for media is to ignore its implications for natural resources, ecology, labour and waste. It is also to overlook the interaction between media materiality and human embodiment, and to negate a key element in the feedback, feedforward loop between human and media bodies.

The materials that constitute the physical hardware of media technologies are often upstaged, even obscured, by the wizardry of the media interface. The various layers of visible surface content keep us further and further from the hardware and computational machinery that fade into invisibility. In 1995, Friedrich Kittler wrote an essay titled "There Is No Software', arguing that human-generated texts have vanished, existing only in the cells of computer memory. Twenty years later, Lev Manovich asserts there is nothing but software; that software has taken command. He asks, 'What about the physical materials of different media?' and answers that 'in the process of simulation they are eliminated' (2013, p. 201). Software simulation, he suggests, 'replaces a variety of distinct physical materials and the tools used to inscribe information' (2014b, p. 201). But while software inevitably plays a crucial role in our media interactions, software code is reliant on broader technical, cultural and material formations that facilitate it. Software obscures hardware, but it depends on 'hard' materials and tools, so rather than 'replace', it hides them. At its most basic, there is still a reliance on electricity, silicon and other essential materials.

A further problem with denying the existence of hardware is that it limits user knowledge, choice and potential creativity. As media archaeologist Lori Emerson suggests, it 'denies access to digital tools for making, thereby predetermining choice' (2014, p. 3). Emerson claims that the breathtaking technological feats of our devices deliberately divert our attention from how closed they really are, stifling user agency and creativity. In her book *Reading Writing Interfaces: From the Digital to the Bookbound*, Lori Emerson emphasises the material basis for media, asserting, 'The dream in which the boundary between human and information is eradicated is just that, a dream the computing industry rides on as it attempts to convince us that the dream is now reality through sophisticated sleights of hand that take place a the level of interface' (2014, pp. x–xi). With the advent of so-called interface-free devices, what's at issue, suggests Emerson, is what is revealed through what is concealed. Contemporary marketing continues to tout 'natural, intuitive, invisible, and even "magical" interfaces' (2014, p. 4) that supposedly provide us with a more direct and fundamentally better way to engage with computers. However, although the interface enables access, it also acts, in Emerson's words, 'as a kind of magician's cape, continually revealing (mediatic layers, bits of information, etc.) through concealing and concealing as it reveals' (2014, p. x).

Emerson takes issue with the principles of 'invisibility' and 'user-friendliness' as deployed in the media industry as deliberately bending the truth in their implication that this very specific understanding of user-friendliness is indeed the only possible one. This promoted notion of the user-friendly device is problematic, Emerson claims, because not only does it promote 'the way in which not only hardware/software is now utterly black-boxed but its closed architecture is being marketed as a feature' (2014, p. 3). The sleek, compelling surface of the interface serves to distance the user from accessing the underlying workings of media. When the prioritisation of transparency actually obscures the physical materials and tools, we become consumers and not producers of content. The desire for invisibility, Emerson suggests, 'turns all computing devices into appliances for the consumption of content instead of multifunctional, generative devices' (2014, p. xvii), turning users from active producers of content into passive consumers.

Artists, writers, and theatre makers, are potentially in a strong position to question the magic of media. Although the theatre has always staged the amazing, using the most sophisticated technology to create mesmeric effects and produce illusionary environments, there are also intermedial productions that reveal, rather than conceal, the mechanics and materiality of media, drawing attention to the media object. While *The Tempest*, following in the footsteps of Jacobean masque and Restoration spectacular, presents an aesthetic of mixed reality and media magic, these productions place the media object centre stage and make clearly visible its processes of mediation. The focus of the remainder of this chapter is not on the staging of digital effects, but on the staging of what Lars Elleström (2010) has called 'the material modality' of media technologies; on the technical media themselves, rather than on their perception. Technical media, according to Elleström, are the physical basis for media communication: 'the technical media of distribution of sensory configurations or technical media of display' (in Mark's introduction).

Various recent theatre productions have exhibited a dismissal of 'digital wizardry' and embraced the low-tech, the analogue, the ordinary, exploring how media objects and tangible technologies are staged, engaged and deconstructed. These works, rather than showcasing what Elleström (2010) labels the 'qualified medium' of, for example, film, instead stage the video camera and its component parts, the screen and the projector. The emphasis here is on media form rather than on informational content; on the physical presence of technology (machinery, equipment) and the media modes rather than on the processes or patterns of meaningful mediation. Although theatre may not be in quite the same position as Lori Emerson's digital literature to directly tackle the invisibility of digital interfaces, like digital literature, theatre and performance can, to quote Emerson, 'embrace *visibility* by courting difficulty, defamiliarization, and glitch' and stand 'as an antidote to ubi-comp and this receding present' (2014, p. xviii). One area of performance manifesting an insistence on the materiality of media, through the use of a notably analogue aesthetic, is the field of audio theatre, which involves the use of sound technologies to place auditory experience at the heart of both the form and content of the performance. It is not just that these works are using analogue rather than digital technologies, but that they are doing so in a way that makes visible the often hidden mechanisms of media and that reassert the physical materialities of media objects onstage.

STAGING MEDIA MATERIALITY

The use of analogue audio tech in performances such as Daniel Kitson's 2014 show *Analog.UE* stands against the seduction of the wonder or magic of digital media. In *Analog.UE*, Kitson uses forty-something large cassette and spool-to-spool tape players that, at the beginning, are piled on top of each other at the back of the darkened stage. In a work that owes much to Beckett's *Krapp's Last Tape*, Kitson never actually speaks directly to the audience. Instead, he carries and drags each of the ragtag audio-players to the front of the stage, plugs them in and presses 'Play', before heading back upstage to repeat the process; we hear him talk for nearly an hour and a half without seeing him speak a single word. Kitson travels back and forth lugging cumbersome sound equipment in a race to place one machine and press 'Play' on the track just as the previous track finishes.

The recordings, which obviously have to be played in a specific order, weave together various narratives, our interpretation of which are influenced by what we see; as the stage slowly becomes a sculptural mess of interwoven extensions leads, tape machines and slide projectors showing dusty family photos, so we start to connect the various threads of narrative. One strand involves an elderly man called Thomas, who, in 1977, is seated in his garage, recording his memories at the request of his wife, Gertie. Another introduces us to Trudy, a call worker, who has heard one of Thomas's tapes and is keen to hear more. Kitson also weaves through his own reflections on being a single man in his mid-thirties and his process and thinking behind the show, including ruminations on the need to preserve moments for posterity.

Some of the machines are enormous and clearly heavy. Kitson must set them up, plug them in and battle the clunky mechanisms, navigating, cords, plugs, spools, tape and play buttons in order to produce sound. It is a repetitive performance of human exertion and places emphasis on the sweaty materiality of the body just as much as on the scratchy analogue recordings and dusty objects onstage, and there is a clear visual connection between human labour and media output. The machines whir and whine, with a different sound quality to every single one. We can hear the frailty of the analogue tape, as it clicks and stretches through the machines, adding a dramaturgical connection to the frailty of Thomas's memory and a reminder that these clunky mechanical objects are machines for recording and mediating memories. While the stories are evocative and engaging, the machines take centre stage, each individually lit to ensure the audience not only hears but also sees the means of mediation. The stage and lighting remediates the media objects, and it is their performance, rather than Kitson's that is presented. Kitson beavers away with a torch between his teeth, very much a stagehand rather than a performer.

Another audio theatre production that places technological media centre stage, and emphasises the materiality of both the body and media objects, Complicité's *The Encounter* (see Chapter 4 for full description of the production) combines old and new media to mix and layer live and prerecorded sound accessed via headphones. Simon McBurney is the only visible performer in a sparse and almost entirely functional stage space, and he performs a two-hour feat of dynamic storytelling using live binaural sound created making use of a dummy head onstage with microphones in each of its ears (the Neumann KU100), various other microphones onstage, Foley effects, prerecorded binaural sound and cinematic background music. He begins in stereo sound, introducing us to the various microphones and loop pedals, and explains how binaural sound works: "Here I am somewhere in your head', he says, before 'walking from one ear, across the electrified pate of our brain, to lodge behind our frontal lobe'. He offers a preface about the nature of the 'common imagination' and the way we all regularly discover that what we think to be real is in fact a story. He tell us that the function of stories are for the listener to enter into the consciousness of the protagonist, and in the ensuing tale that McBurney weaves, the use of binaural sound places audience members at the centre of the protagonist's world and sonically renders their immediate environment.

McIntyre's encounter with the Amazon and its people is vividly constructed through sound (designed by Gareth Fry). McBurney, speaking to us mostly as a kind of narrator, skilfully uses materials he has onstage to create the sounds of the jungle. Slowly shaking a large water bottle around the dummy head creates the sounds of a river lapping around us; a crackling crisp packet becomes the cackle of the jungle fauna; and by trampling a pile of old recording tape, McBurney creates the sounds of crunching leaves underneath our feet.

As the production blends the live and prerecorded, so the themes explore the experience of time. At various points, McBurney's voice comes to us from the past, recorded six months ago in his flat, to speak to the live McBurney. Another prerecorded voice, the Oxford Professor Marcus du Sautoy, tell us that the perception of the linearity of time is an illusion, and explains different models of time; the Mayoruna tribe have a cyclical understanding of time and believe that theirs is a journey back to before time. McBurney moves between narrating the story, which is of long-past events made immediate through McBurney's world building, to playing documented conversations from his past off his phone, for example with his daughter in his flat, that are also of the past, but a different past.

As the protagonist of the story, Loren McIntyre, enters into the Amazon rainforest, the stage lights fade so that the stage actions are less prominent, less dominant over the world of the auditory. But our eyes soon adjust, and the performance of McBurney and the media onstage is never concealed. You can control your own degree of immersion; while the sound is immediate and pervasive, you choose whether or not you want to look at McBurney and the mechanics of the sound production, or let your vision become unfocused and tune in to the world created through the binaural sound.

As in Kitson's *Analog.UE*, the aesthetic places emphasis on the performer's physical efforts and the presence and individual materiality of the media onstage. The objects of mediation are clearly displayed, and there is interest in seeing the different microphones behind the variations in tonal quality. Many of McBurney's descriptions are of things happening to the protagonist's body – cut skin, burning feet, breath, dehydration, eating, indigestion – which draws our attention to both his and our physicality, and as McBurney's exertions lead to sweating and heavy breathing, the labour of his efforts in creating the fictional environment is made ever more visible. Though clearly explained to us, there is undoubtedly audio trickery through the use of binaural sound. However, it is clearly effort, and not magic, that brings us the sonically rendered story world.

Moving away from the arena of audio-theatre, the Belgian filmmaker Jaco Van Dormael and choreographer Michèle Anne De Mey's *Charleroi Danses: Kiss and Cry* (2011) also makes prominent the physical objects of mediation, this time in the form of the camera. Headlining the London International Mime Festival at the Barbican in February 2017, the production draws on filmmaking, dance, puppetry and storytelling to create a show that stages the live creation of analogue visual effects. Above the stage hangs a large screen, onto which is projected the live feed from the onstage cameras, which are continuously worked by numerous camera operators who also double as stagehands and puppeteers. The stage is full of moving cameras, cords and detailed little models on tables that appear as a film set in miniature. The story is told by the performers Michèle Anne De Mey and Gregory Grosjean, using only their hands filmed in close up, which perform sophisticated choreography and interact with the miniature sets and doll house props in a way that suggests dancers' bodies and evokes emotional and material worlds (Figure 5.1).

Figure 5.1   Michèle Anne De Mey and Jaco Van Dormael, *Kiss and Cry* (2011). Photographer: Maarten Vanden Abeele.

The focus on the dancing hands develops dramaturgically from the narrated story at the heart of the production. Giselle, a lonely elderly woman remembers her five past lovers; the first, the most memorable, lasting only briefly when she brushed hands for a matter of seconds with a boy on a train. The hands then become the medium for communication, expressing the flirtation of early love, the comfort and intimacy of developed relationships, the elation of dancing, the anger of rejection and the desolation of abandonment. The hands waltz, ice-skate, swim through cloudy water and swing from trapezes, accompanied by music, atmospheric sounds and voice-over narration. Images of Giselle, suggested by a tiny toy figure sitting on a bench, evoke a powerful sense of nostalgia, and the oscillation between Giselle in the present remembering the past, and images evoking her memories, reinforce a thematic concern with the interrelation of time and memory.

The audience is faced with both the live creation of the film and the film itself; the techniques and tricks used in film-making are exposed, and though the audience's attention is split between stage and screen, it is the relationship between the two that is most revealing. In one early moment, the screen shows a speeding train from the perspective of a passenger, whilst onstage we see a working model train pootling about its model track; the screen image shows the feed of the camera attached to the train, revealing the function of the camera to frame perspective. There is undoubted artifice; the performers literally use smoke and mirrors to create the onscreen effects. However, the labour of the performers, stagehands and camera operators in the process of image creation is emphasised, and the enabling materials, objects, media and technology are ever present. In one particularly memorable moment evoking the sadness of a failed relationship, the screen shows hands dancing a complex, intimate choreography, but while the screen shows only the seemingly disembodied hands, onstage we see the two black-clad bodies attached to the hands dancing a complex, full-bodied pas de deux. While the screen image is compelling, the staging of the process of its creation and the bodies and technology implicated add visual interest and works dramaturgically to reinforce the constructed nature of memory, time and perception.

These productions reclaim the often invisible materiality of the machine and explore the physical presence of media technologies. They undermine the 'magic' of media, presenting the output of technological media not as magical, but as fundamentally embedded in material forms and human labour. In all three productions, there is an emphasis on revealing how the media work both in their mediation of sound and imagery, and at the level of mechanics. At the beginning of *The Encounter*, McBurney specifically introduces us to the workings of the onstage tech. In *Analog.UE*, it is significant that we can see and not just hear the tape moving across from one spool to the other, the operational mechanics clearly displayed. In *The Encounter* and *Kiss and Cry*, the audience is presented with both the media product and the process of its production, positioning the audience not just as passive consumers of content but also as having to choose between focusing on the immediate media output or on the mechanics of its production. In *Analog.UE*, though we do not see Kitson recording the tapes he plays to us, the process of recording is presented as part of the story, with both Kitson and the character Thomas explaining the context and thinking behind their recording of the tales on the tapes.

PERFORMING A POST-DIGITAL AESTHETIC

These works do not just present media objects but also stage the performance of the mediating process, of the technical medium's "distribution of sensory configurations Elleström (2010, p. 30–37). The practice of the theatre revealing the mechanics of media production onstage is of course nothing new; it has been a feature of the work of various postmodern theatre companies such as the Wooster Group, who have frequently used television sets onstage to thematise processes of mediation and communication in a televisual society. In light of the seduction of today's digital media, the choice to eschew the vast array of technology on offer, or instead to focus not on what such technology can do but on how it works, how it takes up space, how it affords interaction, how it conveys meaning, aligns such contemporary productions not just with a postmodern aesthetic but with a *post-digital* aesthetic as well. The term 'post-digital' has been used across various areas of discourse and developed a multiplicity of meanings. Most notably for this discussion, the post-digital has been invoked to describe a condition of contemporary society in which the magic of media technologies has faded.

In their edited book *Postdigital Aesthetics*, David Berry and Michael Dieter explain the postdigital includes 'a shift from an earlier moment driven by an almost obsessive fascination and enthusiasm with new media to a broader set of affectations that now includes unease, fatigue, boredom and disillusionment' (2015, p. 5). Florian Cramer, writing in Berry and Dieter's edition, echoes this definition, explaining, 'the term "post-digital" can be used to describe either a contemporary disenchantment with digital information systems and media gadgets, or a period in which our fascination with these systems and gadgets has become historical' (2015, p. 13). I would hesitate to suggest that any of these artists discussed are disenchanted with, or opposed to, the digital; the digital is, as Florian Cramer reminds us, 'routine or business as usual'. Although we may indeed, as Matthew Causey argues, now think digitally, and though 'artists and researchers of postdigital culture are fully embedded in the aesthetics and ideology of the digital' (Causey, 2016, p. 432), a theatrical post-digital aesthetic is manifesting in the works discussed here in a way that promotes an understanding of media as materially grounded and as counter-narratives of media wizardry.

In his article *Perspectives on the Postdigital: Beyond Rhetorics of Progress and Novelty* (2016), Sy Taffel helpfully maps the various definitions ascribed to the term 'post-digital', which he explains refer to

> (1) a return of the analogue or move beyond discrete samples, (2) the revelation of seams and artifices within the otherwise smooth spaces of the digital, (3) the historical phase of technocultural development occurring after the digital revolution, (4) the rematerialisation of digital technology and its integration into urban environments; (5) a way of escaping the fetishisation of newness and upgrade culture (p. 325).

In the theatre productions discussed here, these definitions of the post-digital are deployed as some of the strategies used for performance; these productions engage with analogue technologies, reveal artifice, rematerialise media, and eschew the fetishisation of the new that is typical of digital culture.

The most obvious post-digital strategy manifest in these works is the revival of old or analogue technologies that emphasise, instead of disguise, media mechanisms. Cramer links the post-digital to ideas like the 'off-internet' and 'neo-analogue', and likens the post-digital to the 'contemporary maker movement', referring to a contemporary subculture focused on technology-based 'DIY'. *Analog.UE*, with its junk-shop aesthetic and second-hand analogue tape players, which Kitson explains took a year of gathering from eBay, can particularly be linked to a neo-analogue aesthetic. In *The Encounter*, McBurney uses an array of different standing microphones, is particularly industrious with a loop pedal and uses materials in a manner for which they were not originally intended; McBurney's Foley effects use water bottles, crisp packets and videotape creatively to suggest other objects. The most astounding element of *Kiss and Cry* is the simplicity of the film-making strategies it uses to create its projected imagery, and the doll's house furniture and sometimes mismatched figurines lend the aesthetic a DIY look.

Like the post-digital more generally, *The Encounter* and *Kiss and Cry* combine old and new media. McBurney draws on different devices, including his mobile phone, to achieve different functions and qualities, which is a strategy Florian Cramer identifies as being particularly post-digital. He refers to the 'post-digital hybridity of old and new media and explains 'post-digital choice' as involving the use of the most appropriate technology for the job, rather than defaulting to the latest and most dazzling digital device: 'Young artists and designers choose media for their own particular material aesthetic qualities (including artifacts), regardless of whether these are a result of analogue material properties or of digital processing' (Cramer, 2015, p. 24). McBurney uses different microphones for the various quality of the sound they produce, and brings together the remarkably low-tech with the high-tech live binaural sound and headphone system.

In post-digital art-making, according to Cramer (2015, p. 22), there is a tendency 'to focus less on content and more on pure materiality, so that the medium, such as paper or celluloid, is indeed the message – a shift from semantics to pragmatics, and from metaphysics to ontology'. Although all three productions involve visceral storytelling using narration and imagery, the specific materiality of the medium, from scratchy magnetic tape to sophisticated video cameras, is exploited, emphasising the ontology of the medium. In all three productions there is an emphasis on revealing how the media work. At the beginning of *The Encounter*, McBurney specifically introduces us to the workings of the onstage tech. In *Analog.UE*, it is significant that we can see and not just hear the tape moving across from one spool to the other, the operational mechanics clearly displayed. The mechanical is staged as an aesthetic event, every click, whir and turn a part of the performance. The slide projector images that Kitson presents are often blurry, with the image off centre on its projection screen, which contributes to making visible the elements involved in the process of mediation. In both *The Encounter* and *Kiss and Cry*, in staging both the means of mediation and the media product simultaneously, the audience is not only invited to make clear connections between the media content and its material basis, but also to identify the processes behind achieving sonic and visual trickery.

None of these media mentioned here produce content without human intervention, whether it be pressing buttons, determining camera angles, providing sound and visuals for cameras and microphones to mediate or physically moving devices across the stage. A further post-digital theatre strategy in these productions is the emphasis on human labour in preparing and operating media. Kitson and McBurney end their solo performances sweaty and clearly exhausted, but whereas McBurney's efforts are largely towards the creation of sonic content, Kitson's are limited only to the transportation and operation of the tape players and slide projectors. There are times when the machines falter and Kitson has to return to a machine more than once to correct the playing mechanism and, on at least one occasion, restart the recording. In *Kiss and Cry*, the two dancers provide the on-screen choreography, but alongside them are a team of camera operators and stagehands who move according to their own choreography to ensure particular shots, manipulate props, manoeuvre machinery and cables, and operate lights.

It is not the focus of these works to explicitly engage with digital interfaces or software; perhaps future performance will see the hacking, deconstruction and reconstruction of digital devices. However, in the way that *Analog, UE, The Encounter* and *Charleroi Danses: Kiss and Cry* dismiss the fetishisation of the new, and through the productions' emphasis on materiality, mechanics and human effort, they stand against the perception of the 'magical' media device. By employing post-digital strategies such as deconstructing, simplifying and repurposing media, and emphasising media materialities, physical objects, human labour and machinic operations, theatre may perhaps stage a resistance to the misdirection of media magic, the growing obscurity of media mechanics and our apparently increasing and commercially prevalent willingness to be guiled into illusory acceptance of convenient software-mediated realities.

Practical ideas

1. **Media Tales Version 1**
   Select one of the media objects you engage with, and investigate the vital components of the hardware. Undertake research into the material and minerals that make up the medium's different components. Where do these materials come from? How are they manufactured? Who are the people and what are the processes involved in their production? Find the potential stories in the manufacture of the media object, and use these as the basis for generating written or devised performance. Tell the story of your media device and of the people and materials involved in its production.

2. **Media Tales Version 2**
   As in Version 1, select one of the media objects you engage with, and investigate the different components of the hardware. Think about what will happen to the device when you replace it. Where will its components end up? Research the life and death of such media objects, and tell the story of their elements once they leave your possession. What further impact will they have on the world?

3. **No Signal**
   Use a live-streaming platform such as Skype or FaceTime to connect with someone in a different space. Although a live connection can work smoothly, there are inevitable interferences – lags, frozen pixels, jumps and so on. Rather than seeing these 'disruptions' as a negative disturbance, try to find them; embrace the lag, the freeze, the jerky, the pixelated. Try different gestures and degrees of movement.

Work with both dialogue and physicality to explore the aesthetic of the glitch. How can you replicate this aesthetic through movement, through voice? How can it be used creatively?

4. **Machine Music**
Source any analogue media technologies you can get your hands on. These may include overhead projectors, tape players, slide projectors, film projectors, dictaphones, typewriters. Discover the various sounds these machines make as they function, both deliberately crafted sounds (e.g. playing back recorded sounds) and the incidental sounds of the machinery. Explore the potential dramaturgy of these sounds. How do the sounds of the machine articulate their function (or not)? How do the sounds work thematically? Aesthetically? Sonically? Develop a performance in which the functional sound of the machines takes centre stage. Make a point of plugging the machines into an electricity source, of not hiding the process of starting up the machine or unwinding cords; make the material and mechanical processes a feature of the performance.

5. **Push the Button**
For this exercise you will need to develop some text: tell a story, recount a significant event, or use some existing dialogue. How many different forms, formats, media interfaces, audio devices, can you use to record and play back your speech? Some examples might include different phone-based apps, digital or analogue dictaphones, old cassette tape machines or answering machines. Record short bits of text across these devices and experiment with playing back the recordings; you may choose to keep the order of the text the same or experiment with the order. As in the previous exercise, play with making the material and mechanical processes of the media an aesthetic feature, plugging in and powering on the devices, making visible the opening of software programmes, unwinding cords, pressing buttons and rewinding tracks.

Development: Think about the dramaturgical implications of the different media materialities in relation to the story content. Analogue tape is fragile, like the memories it records. It deteriorates with repeated use. Digital code enables endless repetition. Media may evoke dramaturgical connotations relating to nostalgia, intimacy, ephemerality or issues around privacy, authenticity and temporality. Work to contrast or connect the dramaturgical implications of the media with the details of the text.

Variation: The same exercise could be undertaken with visual recording devices or a combination of both visual and audial devices.

6. **Digital Gestures**
Media devices afford a variety of physical interaction (even voice activation can be thought of as a physical interaction). Different physical and vocal gestures are used to activate, instruct and engage with media devices. Select a particular device you regularly interact with, and deconstruct the gestures you use in your interaction

with this device, using them as the basis for improvised movement (using a background soundtrack may help with this). Try performing with and without the object. Think about varying pace, scale; allow gestures to manifest as small and massive, in the tiniest of body parts and throughout the whole body. Work from the specific to the abstract. Develop your improvised movements into rehearsed choreography for performance.

7. **Rethink, Remake**
   Can you get your hands on a redundant computer? Tablet? Smartphone? Or even an old tape player, answering machine or video recorder? Take it apart slowly and carefully. Consider the components in terms of weight, texture, sheen, colour, shape. Rearrange, reconnect and remake based on aesthetic principles of your choosing.

6 The Audience in Intermedial Performance

Gareth White

This chapter considers some new varieties of spectatorship that are created through intermediality, and the new challenges and opportunities of such spectatorship. Specifically, I examine two aspects of the spectatorship of intermedial theatre. Firstly, as strategies of technological mediation offer proliferating new ways for audiences to participate, how performances figure the audience member as tech user; and secondly, how they thus model human–media relationships in action, including a thematic interweaving of the user-participant with the conventional content of the performance. Through three examples – Rimini Protokol's *Remote London*, Silvia Mercuriali's *Macondo* and Complicité's *The Encounter* – I explore a range of positions, relationships and activities that intermedial performance opens for its spectators/participants. Drawing on Brian Massumi, I consider the role of the body in these interactions, before contrasting this with a reading of Friedrich Kittler's perspective of media users as points in a network, rather than discrete human subjectivities.

THE AUDIENCE IN INTERMEDIAL THEATRE: NETWORKED BODIES

You probably own a set of headphones, quite possibly more than one. What do you use them for? Listening to music or to podcasts, having phone conversations, hearing directions while driving or walking, replaying sentences you have written, or 'reading' audiobooks, perhaps. Turn that question around, and think about what your headphones use you for: listening to products that you have paid for, hearing adverts, following instructions, doing educational tasks. Headphones are tools that we use for their convenience. They give us privacy; they add a soundtrack to mundane life; they help to connect us to people; they make reading and writing easier. But like all tools, all technological objects, they make demands on us. They need to be used – once a task has become easier through the use of an available tool, it is hard not to use that tool and not to allow that tool to use us for other people's purposes (advertisers, e.g.), or simply for the tool's own purposes, its need to be used.

This chapter looks in detail at three performances – Rimini Protokol's *Remote London*, Silvia Mercuriali's *Macondo* and (as in Joanne Scott's and Rosemary Klich's chapters earlier in this book) Complicité's *The Encounter* – which use headphones in clever and original ways, but which also ask questions about the place of technology in our lives. What the chapter aims to show is how foregrounding media technology in performance also foregrounds the audience's interaction with that technology, and our interconnection with technology in general. Along with its apparent subject matter, expressed in the characters, images, words, actions and events, and so on, these performances are also about what we do with technology and how we do it. Where this is most evident, as in these examples, it might be recognised as part of a recent trend to give audiences things to do *in* performance, and to draw attention to the things we do *as* audiences, that shows no sign of abating as I write this chapter. But it is also something distinctive of its own when technology is one of the things that we are asked to 'do' or to do things with. It is, perhaps, the technology itself bringing performance into being; it is about *what technology does with us*.

But let's remember that audiences in intermedial theatre are not always invited to do unexpected things. Sometimes we are required to sit quietly in the dark while a performance takes place somewhere in front of us in the light, taking advantage of, for example, the mediating technology of the theatre building itself, with its organisation of space, acoustics and light. As Mark Crossley has already made clear in Chapter 1 of this volume, theatre itself is a medium, and the implication of the terms 'medium' and 'media' is that the technologies in question mediate the performance – they *come between* the performance and the audience. As you will read in other chapters in this book, this *come between* is problematic: media produce what they mediate as much as they help to deliver something. The questions intermedial theatre asks are often questions about how media do this, how they engage us and connect with us, and how our relationships with them change, reorienting our perspective on the world, ourselves and each other, and challenging expectations about the role of technology in our lives. We are invited to take up familiar devices and use them in surprising ways, or to interact with new devices or new software, or with novel combinations of devices, software and people. These performances produce new relationships with media technology and allow the network that includes both us as users and our media tools to express itself.

The three performances I refer to in this chapter use similar basic technology: headphones worn by each audience member. Through these headphones we hear a performance that is complemented by other performances that we watch or performances that we give ourselves. All three offer curious combinations of listening and watching, tell stories about technology and its users, and place us as listeners and users in complex interactive relationships with devices and the stories told through them.

REMOTE LONDON

Rimini Protokol's *Remote London* is an iteration of a performance that has been staged as *Remote Berlin*, *Remote Sydney* and so on, in cities around the world. For the *London* edition, staged in 2016, I received the following invitation by email on the day of the performance:

> We look forward to seeing you at REMOTE LONDON this afternoon. You do not need to pick up your ticket from Chelsea Theatre – please come directly to the start point at **St George's Gardens** (entrance next to 8 Wakefield Street, London WC1N) at **4pm**. We will be equipping audience with the audio equipment from 3:30pm inside the garden. We ask you to leave a credit card, driver's licence or a £50 deposit for loan of the equipment (returned at the end of the performance), to read and sign the attached Health and Safety Notice, to wear comfortable shoes for walking and to come prepared for all weather conditions. The running time for the performance is 1 hour 50 minutes. The end point for REMOTE LONDON is in a different part of London so we advise using public transport to reach the start point and also to take the following route from Russell Square station to St George's Gardens. (Personal email)

In the email was a link to a Google map, and a copy of the waiver that would have to be signed at the start point when collecting equipment. Before looking in detail at the performance itself, let's pay some attention to this invitation to participate in the performance. It is very explicit: we are told the parameters of what is expected of us in this performance. An arrangement of this sort is far from unusual in contemporary performance, but it is worth noting the care which the producers took to ensure that I understood that I was not to expect a sedentary audience experience and that I was expected to take responsibility for some of their media equipment. Expectations were being managed in two spheres, of audience activity and personal obligation, to ensure that each participant had a good chance of starting the performance appropriately prepared. Helpers were on hand with the portable audio players and headphones that we were to wear through the duration of the piece, and in case of any mishaps or malfunctions. With this preparatory work the performance could begin, allowing the technology through which it was mediated to fade, to some extent, into the background.

INVITATIONS, HABITUS, ENCULTURATION

We can think about how performances like this make an invitation to take up technology and partake of a performance with it as an audience member or an audience participant. In my book, *Audience Participation in Theatre: Aesthetics of the Invitation* (White, 2013), I suggest a framework for thinking about how audiences, as groups of people who haven't prepared in advance to be part of a performance, are sometimes asked to make active contributions to a performance: some of these terms will be useful here. An invitation to participate can be thought of as overt, implicit, covert or accidental (2013, pp. 41–44). A performer can, for example, speak directly to his audience and ask for a volunteer; or leave an empty chair in a room where audiences gather, as a suggestion that someone may sit on it; or play a trick that puts the actions of an audience member 'in the spotlight'; or make a gesture that seems to members of the audience to ask them to respond, when that is not intended.

These different kinds of invitation become more interesting when we consider how these invitations don't necessarily ask for a rational, considered response and, though they might appear to be, aren't addressed to everyone equally. A set of ideas from Pierre Bourdieu's sociology helps to unpack why. For Bourdieu, social interaction depends on who is interacting and what they can bring to situations of the relevant kind. He calls the situation the 'field', and in any field different kinds of social resources (e.g. technical or artistic knowledge, forms of language, ways of dressing in *Outline of a Theory of Practice*, 1977) hold different weight and relevance; he calls these resources 'capital'. How individuals can make use of this capital depends on their learned dispositions, their 'habitus'. In any social situation, our habitus allows us to make use of our capital to our advantage in the relevant field. Most importantly, we do much of this unconsciously: what we should do just feels right, and the situation draws behaviour out of us; or, conversely, we feel awkward, not knowing how to behave, because the field is unfamiliar and there's no appropriate habitus kicking into action to put our capital to work. Crossley has drawn our attention to the idea of enculturation in Chapter 1; Bourdieu's habitus is a particularly strong interpretation of unconscious enculturation in which our first instincts, the way our bodies respond before we think about a situation, are culturally ingrained.

A comparison with computer gaming is instructive: an experienced gamer can become involved in a new game very quickly, adapting to controls, goals and parameters based on prior experience and affinity – these skills are capital, useful in this field but not necessarily in others, and applying them to the somewhat-fresh context of a new game is what the gamer is disposed to do, it's part of their habitus. A non-gamer must work harder for longer to gain a degree of mastery over game controls, so that to begin with their involvement is in *how* to do things in the game, rather than in *what* they are doing and what they are trying to achieve. The same is true of a newcomer to a social situation like experimental theatre, asking themselves 'How am I supposed to understand what's going on here, and how am I supposed to behave?'

Applying this theory in this way suggests that what is happening is an enculturation as well as a learning process; it reads the process as changing the individual's embodied interaction potentials, changing their capacity for action within certain networks of stimulus and response, or risk and reward. It hasn't just given us a new game experience at our disposal, at our fingertips: by altering our habitus it reprogrammes those fingertips and the embodied mind that makes those fingertips work. Crossley has introduced Merleau-Ponty's body schema in Chapter 1, the idea that a blind person's stick, or a game player's joystick, extends their 'world of feel-able things'. It is worth keeping in mind the possibility that the software of the game might also be part of our body schema, along with its control devices; that as well as devices that allow us to feel and do things beyond the limits of our skin, technology has ways of reaching within us and changing what and how we feel and what we do. Why not go further and think of how the software itself extends *into the body* of the player, as a set of instructions that we follow – but that's an idea to return to later in this chapter.

The idea of habitus-field-capital helps us think about why invitations to participate in performances mean different things to different people, but also how when we do engage in an unfamiliar interaction: it brings about small – imperceptible, perhaps – changes in us. The theory can apply to performances where what we are invited to do is something strange and unexpected, or something more familiar and apparently more straightforward – putting on headphones, for example, and listening to recordings while continuing to pay attention to and perhaps interact with the non-recorded world around us. The three examples of this chapter are works of this kind, and I intend to show how they too, in subtle ways, work on our enculturation, and re-enculturate us, reprogramme us for social interaction through technological mediation.

The beginning of *Remote London* seems to have a strategy to allow all to participate, to render the differential capital available to audience members equal: all can be assumed to be familiar with walking around the city; all can be assumed to know how to listen to recorded sound on headphones, with guidance to ensure that any unfamiliarity is glossed over. But nevertheless, the piece makes use of technology that is in the process of enculturating us. It imitates artificial intelligences, and the voices with which they speak to us, on an increasingly regular basis.

AFTER THE INVITATION

When *Remote London* gets under way, we are guided by disembodied voices. The voices we hear are not only disembodied by being mediated through the headphones, but they are also computerised voices, synthesised rather than recorded, and thus lacking a point of origin in a human body. This lack of a body is part of the fictional world introduced by the words spoken, referred to explicitly by the first of the voices, who calls herself Rachel. Rachel, we learn, is a computer, and she speaks with envy of the human bodies that walk together under her guidance. The audience is first invited to wander among the gravestones of St George's Gardens, and to imagine the dead gathered there, and then to gather together as a crowd ourselves before moving out of the park and into the city. As we walk, we are invited to think of ourselves as a 'horde', as a single organism with a shared identity. We are described as if we move as one, and this sense of collectivity is reconfigured in different ways several times: at different points we observe others in the city; we pretend to be a crowd on a demonstration; we dance; we are split up into teams; we race each other. We become 'flaneurs' – idle, wandering investigators of the city's streets – both separate from and among the city's living inhabitants, who seem to perform for us, for example at King's Cross Station, where the architecture of the station entrance is appropriated as a proscenium arch, framing the everyday action as a show laid on for our benefit.

This technological 'mediation' is focused on the use of headphones to deliver artificially produced voices, which interweave with visual, spatial and physical elements to create a set of complex layered experiences. A substantial proportion of what is heard in these pieces is spoken text, addressed directly to the listener to create an imaginative world in which a relationship to technologised life is reimagined. Having outlined how engagement with performance is a matter of enculturation, where invitations to participate can be socially differential, it seems clear that this piece, which invites participation using such generally familiar technologies as headphones, does not draw on obscure or difficult social capital or habitus to engage the participant. It is easy to become involved in; but what I propose is that the process of inducting participants and the appropriation of our familiarity with technology is part of its performative dramaturgy, integral rather than peripheral to them as works of art. It makes a difference that we are probably familiar with navigating the city while wearing headphones, that we may be used to following instructions from computer-generated voices and (in a different way, and not necessarily for all participants) that we are comfortable treating this as an 'art' experience and, for example, reinterpreting the architecture of a station as a piece of theatre technology.

ZUNSHINE AND MIND READING

To unpack some of the layers of what is happening in this way, I introduce here another idea of how we respond instinctively to social situations, an idea of 'mind reading' drawn from contemporary cognitive science. Throughout this piece of headphone-walkabout performance, the participant spectator is provoked, explicitly or implicitly (more often implicitly), to imagine the mental states of other minds. Some of these people are real; some are fictional; and some of the fictional minds are not human. At some points the overlap of fictional and real people creates interesting tensions, and the overlaps of human and invented non-human minds suggests a reimagining of the subjective experience of being a human body in a contemporary city.

For Lisa Zunshine, a leader in the emerging field of cognitive cultural studies, works of art provoke this imagination of other minds in ways that exploit our involuntary compulsion for 'mind reading', an essential part of human psychology, founded on 'neural circuitry that is powerfully attuned to the presence, behaviour and emotional display of other members of our species' (Zunshine, 2012, p. 4). This 'circuitry' (its precise structure remains disputed amongst neuroscientists) leads us to perceive in other people's bodies and actions evidence of their thoughts and emotional states; it seems to make perceptible the invisible interiority of other subjectivities. Importantly, these perceptions are not a matter of deliberate enquiry, but of preconscious orientation to everyone that we encounter:

> This attunement begins early (some form of it is already present in newborns), and it takes numerous forms as we grow into our environment. We are intensely aware of the body language and facial expressions of other people, even if the full extent and significance of such awareness escape our conscious notice. (2012, p. 4)

This is a key human attribute that makes culture possible, she tells us, because it allows us to negotiate complex social environments and to represent human beings (and other subjects) as having meaningful, complex interior lives. Think of a figurative picture of a human subject – how much does it tell us explicitly about what the subject feels, and how much do we perceive about those feelings on the basis of facial expression and body language? Think of a character in a radio drama – how much do we perceive about their state of mind because of their tone of voice and manner of speech, in fact how much more do we know through these cues than through what they say? So far, so obvious. What is really insightful in Zunshine's analysis is the identification of strategies of 'embodied transparency' through which forms of representation manipulate this instinct and intrigue us by making us feel that we have been given privileged access to more insight into a subject's secret interior than usual. She describes film scenes in which characters showing apparent restraint under great emotional pressure nevertheless seem to reveal themselves to us; and traditions of painting which celebrated (and proliferated) scenes of people distracted, absorbed, or asleep and therefore unusually unselfconscious; and the humiliations of reality TV with their very direct exhibitions of emotion. All of these are compelling to us because we cannot help but imagine the inner life of a sentient body that comes to our attention, and if context, inattention or obvious activity makes some germ of this inner life perceptible, we will strive to fill in the gaps. What is interesting in the context of *Remote London* is how this is manipulated in a work where the ostensible performers, and key characters, have no body at all with which to create this transparency.

Throughout *Remote London*, I am implicitly led to imagine several different minds and mental states – including the minds behind the computer voices that speak to us. But what kind of mind do I imagine in this case? The mind that is proposed in the text is an artificial intelligence, a computer mind with presumably some kind of computer body. It is, of course, ventriloquised by another intelligence, an author who has invented and typed its words and submitted them to a machine to be generated as sound, then recorded and reproduced for each performance. Nevertheless, I cannot help but imagine the subjectivity and personality proposed by the text – Rachel, and later George – as a presence with me as I walk the streets of my home city. What we can draw from Zunshine and the neuroscience she is inspired by is that this imagining is an unconscious and compulsive activity, not a flight of fancy inspired by conscious thought about the story and characters.

As well as this, I imagine the subjectivity and personality (the mind) of the performance-maker who wrote the text, who conceived the work and who guides my action. I wonder about the intentions of the theatre makers. The feeling of the performance makers as present with me, is powerful. These things work on involuntary responses of mind and body, and are wrapped together thematically, formally and technically in this work.

MANIPULATED MIND READING

This isn't exactly the embodied transparency that Zunshine tells us about: there are no other bodies to associate with the most important characters in the play. But it depends on the same kind of 'mind reading', in the positing of an intelligence and an intention behind action and words, rather than within a human body. It's still, in her words, about 'getting inside your head'. It doesn't present or describe bodies betraying the minds that they contain. But it plays games with conflicting impressions of minds at work: as I participate, I don't only imagine the mind of a character, but also the intelligence behind that character.

As Rachel asks us to move out of the cemetery in St George's Gardens, I feel some irritation. Can we not linger longer here? Can I not stay longer, now that this curious corner of the city has been revealed to me? But she insistently moves us on, and as she does so begins to suggest that our manner of responding to her commands reveals something about our character – are we the sort to dash ahead, or to fall behind? This irritation turns to a kind of delight, however, when it becomes clear that it is written into the performance: Rachel talks to us about our obedience to her voice, and how this replicates the predictability and orderliness that is a requisite of living in a modern city. As she instructs us to perform, to dance with each other, or to raise our arms 'in protest', I join in partly from the sense of fun that being part of the 'horde' brings, but also because I become aware that if I choose not to take part, then my refusal only illustrates what Rachel has been saying about cooperation. If I don't play my part, the performance as a microcosm of the city, begins to break down.

Thinking about how my participation is being manipulated, I grow to admire what the performance is doing with me, and aware of the performance makers as being on the journey with me. There is a technical cleverness to giving the impression that Rachel – who must be a prerecorded voice, mustn't she? – is watching us as we wait at a pedestrian crossing, timing her instructions perfectly to our permission to cross. There is also a cleverness to the script that seems one step ahead of my thoughts about what it asks me to do. Just after we have formed an audience to watch the bustling crowd at King's Cross, where the commentary about what people are carrying is uncannily accurate but where I feel self-consciousness at stopping to stare at passers-by, we are asked to stop again to look at our reflections in the plate glass of a restaurant. We can see ourselves as the strangers at the station saw us, an odd group huddled together wearing identical headphones; but then I see the people on the other side of the glass, noticing us and looking back. What do they think of this strange crowd? How many times have they (especially the restaurant staff) seen a crowd like this today? 'Good move', I think before Rachel takes us somewhere else. 'What have you got next?' – or something of the sort.

The performance asks me to get inside the heads of other people, and it gets inside my head too. We might think of this performance as working with a *disembodied* transparency, working as it does with voices that have no bodies, both because they are themselves actually computer generated and because in the fictional world of the piece they are computer minds, without human bodies. It is one of the tricks of the piece to lead us to attribute feelings to a (fictional) machine mind that cannot have feelings like ours and to allude to a host of other non-human minds inhabiting the city with us, as a subtext to our movement around a contemporary city as fleshy human bodies. As 'normal' human minds, we cannot help but feel curious about what motivates these minds, about what they might conceal, when on reflection we can imagine that their inner lives would have to be utterly foreign, impenetrable except to (fictional) computer scientists responsible for their self-generating, emergent cognitive systems.

The authors of the work are disembodied too. We hear voices that speak words that they have written; we follow instructions that they have invented; and though they are not with us to display the outward symptoms of their inner lives, we will still 'read' into these manifestations of their controlling agency for what is in their minds as they interact with us from several removes. We are interested in their authorship of our experience, when they are not with us in the flesh. I feel – or imagine that I feel – what the strangers I encounter on the street feel and what the other participants feel, and it provokes my own affective states. I go through a number of relationships to how I imagine their thinking, ultimately coming into a fairly complex orientation towards what I think is intended for me and for other participants by the performance makers.

Our orientation to the work leads to how we participate in it. Follow the metaphor – how we turn to face it initiates and is part of our repertoire of action when invited to participate. And our orientation is dictated by how we imagine and feel the other minds present to us. I am disposed to respond, to take up a relation in certain ways. In part, I am consciously orienting myself towards an evolving set of 'other minds' as I perceive them in this network of activity. And in part I orient myself unconsciously: my dispositions don't manifest in my own mind as conscious thoughts. To put this strongly, they are pre-subjective or intersubjective. This line of thinking helps us to explore how complex affective processes arise out of relatively simple participatory strategies that depend on and exploit our embodied mind: we are bodies that encounter other bodies, rather than just minds aware of other minds.

MACONDO

Another example can help to further unpack this idea of embodied orientation and how it is exploited in performance. In Silvia Mercuriali's *Macondo*, a seated, headphone-wearing audience are invited, one by one, to take roles onstage, to act out a 'play' whose cast has, apparently, gone missing. The play is based on Gabriel Garcia Marquez's *One Hundred Years of Solitude* (2007), with its extensive cast of characters and epic themes, but the headphoned audience, instead of seeing the play conventionally staged before us, hears the backstage crew bickering and trying to solve the peculiar situation of the absence of the actors that should be bringing the story to life. We are spoken to via the headphones, individually and as a group, brought onstage and instructed to strike poses, speak short scenes, and dance. As audience participants giggle and grimace their way through their tasks, they also fleetingly capture the sense of the story and the characters. As well as sympathising with their embarrassment and confusion, as audience members we might find ourselves 'reading' them as the characters, attempting to assemble the story out of misshapen fragments and to enjoy an incompetently assembled spectacle.

Mercuriali works with our orientation to the performance by assembling us first as a conventional audience, our gaze directed towards an empty stage, but then interrupts this with disembodied voices that direct our attention to other unseen spaces, an imaginary backstage milieu of theatre's unseen workers. Again we imagine characters who are invisible to us; they are disembodied in the sense that we cannot directly share space with them, see them or relate to them physically, though unlike the computer voices of *Remote London,* they are spoken by actors and are ostensibly human characters. The additional layers of this performance come from the performances given by audience participants, by the other people we watch and the performances we give ourselves. On the occasion that I experience *Macondo*, the audience participants appear to obey the instructions they are given. They step onto the stage with differing amounts of boldness or self-consciousness; they cooperate with each other to show us tableaux of murder and heroism, costume themselves or become 'the director' ordering others around. What's going on for us here is not the familiar situation of watching a show at the safe distance facilitated by the architectural technology of the theatre, but experiencing something emerging that involves us in it. We seem to be disposed towards obeying instructions given through headphones, perhaps because we have come to a performance that depends on them, but also perhaps because of the familiarity of that relationship to technology and of the habit of doing as we are asked, an orientation to disembodied voices that disposes us to trust them. So we find ourselves disposed to step into the light of the stage, to become part of the show, and so the show becomes what we do as well as what we see. And what the show means also comes to include how we feel about what we do, that we might have found ourselves doing without quite knowing why.

AFFECT AND EMBODIED MEANING

Mind reading, as Zunshine borrows it from cognitive psychology, can be read as an aspect of embodied meaning-making. This is a set of propositions about how our interactions and responses to events and the world around us are led by the physical body rather than a disembodied consciousness. Embodied cognition says that meaning constantly emerges from the body's embeddedness in its environment, and that this where-am-I-and-what's-going-on meaning provides the basis of all our conscious thinking. It's not that we are merely instinctive animals, acting without thinking, nor are we automata, doing only what we are programmed to, but that thinking is not necessarily (or even often) the most important element of how we understand and act in the world. A more embodied interpretation of the mind-reading phenomena discussed in Zunshine's work would cast it as a mind feeling, as the body's awareness of other bodies present at a precognitive level, that comes to mind as observations of how those bodies orient toward it. Mark Johnson describes it in this way:

> An embodied view of meaning looks for the origins and structures of meaning in the organic activities of embodied creatures in interaction with their changing environments. It sees meaning and all our higher functioning as growing out of and shaped by our abilities to perceive things, manipulate objects, move our bodies in space, and evaluate our situation. (Johnson, 2007, p. 11)

Though the architecture of embodiment theory is often built on the young child's interactions with simple objects and spaces, and of the adult's orientation to other people, it is not hard to identify in Johnson's 'situation' that there will be technological things, objects, environments and means of moving in space, playing a part in the meaning of any contemporary human existence. Embodied meaning is the meaning of the technologically engaged body. This moment-by-moment flow of engagement, interpretation and response is sometimes called *affect*, a term drawn from psychology, where it is closely connected with emotion. An affect is a felt response that hasn't yet reached conscious awareness; it is the bodily state that sets the scene for our conscious feelings of fear, comfort or curiosity. A simple way to understand the relevance of this is to consider that things that come to our attention must have already been happening before we became conscious of them, happening to the body:

> The idea is that whatever becomes noticeable must already have been affecting one and must have some kind of affective force or allure, or affective 'grabbiness', in relation to one's attention. (Thompson, 2007, p. 263)

For Brian Massumi this not-yet-known meaningful orientation to the world is an area of great potential. What we know and what we do emerges from it and returns to it – it is a field of energy that connects us and one another, a flow. Massumi is a philosopher at the forefront of connecting cognitive philosophy and affect with critical social theory (and not without his detractors), exploring how politics at the macro and micro level is a matter of affective dynamics: think of how a political demagogue convinces his followers, or how an individual is browbeaten into conformity. The theory of the habitus outlined earlier might be recast as a theory of embodied cognition and affect in this mould: the body that has learned how to interpret a social field, and is disposed to respond appropriately, has been shaped and habituated into an affective dynamic that allows it to function. A social situation is matched in the body by an appropriate affect, which drives a response-choosing moment, more conscious or less conscious as the situation allows.

In *Remote London*, there is an explicit coming together as a group, with references in the spoken text to what it means to live together, and shared actions undertaken by the participants, who themselves act as a commentary on what it means to share space and negotiate the sharing of space. This is affective life at a thematic level, part of the subject matter of the piece. The bodies that inhabit the city that Rachel tells us about derive their predictability, mutual trust and interdependence from affectively orienting themselves to each other. In *Macondo*, the coming together is less explicit, though by the end of the piece the whole audience is onstage moving together as a dual community – both the village of the story and the actors telling it. It is potentially more affectively challenging, in the sense that there is more potential to feel conflicted about whether and how to participate, a potential to feel conflicted while participating, to feel that we are doing things that are not our own, but that perhaps we are moved to do those things without knowing why. What each of these performances means to us will emerge from moment-by-moment experience rather than from the reception of a pre-planned performance, from being bodies in motion and in relationship with other bodies and the minds we imagine in them.

MEDIATED LIFE

What has this to do with intermedial performance, particularly? It may seem like a long-winded way of fleshing out what is going on when we make decisions in the kind of performance that gives us space or makes demands that we do so, how we don't select our options or express ourselves as rational subjects, but foremost as embodied minds that make a situation meaningful, with a felt, affective interpretation coming before all else. But what this kind of thinking directs us to is to think about the roles that technology plays in both presenting this in-the-world situation to us and in shaping our embodied cognitive response to it.

Think of how you use your mobile. If you're in the habit of using its maps and route-finding functions, you may have found yourself becoming dependent upon them. You may find that you habitually reach for your phone whenever starting a journey, when you know the route and could find your way and estimate your time of arrival without it. But this does more than simply reduce your ability to navigate independently while enhancing your ability (when equipped and connected) to find your way. It changes your embodied understanding of geography and space. The phone, and its map, extends how we move and becomes an extension of us. As Massumi says, it is a kind of prosthesis (Massumi, 2002, p. 96).

In *Remote London*, we are told a story (in a sense) of non-embodied minds, enquiring about the experience of a group of embodied minds as they negotiate the vast complexity of a modern city. The prosthesis in this case is not our own phone, but a GPS-enabled audio player. It serves to separate us from the rest of the city while connecting us to it in an alternative way (as discussed above) and also connecting us to a smaller group of co-participants. We are used to headphones; we don't have to be newly acculturated to putting them on and moving around while wearing them. We aren't surprised by the voices that appear in our heads or the presences of other minds to us; we slip seamlessly into the symbiosis of the technology with ourselves. The elements become a system:

recording, headphones, ears, eyes, legs. We look and walk as directed, affectively orienting to the combined situation of city streets and the words appearing in our heads, consciously monitoring and occasionally choosing what to do (Figure 6.1).

Rimini Protocol has said that part of the inspiration for *Remote London* is the growth of computer-generated voices mediating our lives, particularly as we get used to GPS devices aiding our navigation, and that we grow used to taking instruction from these voices. *Remote London* not only shows us this but also puts it into action through our own bodies, and manipulates our body–mind and its responses to voices of this kind, to other bodies and to urban space. Mercuriali, too, has created a series of works through her companies Il Pixel Rosso and Rotozazza, which are described as Autoteatro, performances that are initiated through instructions given to audience members, usually through recordings heard through headphones. The performances of Autoteatro emerge 'automatically' through instructions only, with no further input, relying on the way we respond to instruction and play – often with other people – with this invitation. Both the Remote series and the Autoteatro are collections of affective works in the way they work across the affective connections of body to machine and body to body.

Figure 6.1   Rimini Protokol, *Remote X* (2016). Photographer: Mike Vonotkov.

THE ENCOUNTER

In Complicité's *The Encounter*, we are also invited to put on headphones to hear the performance, though in this case we have been invited to take seats in a theatre auditorium and asked not to leave them or do anything else unusual during the performance. The innovation, in this case – and perhaps the surprise – is that the technology of the auditorium as an acoustic device is not put to use: we hear the performance entirely through our headphones while we watch the performance onstage in something like the usual manner. The performance begins with Simon McBurney, the only performer, explaining the equipment onstage, a binaural microphone

> which imitates the human head. It places you aurally right here on the stage. As if these ears were yours. It's as if you were standing on stage with me. . . . Now what I would like you to do is close your eyes. I'm going to take a little walk, around your head. You should have the impression that I really am beside you. This is not digital manipulation, this is what I'm really doing. (Complicité/McBurney, 2016, p. 9)

As with *Remote London*, the technology itself is to be a character in the play, though this time in a more direct way, not disguised in the portrayal of a technological character, but foregrounded as the impetus behind the action in one of the play's two layers of narrative. McBurney's domestic exploration of binaural technology inspires him to devise a way of telling an untellable tale, of another exploration and discovery, but in this case one that is radically anti-technological. As the play continues, a second narrative emerges and becomes dominant, as a distorting mirror to the discovery of the potential of binaural technology. McBurney tells us of his fascination with the story of Loren McIntyre's odyssey in the Amazon rainforest, in which the photographer – a man in a quintessentially technological profession – becomes lost when pursuing pictures of the Mayoruna, a rarely seen Amazonian tribal people, only to be rescued by one of these communities and taken on an even more disorienting journey of exploration, within himself and, it seems, out of the stream of ordinary time, and back to 'the beginning'. The tale is told with McBurney's progressively more elaborate use of visible onstage Foley techniques producing diegetic sound and atmosphere.

In Chapter 4, Joanne Scott has described in detail how the play manipulates several streams of time and is able to do so because of the recording and sound-creation technology it uses; I am more interested in the relationship it creates with its audience and how the theme of societies that are or aren't dominated by technology weaves through the performance and the way that we engage with it. This performance doesn't ask us to 'do' anything; we are a 'passive' audience. But if we agree to take part on its terms, not only to put on the headphones and listen, but to imagine what is described to us, playing along with McBurney's scheme of matching unexpected objects to the sounds of the rainforest and the gradual sensory derangement of the story's protagonist, then the story and its technique will begin to work on us. We will participate in the performance by doing the work that it asks of us, synthesising the aural environment with the textually described one and divorcing it from the inconsistent stage picture. But the performance 'gets inside your head' in another way, using technology and technique that offer a performance that can only be brought together in our heads by the peculiar neurosensory dynamics that binaural recording appropriates. The performance not only feels as if it is up close and all around, as McBurney seems to encircle each of us in our seats as he walks repeatedly around the stage, but it is also happening inside our heads as our aural-neurological system does its work.

Though McBurney is the only performer, he performs a number of character voices, and other recorded voices are heard, including those of Petru Popescu, the author of *Amazon Beaming*, on which the play is based; a number of experts on tribal people's rights, psychiatry, neurobiology and the mathematics of time; and McBurney's five-year-old daughter, Noma. As Scott notes earlier in chapter 4, a joke plays out where the onstage McBurney argues with a recorded McBurney about who is in the past, present or future; the absent daughter has conversations with the present father; and fragments of interviews with experts interrupt and overlap with each other. The very simplest potential of recording technology, to make absent people present, is exploited to foreshadow the existential confusion to follow.

McIntyre's journey into the forest is also a journey away from technology: he arrives by aeroplane but soon becomes lost and unable to navigate. Then his watch, Nike trainers and camera are destroyed, whereupon he is 'reduced to just a body' (Complicite/McBurney, 2016, p. 33) having to live by 'nature's clock' (p. 34), as the Mayoruna do. He bonds with them by weaving a belt out of palm twine, and comes to rely on their medical techniques, but in a climactic scene there is a ritual destruction of the Mayoruna's own equipment:

> They carry their belongings and pile them next to the fire. Axes, manioc graters, calabashes, fishhooks, personal belongings. Another great mound of objects is forming. Painstakingly crafted objects, critical for the tribe's survival, things they would never mindlessly abandon. (Complicité/McBurney, 2016, p. 46)

All of these things are burnt, apparently releasing the tribe to return to 'the beginning'. As with *Remote London*, the events of the play and the form of our engagement with it refract its concern with technology differently. McIntyre's odyssey away from the modern world is inverted in the intimacy that the headphones give us with the rich binaural soundscape of the performance and with the technology itself. McBurney's exposition of the technology, and the stage setting ('prosaic to the point of dullness' [2016, p. 6]), expose the performance mechanics and foreground the technique and equipment: there is a strategy to deliberately make the technology a feature of the play. The objects used to make sounds onstage are distinctly visually un-evocative of the environment they portray: water bottles, crisp packets, handheld recording devices, mobile phones. The virtuosity of generating soundscape with these means (though there are progressively more authentic recorded sound and voices played by the two onstage sound engineers as the play progresses) is celebrated, but the contrast of two worlds is also accentuated by this strategy.

There is a conversation threaded through the play between McBurney and his daughter, facilitating his reflections on how contemporary technology reshapes our experience of time and how we carry hundreds of photographs and can record and relisten to our loved ones (even stage conversations with them); the past can be made present, and the present cast forward into the future. This serves as a contrast to the Mayoruna's desire to leave behind a life – and time – shaped by technology, to return to the beginning.

EXOTICISM AND DERANGEMENT

The play has a colonial dimension, portraying a distinctly exotic, uncivilised 'other' to reflect the anxieties of a privileged contemporary perspective. The Mayoruna have abilities lost to modern people: they can communicate telepathically and ritually manipulate time, and can reveal to McIntyre (and tantalisingly hint to us as we experience the story) the potential of a non-technological life. They serve as a refracting mirror on modern life, cyphers rather than fully drawn characters. But as with *Remote London*, it is the way the technology and technique of the play itself are integrated with this theme that is interesting in this context. In a self-consciously technological work, the climax is a celebration of the 'primitive', where an alternative shamanistic technology of ritual derangement leads to an out-of-body experience. The in-body technology of binaural audio invites us to our own derangement, a feeling that we may be out of body ourselves, along with McBurney/McIntyre. As well as the delight provided by hearing so much out of so little, as we see everything McBurney uses to create a rainforest adventure for us, there is a kind of ambush: apparent theatrical minimalism (a stage with one man, a head-shaped microphone, a table and a few household objects) overwhelms us and conjures up its opposite. The play culminates in an excess, visual as well as aural, with chaotic images of the performer at work onstage and the debris that gathers around him. If we keep up, don't remove our headset or look away, we may begin to feel similarly transported, or at least distorted. It may be that McBurney is interested in the shamanic roots and potentials of theatrical performance. If so, he has chosen in this piece to look backwards to it through cutting-edge tech. This formal/thematic relationship is not accidental, but structural.

Just like *Remote London*, *The Encounter* is about us as users of the technology and about technology in everyday life. It's even more thematically reflexive, as it wraps the problem of the destruction of technological objects and the escape from modernity into the plot at the same time as the tech we are using becomes increasingly immersive. The escape from modernity is also an escape from mediality and an escape to a space of potential. It shows us how our meaning-making is historically (i.e. in a way that is connected to things as they are right here, right now), wrapped up with tech, including our longing to be without it.

THE GOD OF EARS

Early in the play, immediately after McBurney has asked us to put on our headphones, he says:

> So now instead of shouting I can be as close to you as I am to my children. Closer in fact, because now, instead of whispering in your ear, I am in the middle of your head. (Complicité/McBurney, 2016, p. 7)

He thus demonstrates something that headphones can do that everyday sound production cannot – it can make us hear sounds and voices internally. Most of the play makes use of the capability of the binaural microphone that is onstage throughout, to give uncannily precise directional sound. But this reference to a voice 'in the middle of your head' prefigures a telepathic voice that McIntyre will hear later in the play, and his descent into a kind of madness.

In an essay called 'The God of Ears', media theorist Friedrich Kittler riffs on the theme of hearing and madness (Sale and Salisbury, 2015, pp. 3–17). The essay is partly a fan letter to Pink Floyd's 'Brain Damage', the penultimate song on *The Dark Side of the Moon*, itself an elegy to their erstwhile singer Syd Barrett, lost to the band through mental illness some years before this record was made. For Kittler there comes together in this song (and the album as a whole) the realisation of the promise of stereo recording and a lyric that makes incipient madness a matter of aural disconnection, of what is heard and not heard.

So, in the age of its possible technical impact, the history of the ear is always the history of madness, too. Brain damage music renders true what, in the form of dark anticipations, has been stalking many minds as well as the corridors of mental asylums. According to a dictionary of psychiatry, 'the sense of hearing is, more than other senses, affected by hallucinations'. Purported acouasms, perceived or caused by delusion, range from white noise, frizzling, the sounds of water drops and whispers to talking and screaming. It reads as if the dictionary of psychiatry wants to list Pink Floyd effects (Sale and Salisbury, 2015, p. 10).

The Encounter adds overlapping babbles of voices and the sounds of the rainforest to the water drops and whispers. Kittler's concern, it seems to me, is with how technology changes what we hear and how we hear, with what sound and hearing are, for us, as an extension of ideas about hearing that predate sound recording and reproduction. The god he refers to in the essay's title is Pan, Greek god of nature and the wild, of wooded glades, and who also gives his name to the word 'panic': the coincidences with the subject matter of *The Encounter* continue. If our language is shot through with assumptions about hearing voices, hearing is our frontier with insanity. Modern aural experience is enhanced by recording and playback, but it is also interpenetrated by sounds beyond our control, a host of voices from bodies that are not present, from which we cannot hide: the everyday soundscape is *mad*. Sound art, then, is where tales of madness will be told, and *The Encounter* is a piece of sound art, doing what it should: making disembodied voices appear in our heads.

But for our purposes Kittler's example is hopelessly out of date: *The Dark Side of the Moon* was released in 1973, its recording techniques, and their integration with its songwriting, were cutting edge at the time. The intervening years have seen an enormous proliferation of such techniques, along with the musical forms that make use of them. Just as important is the proliferation of the means of listening: recorded sound is portable, accessible, available, and the means that it becomes so progress every year. With the technology in my pocket, I might skip from *Brain Damage* to Gnarls Barclay's *Crazy*, and on to Dizzee Rascal and Armand van Helden's *Bonkers*, without pause for thought, or my streaming service may shuffle its way to a sequence that seems uncannily to speak to me, with secret messages in the happenstance order of songs.

156 *Intermedial Theatre*

In an essay on another proliferating recording technology, the cameras integrated into mobile phones, Caroline Basset tries to follow through one of Kittler's theoretical innovations: that the meaning of technology is not necessarily to be regarded as its meaning for us, its human 'users'. Technology 'increasingly orders our world with no reference to humans' (Bassett in Sale and Salisbury, 2015, p. 193), as computers talk to each other at speeds beyond our comprehension. Though camera phones reference humans frequently – incessantly – as snaps and selfies are taken, uploaded and shared, Basset speculates that the process has taken on its own logic, to the extent that 'now that human mobile cameras are taking pictures, humans could take on the role of being mobile', and 'humans are thus reduced to fleshy carrying pouches' (p. 202). Taking pictures, then, is what the network does more than it is what we do, and we slot conveniently into the system. Is this a crazy idea? In two of my examples, we might see it being examined through performance – performances that depend on our following instructions via headphones and mobile audio players. The performance happens because we follow instructions delivered directly into our ears. We are the medium through which the performance happens; we serve it in a way that might replicate how we have become the servants of technology. How seriously should we take an idea like this? We don't need to credit technology with an independent intelligence, only with having gained independent, self-serving but unconscious purposes of its own, as a network of devices that demand to be used. The artists are collaborators in this, wittingly or otherwise, and commentators on it, also wittingly or otherwise.

DISCOURSE NETWORKS

As well as historicising the mythos of technology, in which the stories that we have told ourselves about it as it evolves around us intertwine utopia, psychic inheritances and violence, Kittler charts its inroads into our subjectivity (Kittler, 1999). For Kittler our devices are not mere adjuncts to human agency; they are points of activity within discourse networks. The idea of the discourse network is about the frameworks through which meaning can emerge. In Kittler's work, initially this is the meaning that can be found in texts, as the technologies of writing change historically and allow very different relationships of the word to the hand that writes it, the page on which it appears and the voice that speaks it. But it becomes clear as Kittler's thesis is developed that the proposition is much broader, not limited to the specifics of media and how they each shape meaning (though he is spectacularly well informed on these matters), but about how, in Welberry's phrase, 'mediality is the general condition under which, under certain circumstances, something like "poetry" or "literature" can take shape' (Kittler, 1992, p. xiii).

Obviously, a genre such as 'headphone performance' can only emerge when we have headphone technology and the recording, synthesising and editing technology to go with it. But the point is broader and more interesting than this. Meaning itself is a product of the media available and at work, not of the conscious choices of the artists who make it and the audience who listen to it. One of Kittler's most striking turns of phrase is to refer to the human agent in the age of media as 'so-called Man' (Kittler, 1999, p. 16), expressing a pithy scepticism about the relevance of an independent category of human subjectivity, preferring to see a discursive formation that changes with each emergent landscape of mediality. In other words, what it is to be a human being is significantly shaped by and inevitably intertwined with the devices that share our lives. The points of intersection within the network, between which the discourse spreads and reproduces itself, don't just include inanimate devices. People, too, are part of the network, responding to its demands and reproducing, distributing and reinforcing its discourse. The elements of the network can be considered horizontally, without privilege: we are as much at the command of the network as our devices are. This may seem like a familiar argument about insidious digital devices, relegating their human users to subservience, but it is not inspired by technophobic dystopianism. In the idea of a discourse network, technology and technique are themselves as likely to reproduce assumptions and associations about themselves as to transmit messages thought up independently by human subjects. Human subjectivity is reshaped by being part of these networks – it always has been imbricated in discourse networks, but now the networks are richer, more complex and more independent. What we find in intermedial art is an investigation into these discourses and how we – as audiences engaged by the work's networked possibilities – are and can be networked ourselves.

This is a digression from the matter of intermedial headphone performance and audience interaction, but with a purpose. My purpose is to elaborate how the very engagement of technology in performance can complement performance's thematic content to address our interconnectedness with objects (including technological objects) and with other people. Technological objects extend our perceptual and physical capabilities. They make us more than we are without them, to the extent that some people have begun to think that we take them so much for granted that they are effectively part of us, that we are becoming 'cyborgs', habitual hybrids of human and machine. As with Friedrich Kittler, thinking in this way requires an effort to consider the human and the non-human on an equal footing, not to take human thought and action as the point of origin of this interconnected activity. We are 'programmed' to respond just as our computers are, or at least, interconnected action will entail complementary responses from within a predictable range. Our actions do not begin within us, but elsewhere, in the myriad of stimuli that our body–mind is processing continually, both within and beneath awareness (and as these stimuli are themselves produced by other events, and so on regressively and ad infinitum, they can hardly be said to have beginnings at all). When you are asked to take up a technological object and to hear the world differently through it, you are being asked to become part of the world in a different way. Your position in the network alters; your availability as a channel in the flow of feeling, ideas and action is modified. When or if you reflect on this experience, you might be led to think consciously about how the technique and technology of attention changed what you attended to and how.

CONCLUSION

What the various theories I have drawn on in this chapter have in common is an interest in meaning-making, in meaning not as something that we find articulated in a performance, waiting for us as an audience to come along and receive it, but meaning as something that is continually happening to us. I have referred to a mixed bag of social theory, cognitive psychology and affect theory, all of which focus on the body as the site of emergent meaning, rather than the disembodied rational mind or the messages it sends. This perhaps unexpected perspective from which to consider the audience in intermedial theatre is chosen deliberately to direct attention to what lies beneath the surface of social life, to where technology engages with human bodies in the meaning-making process. The performances I have discussed are both reflexively playful in the way their audiences are engaged with technological devices and in ways that refract the critique of intermediated life in their thematic and narrative content. As audience members for these pieces, we are active parts of the show, not as agents of our own creative will, but as the place where the performance happens through us, as the terminal point of the network.

What should you take from this, as a performance maker? Not, I would suggest, an instruction to go and make reflexive performances about the discourse network, but rather an invitation to allow yourselves to be led by your technology as a collaborator in your making process, to let it lead you (and the rest of us, as your potential audience) into new ways of engaging and new networked ways of being. This doesn't mean imagining that we must absent ourselves from saying what we want to through performance, or that the machines are now in control, but rather it is about being interested in the way that what we want to say is shaped by how we say it, and what we hear (see, do, etc.) is shaped by how we hear it. Working with media is being interested in how media reshape our thinking and our doing, and being interested in what emerges from this reshaping. And as critical audience participants, the invitation is to pay attention not just to what the performance does, but to what the performance does with us, as networked subjects, where meaning emerges in action, interaction, feeling and thought.

Practical ideas

These three exercises use the same equipment and can be done separately or one after the other, in no particular order.

For each exercise, you need several mobile phones, with plenty of call time available, and several pairs of headphones. Each exercise should be given at least an hour and could be given much longer. Each needs at least two paired groups, creating experiences for each other, or more paired groups. Group numbers might be from two to five or six; perhaps they could be exercises for individuals. Each exercise needs you to devise a performance for your paired group, to be shared with them via your phones and theirs, and their headphones. In each you should try to use your phones as a one-way transmission device – when you are the audience, don't answer back!

1. **Improvised Foley**
   Use everyday objects to create a soundscape to be heard through a mobile phone. Spend ten minutes gathering things that can make noises: things you have with you or that are in the room, or things that you can quickly find and fetch – coffee cups, water bottles, cans, etc.

   Think of a scene from a story or a film. Create the atmosphere of that scene or a moment from it. Then explore how the sounds you are working with are heard from one phone to another. Explore volume and proximity – can you combine and balance sounds so they are heard in interesting ways through the receiving phone.

   Try it out by phoning one of your paired groups, to listen to your composition through their headphones. See how they respond. Make it better. Try again.

   You won't be making binaural sound, but you will be exploring how to create aural environments that play on your audience's disposition to imagine an environment.

2. **Audience as actor**
   Take a scene from a play you know that has an appropriate number of characters for your paired group. Develop a set of scripts that you will speak separately to

the members of the other group – that is, one script for each of you to speak to a member of the other group. Your aim is to devise instructions that will invite each of your *instructees* to play their part in the scene. Aim for about 2 minutes of action to start with.

You are not acting the scene; you are instructing someone through your phone and their headphones, giving them things to do and things to say so that they act the scene.

Aim to be economical. Write what you think are enough instructions to make the instructee's performance interesting, and then reduce them by half, keeping the most interesting elements, and leaving the group to fill in the gaps. Think about how you give instructions that work with your colleagues' instructions, so that you build up a scene together using your different instructees.

Try it out: phone your instructees, give them instructions (keeping to your script – don't improvise) and see what they do. Make it better. Make it stranger. Try it again.

3. **Guide character**
Work together to devise a persona who speaks to members of the other group. Think of reasons a person – or a non-human personality – might need to communicate through headphones rather than face-to-face – anxiety, secrecy, to threaten anonymously and so on. Experiment with one another, improvising as a character who has a reason to reach out to people through the phone. Script something that you can speak to someone from the other group, either individually or as a group. Aim to be economical: cut back the script so the listener has gaps to fill in.

Try it out with your paired group. Phone one of the group members and speak to them as the character. See how they feed back to you. Try again, refining the character and the script to be more intriguing and compelling.

Further developments

1. How can you bring these three exercises together? Make a performance that is given for and with another group or an individual from that group, under your instruction. Focus on what has been most intriguing or exciting, and concentrate on how to develop that using the other things you have discovered.
2. Refine your scripts and record them. Can they be refined well enough that they create experiences and performances for your audience participants entirely through the headphone experience?
3. Or instead of moving towards recording, move towards dialogue. What happens if you move through this kind of development of a script and then allow and invite moments of dialogue? See how your audience participants answer back to the characters, environments and performances you have drawn them into.

7 Practitioner Case Studies

Introduction by Mark Crossley

This chapter is a collection of practitioner accounts written by nationally and internationally known theatre makers in their own words. They were asked whether they could reflect on the thinking behind the making of their intermedial practice, the devising processes involved and the performance modes adopted. They all have their own distinctive style of writing about their work, from academic analyses (several of the contributors work in academia alongside their practitioner personae) to musings of a more poetic or practical nature. Wherever possible, the format of the writing as it was presented for publication by the author has been retained, in terms of punctuation, grammar, stanzas and the like, in order to capture the rhythm of the practitioner's expression. Some are long; some are short; some have images, depending on what needed to be conveyed. Each case study is listed with the practitioner's name alongside any institution or company name, the specific production(s) (if relevant) to which they are referring and a short *Background* section to contextualise their practice.

The practitioners in this chapter represent the molten present of contemporary theatre making in their crossing or diffusion of borders between media, modes and genres. They reflect intermediality as it manifests itself today across a wide array of practices, but equally there are many aspects or forms of intermediality that this text did not have space to accommodate. There should be no assumption that the term 'intermediality' is used on a regular basis by these theatre makers, or others like them (even though some make it overt), as it is a term that to some extent remains a conceptual framework rather than a mainstay of practitioner methodology. For the record, only Tristan Sharp, Andrew Quick with Pete Brooks, and Craig Vear make direct reference to 'intermediality' as a term. Perhaps this book will hasten the ubiquity of the word, if such a thing is necessary. Whilst it will of course be left to readers to find their own themes within this final chapter, and any resonances between the chapter analyses and the practitioner voices, I have nonetheless taken the liberty of offering a few initial thoughts that may serve to frame the case studies.

Site is a recurring theme in several of the studies, with Tristan Sharp, Zoo Indigo and David Pledger focusing on this in particular. In this context, architecture and landscape may be considered as media, with their own specific modes of scale, light, acoustics and so forth, alongside the unique contextually qualifying aspects found in each location (hotels, warehouses, forests, etc.). Sharp's is the first study in the chapter, and it may be noted how his company, dreamthinkspeak, experiment with disrupting the modalities of site through their use of miniature models of spaces and rooms the audience have just visited, immediately reframing our experience of them. Russell Fewster reflects on the hypermedial qualities of theatre, and his analysis offers some parallels and contrasts from my earlier review of the term. There are also resonances, from Fewster's exploration of Walter Benjamin's life, to Klich's reflections on magic and illusion, as the production in question sought to evoke Benjamin's maze-like, often hashish-fuelled, experiences and writings through a complex system of 'mise en tech'. Andrew Quick and Pete Brooks from imitating the dog alight upon several of the topics covered in Chapter 1, notably transmediation, representation, transformation and signification in their consideration of the alchemy within the 'screenic' space where the live and the filmic meet. Zoo Indigo's poetic essay on their 2017 production *No Woman's Land* resonates with the themes of forced and enforced migration, which Lavender considered in Chapter 2: intermediality as a lens on history and as a response to global crises. The essay that follows from Dries Verhoeven likewise carries the theme of globalisation and, echoing the thoughts of Scott and Barton, contemplates what may be possible in the intimate, liminal space between screen persona and live participant. James Yarker from Stan's Cafe is engrossed in time – the lack of it, the expanse of it, the elasticity of it and the disappearance of it – in reference to the company's 2016 production *Time Critical*, which involved a series of thematic and performative challenges for the company that the reader may wish to correlate with Scott's impulsion, discussed in Chapter 4, for intermediality to disrupt and reveal time. Stan's Cafe and Zoo Indigo are also notable for their elevation of everyday objects to theatrical signifiers: a chess clock timer in *Time Critical* as a marker of personal, political and mortal time, or a gym treadmill in *No Woman's Land* as a physical representation of migration and sacrifice; the prosaic signifier immediately represented as heightened sign within the qualified medium of theatre. Craig Vear's essay on intermediality in sound composition frames itself within a planetary analogy, considering space and time but also the relationship between sense data and sensations within what Vear refers to as a *Gesamtkomposition*. The final contribution, by David Pledger from the Australian company not yet its difficult, considers the convergence of performance, installation and site in a work entitled *v:Hotelling*, staged in a hotel in the Australian city of Gold Coast in 2016. It ruminates upon the collision of contemporary performance with the commercial reality of such a site and the audiences that knowingly or unknowingly tangent with it.

TRISTAN SHARP: ARTISTIC DIRECTOR, DREAMTHINKSPEAK, UK

Absent (2015)

> **Background**
>
> Dreamthinkspeak, led by the artistic director Tristan Sharp, was formed in 1999 and creates and produces site-responsive performance across the globe. Its practice uses live performance but fuses this with film and installations to create worlds and journeys that an audience can immerse itself in. Its work is noted for the grand scale of productions but also the attention to detail, with settings, narratives and personae often evoked within theatrical dioramas. Productions have been created for such diverse sites as a department store in Brighton, an abattoir in London and a paper mill in Moscow. Often the company's work is inspired by classic texts. including *Who Goes There?* (1999–2002), a deconstruction of *Hamlet*; *Before I Sleep* (2010–2011), inspired by *The Cherry Orchard*; and *In The Beginning Was The End* (2013), which draws upon *The Da Vinci Code*'s the Book of Revelation. *Absent* was created for Shoreditch Town Hall in London and restaged at the Winter Gardens in Blackpool.

Site-specific, site-responsive, site-sympathetic, installation, immersive. These terms get used a lot but don't clarify what I do:

> I create work in buildings that aren't theatres.
> I began working like this in 1994, forming dreamthinkspeak in 1999.
> My influences are architecture, film, visual arts.
> All my work springs from ideas and feelings close to my head and heart.
> Each work is more a meditation or visual poem than a story.
> I don't create work that narrates the history of a building.
> The building is not a setting for a theatrical performance.
> The themes are always about the world we all inhabit beyond the building.
> I look at the world outside through the prism of the building and vice versa.
> The idea is the starting point.
> The building is the catalyst for developing and making the idea concrete.
> My work is part construction, past excavation.

I construct within the building, but I also try to reveal the building in a new light.
The buildings' fixtures and fittings are often embraced and included as part of the work.
The idea and the building become synonymous. You experience both simultaneously.
I always rehearse within the building.
The performers are encouraged to *inhabit* the building, not to use it as a backdrop against which to act.
The rehearsal process is through workshop and improvisation.
Performers continue to improvise during performance.
The above list is not a method statement, but a distillation of what I've discovered since 1994. It is not exhaustive, and not all of my work embraces all of these statements.
The only way I can clarify what I do is by doing it.

That doesn't mean there is no planning. The work is intuitive, but very thorough. Everything is in the right place and there for a reason, even if it cannot be immediately articulated.

Audiences go through the same process. Once you've experienced the work, it will start to release its meaning. The best way to convey this is to take you through a journey of a recent small-scale project called 'Absent'.

'Absent' comprised two 'protagonists'. The project premiered in London 2009 and has been redeveloped twice since then, at Shoreditch Town Hall and then in Blackpool at the Winter Gardens.

This is an overview that relates to the latter two sites.

The publicity blurb and programme states:

The Duchess of Argyll booked into a central London hotel in 1978 and was ejected several years later, having finally run out of friends and credit. In Absent, she is surreally reimagined entering a hotel as an optimistic young woman in the 1950s and being evicted in the present day, into a modernised and radically changed world.

In contrast, the hotel is in the throes of much-needed renovation and commercial development. Recently taken over by a large and respected conglomerate, the business is back in profit and contributing significantly to the economic regeneration of the area.

This is not what the show is *about*. It is only a doorway into the experience.

The woman is a fictional representation of a notorious socialite. The conglomerate is embodied by the CEO. On arrival in the foyer, we see a slick video of him promoting the company's work, filmed in various locations of the surrounding neighbourhood, flagging up local regeneration. He is smart, confident, friendly, articulate, visionary.

His company is a global brand, driving property developments across the world. There are architectural plans in the foyer, showing how the hotel entrance will look post-development. They use an increasingly popular form of modular construction, where everything is prefabricated, then put together like a model kit.

The site itself could easily pass for a once-grand hotel. It's old, faded, romantic, filmic, impractical, dilapidated – the opposite of a modular-built budget hotel. With new owners, there is now a budget-style website through which you book.

After checking in, you are led into a basic budget room. Through a series of two-way mirrors, you see a short scene of the woman's older self, packing in her room prior to departure. She is drunk, mouthy, dishevelled, interesting, spirited, messy, chaotic (Figure 7.1).

Figure 7.1   Dreamthinkspeak, *Absent* (2015). Performer: Pip Mayo. Photographer: Jim Stephenson.

A door opens onto a long corridor, and your journey begins. You move at your own pace, unguided. There are occasional ushers, very discrete, neatly dressed as budget hotel staff.

From this point, you don't see either 'protagonist' again except in filmic sequences embedded into the architecture and fittings of doorways, shelving, windows, mirrors.

From now on, the two 'protagonists' are opposing forces that have been woven into the architectural fabric of the building and the construction through which you journey.

It is now about you: your journey through the building and between these opposing philosophies. The intermedial impact is between architecture and audience.

Your journey continues through freshly painted budget interiors, with the same four Impressionist prints repeated endlessly. If you look through the peepholes of the rooms as you pass, you will see miniature dioramas. One is of the budget room you have just left, with a model of her older self on the bed, with suitcase packed for departure and a wall-mounted TV playing a sepia sequence of her as a young woman unpacking in a swanky 1950s suite on her arrival. Another is a model of that very same 1950s room, with a model of her younger self having untidily unpacked.

Midway through the journey, you arrive at a series of multiple modelled budget rooms of various scales.

You enter a budget room exactly like the first, but strangely smaller. Stranger still, there are architectural models of itself in each of its' fixtures and fittings: small models in shelving units, plan-view models in the wardrobe, and large models set behind the mirror, TV and picture frame. All models have sepia film sequences from the period of the woman's arrival at the hotel, playing within their own fixtures and fittings (Figure 7.2).

Even the room you are in feels like it might be a giant model version of the real thing. Maybe the 'real thing' was also just a model.

This spatial disorientation intensifies as you enter a dizzying series of rooms that comprise a giant deconstruction of the room above, including all the models embedded within it. In effect, you walk through large-scale versions of the fixtures and fittings of the budget room, deconstructed and laid out on a single level: the shelving units, wardrobe, mirror cavity, plasma TV and picture frame.

The homogenous world of modular construction is dissected thrillingly in a multiplicity of modelling madness, like a claustrophobic hall of mirrors.

The impact is multiplied further when you are confronted by a wall of hundreds of small shelving units, each one with a miniature-scale identical model of exactly the same room.

Practitioner Case Studies 167

Figure 7.2   Dreamthinkspeak, *Absent* (2015). Photographer: Jim Stephenson.

After, there is corridor with a mirror in the left-hand wall. As you approach, you expect to see your reflection, but instead you see a seemingly endless series of empty mirror frames, each reflecting itself, but not you. In effect, the 'you' has been effaced (Figure 7.3).

It is a key turning point. From here, the modern renovation, all of which has been in the same design and colour scheme, starts to split and fall away to reveal the former interior of the building through layers of peeling paint, plaster and old wallpaper.

Are you walking in the present through old rooms yet to be renovated, or have you slipped into the hotel's past? Time is becoming ever more uncertain. At one point, you even slip into the future, passing the entrance of the building concreted over, exactly as the architectural plans you saw in the foyer predicted.

In a storeroom, modular wall panels and paint pots are left unpacked and unopened, as if ready to assemble and apply. On closer inspection, these are dreamthinkspeak set-building materials: the paint is (environmentally friendly) theatrical paint from Flints.

Figure 7.3   Dreamthinkspeak, *Absent* (2015). Photographer: Jim Stephenson.

Soon, the rooms are left stripped and empty, revealing old brickwork and foundations. They are blank canvases. If you spend time in them, you may make out the unique features that each one possesses. These rooms exist for themselves, unrelated to the renovation, the notion of a hotel or even the dreamthinkspeak production.

There is one final intervention. Within the cavities of an old Aga-style stove, there are several scale model rooms. These are the rooms you have just been walking through, each one unique and painstakingly modelled, including every blemish and piece of rubble, in stark contrast to the profusion of the modern interiors.

Only one model is of a room you haven't entered. It is the ballroom where she arrived on her first evening, filled with fashionable guests. It has film cut into the back of it. The film tracks her grand entrance as she threads her way through tables and admirers, and finishes with a close-up of her face. A seamless dolly-back shot suddenly reveals the room as completely deserted save for the young woman herself, alone amidst the debris of the night before, as if the whole thing was a dream. The model is laid out inside exactly like it is at the end of the film (Figure 7.4).

Figure 7.4 Dreamthinkspeak, *Absent* (2015). Photographer: Jim Stephenson.

When you open the double doors nearby, you find yourself in the very same ballroom, laid out exactly as it is in the model. You are in the present, apparently walking into the past of her arrival. Or maybe the room has been left untouched for decades, and both you and the room are occupying the present. The large amounts of dust suggest the latter, but the potted plants are still green, and the fabric of the room is in good condition. It is unclear if this room is real or mythical or if it is in fact just another large-scale model (Figure 7.5).

So, what is this piece trying to *say*?

It is not trying to relate the history of the building or tell the story of the woman or tell an audience what to think or feel.

Is the piece portraying the woman and the values of the past as an expression of humanity and distinctiveness, whilst the globalised present champions economic development and homogeneity that essentially effaces our individuality?

Figure 7.5 Dreamthinkspeak, *Absent* (2015). Photographer: Jim Stephenson.

This is certainly one of my preoccupations and one of the key themes that visually underpins the entire journey and brings an emotional kick to the experience.

Yet the production also questions itself and its premises.

The past is not put on a pedestal. It is seen as an unreliable notion – a vivid perception, but also an illusion that exists in the imagination. The idea that the past was beautiful and the present is drab is perhaps as fictional as the idea that the building really was a grand hotel or that the woman ever really existed.

The great modular vision of the conglomerate is also a kind of illusion. The homogenous interior fittings of the new construction are hiding an already existing building. Is this new construction any more 'real' than the existing building? It's not even a genuine construction. It's a temporary installation created by dreamthinkspeak.

Once you peel away all of these layers – the existence of the woman, the narrative of the Shoreditch Group, the fiction of the hotel, the physical layers of interior construction and the digital theatre system (DTS) fabrication of this construction – all of which are also important themes of the production – you end up with the building itself, warts and all.

Is this the reality? Even the building has its own fictions and accretions. It has been through several reinventions and renovations beyond the dreamthinkspeak makeover, glimpsed through those layers of wallpaper and plaster.

In this way, *Absent* is as much an excavation as an installation. An attempt to peel away the layers to reach something that is difficult to put into words, including 'site-specific', 'site-responsive', 'site-sympathetic', 'installation' or 'immersive'.

RUSSELL FEWSTER: UNIVERSITY OF SOUTH AUSTRALIA

Walter Benjamin – A Life in Translation (2016)

Background

Russell has directed theatre for over thirty years, including work with professional actors, acting students and young people. He studied at École Jacques Lecoq in Paris in the early 1980s, thus beginning his theatrical journey. In 2000, he completed a Masters by Research in rehearsal decision-making at the Centre for Performance Studies at the University of Sydney. In 2010, he completed his Ph.D., examining the use of video in performance, at the University of Melbourne.

He is now a senior academic and theatre maker based at the University of South Australia.

Context

Walter Benjamin is a key philosophical figure of the twentieth century, and his ideas on art, theatre, film, mass media, popular culture, consumerism, fascism and war remain influential today. A two-week creative development sought to explore how Benjamin's life and ideas might be translated theatrically. The artists involved included new media artist Simon Biggs, actor Glenn Rafferty, musician Richard Chew, lighting designer Nic Mollison, and myself as dramaturg and director. A work-in-progress showing was held on 23 July 2016 in the Hartley Playhouse, University of South Australia, Magill.

Beginning with direct quotes from Benjamin's writings, the intention was to theatricalise his life via the following means:

- *Immersion:* The actor performed between a scrim (downstage) and cyclorama (upstage), facing the audience and creating an immersive environment.
- *Mirroring:* As the actor spoke, his spoken words were captured and projected on both the scrim and cyclorama through a speech-to-text software

program. This, combined with a three-dimensional motion tracking system, allowed the projected words to move with the actor and created a dynamic interaction as Benjamin's thoughts literally moved with the performer.

An Intermedial Approach

The work sought to draw on modernist practices, but from a postmodern perspective, through the play between a single actor and new media technologies – an intermedial approach that acknowledges how contemporary artists refer to modernist practices for constructing theatrical narrative through means such as montage (juxtaposition of images and sounds) and Brecht's Epic Theatre, with its propensity to disrupt conventional storytelling via projections and the actor breaking the fourth wall (see Chapple and Kattenbelt, 2006).

Rehearsal and Performance

The key issue that arose in the development was how to integrate an interactive system, initially designed for a physically interactive dance project (Biggs et al., 2014), with narrative theatre. Simon Biggs's 'mise en tech' was originally developed for a dance work, *Crosstalk* (2013–2016), and in his own words:

> The environment is demanding of the performer and can't be considered as a backdrop or set; it is an active element, as much to the front as the performer. To work well the piece should be developed such that you cannot tell what is the performer and what is the system, physically or in respect of agency. They become a single agent. (Personal correspondence)

In *Crosstalk*, this means aesthetically the performer is barely visible, performing in low light in order to highlight how the projected media responds to his movement and speech (see Biggs, 2016). For Biggs this can be theorised through the 'work of Michel Foucault, whose concept of the dispositif considers humans as elements in complex systems, technical and social' (personal correspondence). Biggs argues that the relationship between performer and technology creates a scenario where we do not consider 'people as individuals but as nodes or elements in a system comprised of social and technical structures' (personal correspondence). Alternatively, one could reframe this so as to consider the performer becoming a backdrop to the technology. Here we have the question of *Liveness*: Phillip Auslander's argument that the performer becomes part of a mediatised framing system (Auslander, 1999). Chiel Kattenbelt argues, on the other hand, that the theatre as hypermedium can treat technology as something that can be incorporated into the theatre event (Chapple and Kattenbelt 2006, p. 24). Theorists such as Benjamin (1969), Patrice Pavis (1992 and in Svich, 2003) and Steve Dixon (2007) and practitioners such as Bertolt Brecht and Robert Lepage, to name a few, have all engaged with this question of what are the implications of staging the performer with technology. The actor Glenn Rafferty had this to say about his approach to working with a large-scale projection system:

> Only that the scrim onstage will be the hero in its size and, once used, the audience will be hypnotised by the magic. And really this an illusion of sorts. By looking at it yesterday, I was transported as soon as the scrim came to life. (Personal correspondence)

That is to say, the visual power of digital media provokes a need for the actor to reassert his presence. For Biggs, 'As individuals we become fragmented, distributed and blurred and, effectively, it is what makes us (post-) human' (personal correspondence), as proposed by Donna Haraway (1991). When the performer is thus absorbed into the new media work that Biggs's theorises and practices, theatre's traditional demand that the audience see the live human body as well as hear the text is challenged. A key to how the author and actor adapted this interactive dance system for theatre is how the text and the body together demand different spaces in order to engage with the audience.

Rafferty felt that for the audience to connect with the character, alternative staging needed to be considered. He proposed that there be a number of spaces outside the scrim that he, as Benjamin, could move to. This included moving his desk from inside the scrim to outside, using a lectern and directly addressing the audience from within the auditorium itself. This was a radical departure from the originally conceived stage design by the author, which had placed all set pieces behind the scrim. However, Rafferty's suggestion corresponded thematically to the different texts the author had chosen from Benjamin's oeuvre and provided different ways of interacting with the audience: reflective, from the desk, as Benjamin wrote and mused on his writings from a personal perspective; expository, via the lectern, as he outlined some of his key theories and principles; and direct address, in an almost cabaret format, as he regaled the audience with his equal penchant for both 'books and harlots.'[1] This staging meant that the performer moved from audience to desk, to scrim, to lectern – in a circular motion; a mini promenade that gave variety to the performance. The circular motion drew on a circus metaphor, evoking Eisenstein's montage of attractions and Meyerhold's episodic structures.

This altered staging meant that the scrim became an interactive place that Benjamin slipped in and out of and became representative of how he was literally immersed in his world of words and ideas; a maze that was both beautiful and terrifying. In Rafferty word's:

> The rest behind the scrim is what he really is as a human. His ideas of what is human and what is community. This is his dream, his nightmare. Chaos is he as a person. The scrim is working out this chaos. (Personal correspondence)

As Rafferty spoke and moved, his projected words moved with him, and this became a metaphor for Benjamin's identity struggling against that dissolution of self that Biggs points to. Some of the key ways in which the technology reinforced the character's narrative were as follows:

- The spoken texts, following the character left to right across the stage, when he spoke of being born under Saturn: mirroring Benjamin's propensity to wander and to adopt the nineteenth-century notion of the 'flaneur' (the stroller)
- The spoken texts following Benjamin, walking back and forth, upstage and downstage, as he described how, in film, association of images function with the spectator; his physical movement and the movement of the texts illustrating a Montage effect
- Mapping out the character's life in terms of creating his favourite places to visit and inhabit, which, as they appeared by name on the scrim and on the cyclorama, created a sense of the maze that he associated his life with
- The colour and intensity of the projected words and patterns that accompanied a monologue on the effects of hashish and which visually expressed the freedom and inspiration Benjamin found in his experimentation with this drug
- The 'gravity function' of the voice-to-text software which enabled the performer to command key projected phrases to fall down the scrim, to be replaced by another phrase and then another, thereby illustrating both the importance of each new idea and also its propensity to be replaced by another

In this way the director and actor, together with the new media artist, made meaning out of this technological system in terms of the character's personal and thematic journey through their world of ideas; in short, a means to dramatise this philosopher's life. Questions of the body and liveness came to the fore, provoking an ongoing exploration that mirrors theories of dissolution of self and articulation of presence within a technological system. In turn, this reflects the creative tension between abstract and narrative pathways that dance and theatre offer when working with new media technologies.

Interactivity: the motion tracking system allowed the projected words to move with the actor. In this image, Benjamin's thoughts on the effects of hashish are reflected in this movement as well as in the colour and intensity of the projections (Figure 7.6).

Figure 7.6 Russell Fewster, *Walter Benjamin – A Life in Translation* (2016).

ANDREW QUICK AND PETER BROOKS: ARTISTIC DIRECTORS, IMITATING THE DOG, UK

The Zero Hour (2013) and A Farewell to Arms (2014)

Background

Imitating the dog (ITD) has been creating and touring original performance work since 1998. Peter Brooks, Andrew Quick and Simon Wainwright are the artistic directors, and their work has built a company with a unique reputation in the UK, Europe and internationally. Imitating the dog creates outstanding work that challenges and connects with audiences, tests theatrical conventions and brings high-end design, technical and thematic ambition to audiences at small and medium scales.

Scenographic Technologies as Metaphor in Transmedial Performance

Imitating the dog has always had an interrogative relationship with scenography. We have always approached the scenographic world we create as a kind of proposal, in terms of process but also as a metaphoric framework through which the audience reads the text, as well as it being a part of the text itself. We have not felt able (so far) to treat digital scenography as simply part of the generalised language of theatrical scenography. It is not a given. The projected image as signifier in the theatre space is for us always more complex than a simple three-dimensional representation. This is partly to do with the digitally projected image's relative unfamiliarity as a scenographic element, in part because it inevitably references other narrative forms (cinema, television) and also because its use inevitably introduces into the performance space discourses about absence and presence and the whole debate surrounding signification and mediation. This said, our engagement with these technologies has not been pursued as a means to deconstruct texts or act as a platform for deconstruction per se, as if this were even possible in performance (performance is not philosophy). Rather, our interest resides in the exploring the relationship between the screened image and the live body, how live bodies somehow realign our relationship with the screened body, and vice versa, when they occupy the same space. In a sense, it feels impossible to think of live bodies occupying a space that is somehow exempt from the interference of the screen and the information that it produces for our consumption, whether this be fictional information, historical information (news reels, etc.) or documentary information in its various forms. Maybe Jean Baudrillard is correct when he describes the world as being screened out (Baudrillard, 2002). If he is, then our work stakes a claim for the live presence of bodies within the screened space, but always somehow in relation to the screen, in the space of 'screenic' production or representation.

The scenographic set-up for *The Zero Hour* involves both back and front projection screens. Onto the rear screen are projected animated environments hacked from computer games and then adapted digitally. The backgrounds are of locations in Berlin in May 1945, both the actual badly damaged Berlin of our own historical reality, but also versions of the city as it might have been had history unfolded differently. As in previous works such as *Hotel Methuselah* (2006) and *Kellerman* (2008), the actors perform in front of this screen, but in this case they are then filmed live by two camera crews, with the film being edited live online and projected simultaneously onto a front projection screen.

Practitioner Case Studies 177

The actors respond to the director's call of 'action' and 'cut', but otherwise there is no interaction between camera crew and performers. The performers behave as if they are responding to some invisible and unspecified imperative rather than the more localised and real environment of the conventional film set. In this case the camera represents the subjective perspective of history, and the material selected, framed, edited and represented to the audience is analogous to the process whereby the chaos of the past is given narrative shape to become history. In *The Zero Hour*, the figures (the director and camera crew) who sculpt this material are Chinese. In this invocation, the twenty-first-century version of the history of Europe in 1945 is being rewritten for a Mandarin-speaking audience.

In *The Zero Hour*, we use film-making as the central metaphor for the way in which we perceive both what is real and also what constitutes historical narrative. What we see in the stage space in *The Zero Hour* does not cohere visually; it is an unconvincing simulacrum of reality. However, filmed, edited and reprojected using a cinematic grammar, the same material becomes a cinematically convincing representation of our experience of the world, even though its means of construction are made visible. So, two performers onstage, facing away from each other, appear, once filmed, to be sitting next to each other in a car. Reality (the stage world) is being tidied up, filmed and edited to become more real. The crew are Chinese; they speak in Mandarin, and although we do not fully understand their conversations, it is clear that the way in which the actors understand their situation ontologically and historically is neither accurate nor within their control. Alone onstage they are alienated and decontextualised: context is being produced by the framing structure of the film crew and the technical operators who sit unseen in the control room.

It became clear to us, when in the latter stages of rehearsing *The Zero Hour*, that one of the key dynamics that the audience would experience in this performance is the moment in which live (living) events are transformed into screened (lived) events. The delay between the live and the screened was small, but it was noticeable, and the disturbance that this interval of transformation created, of course, became meaningful. It seemed that one of the key elements that we were exploring was what constituted the truth in these two modes of presentation. And this question of veracity arose out of a certain tension that takes place when we are forced to look between the live and the mediated image. Both draw the audience's attention in very different ways. For us, the truth of the moment (and perhaps this has something to do with how actors create a sense, a presence, of being 'real' on the stage) flickered between these two states, between actually being there and the mediatisation of their 'theirness' – the screened image that was always larger than life and, when seen, always removed the clutter of its theatrical production. We realised that this tension also connected to one of the broader thematics we found ourselves exploring, one that is a constant in our work: the question of history itself and what constructs or informs our understanding of historical truth.

ITD's production of *A Farewell to Arms*, an adaptation of Hemingway's novel published in 1929, now feels like a natural follow on to *The Zero Hour*. Once again we found ourselves exploring a highly subjective experience that was set in particular historical circumstances – on this occasion, the conflict between Italy and the Austro-Hungarian Empire in World War I. In a way, the novel is structured around how subjective experience traverses and negotiates the tide of history, and during the design and the initial conceptualisation of the project, we were inevitably drawn to how we might find a way to stage this tension between subjectivity and history, using the transmedial techniques and processes we had developed over a fifteen-year period. Eschewing the more abstract cinematic framework that had been a signature of our earlier work (black proscenium arch, often incorporating different aspect ratios, that acted as frame and projection surface), we decided to stage the work in what looked, at first, like a real space: a derelict hospital. The piece opens with actors and camera crews breaking into this space in order to make a version of Hemingway's novel. The material they record is mixed as a layer into previously made graphical material and projected live into the performance space. As in *The Zero Hour*, the central metaphor is related to the production of film-making, but in this case to a kind of pornographic 'snuff' movie, where the actors appear not to understand where the narrative is taking them, and where the cameras and their crews take on the role of a classical Greek chorus, commenting and nudging the action onwards while dispassionately recording the struggle of the protagonists to avoid the tragic fate which the novel has prepared for them. In *A Farewell to Arms*, the camera crews move in and out of the action, alternating the role of technician with that of performer. They are involved in the action, but ultimately they are observers, their privileged position on the other side of the camera providing a seeming immunity from the tragic events that they witness.

In many ways the intermedial aspects of our approach in this work are a metaphor for the process of reading, of how we imagine and bring flesh to the words, in how we picture them, in how we bring them into play with other fragments of information. We read Hemingway's novel with accompanying sets of connections and associations – to the films of the novel, newsreels of World

War I, black and white photos, romantic fiction and so forth. We read through, and with this jumble of information there is not any purity in the text; hence the disruption of the space through the projection, which, like our imagination, transforms the surface, like the page of the book, into our renderings of the text. The hospital is always there, like the novel, but it constantly shifts under our interpretive gaze.

The only place in the performance where the cameras withdraw is in the scene in which the two main characters find some sense of escape from the forces of history that are propelling them towards an ending that we know is going to be painful and profoundly sad. Finding a kind of sanctuary in the mountains of Switzerland, and during the female protagonist's pregnancy, the novel attempts to explore the day-to-day experience of the central relationship. Here the issues of war – of being on the run, of being injured – fade into the background, and the focus is on the immanent birth of the couple's child and what kind of future the child might live in. This might be a moment, in the face of love, where history is forced into the wings or even made to leave us for a while. For although love endures and is a continuous trope in fiction and all its representations, something about love always seems to evade representation and sits at the edge of language and knowledge, reminding us, perhaps, that certain things might evade the operations of metaphor. In a world where we seem to exist in the whirlwind of image, information and noise, this is a sobering concept and one that always ghosts in our work.

ROSIE GARTON AND ILDIKÓ RIPPEL: ARTISTIC DIRECTORS AND PERFORMERS, ZOO INDIGO, UK/GERMANY

No Woman's Land (2017)

Background

Zoo Indigo is a Nottingham-based Anglo-German performance company co-founded by Rosie Garton and Ildikó Rippel in 2002. Productions have included *Under the Covers* (2010) and *Celluloid Souls* (2017). *No Woman's Land* entwines the story of Lucia Rippel and many other walking women at the end of World War II with Rosie and Ildikó's experiences of their own 220-mile walk. *No Woman's Land* is a three-part project encompassing a three-week walk through Poland and Germany; a short film documenting the walk alongside its historical context; and a large-scale multimedia performance work.

No Woman's Land: Borders of time and transportations of digital image

The Act of Walking

In 1945, as World War II came to an end, Ildikó's grandmother, Lucia Rippel, was expelled from her place of birth, Brzeznica, Silesia. After being raped by a group of soldiers, she walked 220 miles to Pulspforde in Germany, dragging her two small children and all of her belongings behind her in a cart. In 2015, Ildikó and Rosie retraced her footsteps, crossing borders, climbing fences, bleeding and blistering, and carrying their flat-pack children. During their walk, developments of the European refugee crisis dramatically brought the *'then'* to a *'now'*, a historical story in a current place, where survival, identity and migration became an urgent currency of discussion:

> We are tired. We are in a forest in Poland; it is 30 degrees; we are carrying 8 kg; we have walked 16 miles; and we are lost. Our exhaustion overrides our fear and transforms alarm into wide, striding footsteps. Our comfort-seeking eyes lurch forward quicker than the feet can move. In four days Ildikó will have four large blisters on her feet. To distract her from the pain of walking, she gives them names – all B's: Bob, Brian, Bruce, Ben. We will call them the 'Blister Boys'. When one pops, we will deliriously laugh that he has left the band. In three days we will stay in a deadly quiet hotel, where we will watch the news, a terrifying escalating refugee crisis, the images amplified by our ignorance of the newsreader's description in Polish. On day 2, a filmmaker will join us on the walk. This day will be the most challenging of the first week. He will hurt his ankle and he will thrust his heavy camera into Rosie's hands in exasperation; his ankle will still cause him pain a year later.

> The more we walk, the more *time* becomes a ghostly rule of the past. We set off in the morning, and we arrive in the evening; our rumbling stomachs, dry mouths and aching muscles are all that tell the day's clock. There is, however, another *time* that haunts our footsteps, snaps at our heels and chases us through the towering woodland. We are unearthing an unimaginable journey across the then-fractured landscape of Europe. Lucia walked 220 miles in three months; we walk 220 miles in three weeks. We are not hiding; our children are flat-pack; and we have supplies. We criss-cross from Poland to Germany, to Poland, to Germany, following the convoluted route Lucia took to avoid further rape and keep her children safe. We cross the borders between 1945 and 2015, through urban and rural pictures where historical

transformation is revealed: visibly in architecture, inherently in our knowledge of shifting geographies, and in more hushed tones in the social identities of the landscape's occupants. And between these borders we walk through the tall grasses of the unkempt areas of no man's lands. These liminal spaces that are saved by uncertainty and a fear of dispute become timeless corridors through a landscape that so clearly shows its scars (Figure 7.7).

Figure 7.7 Zoo Indigo, *No Woman's Land*, 'Ildikó, Ilona, Charlie, Rosie, Dylan and Lydia' (2017). Photographer: Tom Walsh.

The Walking Acts

In 2017, Zoo Indigo presented *No Woman's Land*, a theatrical reaction to the historical story of Lucia and many other walking women at the end of World War II, alongside Rosie and Ildikó's experiences of their own walk. There is an unspoken reference to current plights of many refugees. Created in collaboration with digital artist Barret Hodgson and musician Matt Marks, the work takes its audience on a rhythmical trek through digitally projected past and present landscapes of the post-apocalypse. Emulating the border crossings that Lucia walked and the duo retraced, the digital media and performance text criss-crosses between *then* and *now*, between Poland and Germany. A Weimar cabaret framework is employed, showcasing a series of *acts* that allow the performers to embrace gallows humour as a mechanism to discuss challenging truths:

> We are wearing beards, waistcoats and braces, because we are men. We are the gender benders of the darkened Berlin bars of the 1920s. This disguise is for all of us – our *own* protection and *your* entertainment. We will sing, dance and tell you jokes; we will keep you laughing and clapping until the moment you choke on your sniggers. You find you are giggling at rape as a routine weapon of war. *Ha-ha*. At sausage rations. At Rape Discos. *Ha-ha*. At carts arranged each month to take those tired wombs for abortions. Again: *Ha*.
>
> Don't worry, like Scrooge's ghosts, we will whisk you back to the present. We will sing you songs about how ill prepared we were for this walk, about our failed plans to walk in our new shoes in Derbyshire, or go to the gym, or print maps. About how we find even just the school run tiring. About our warm-up for this show being a coffee and a pain au chocolate. And there we are; we are back in the present, and you're laughing again – this time more freely, guiltless. And so we go on, tripping back and forth. The bearded ghosts of the past, present and future.

The set is a white three-dimensional plywood landscape, like a pop-up book yet to be painted. As the performance duo welcome in the audience and introduce the piece, the white plyboard is gradually animated with digitally mapped projections. Things creep across the tree branches; flickering neon signs appear on the piano cover; a spiralling staircase works its way down the back screen framed by faded theatrical curtains. The audience now sits amid the jaded glamour of a politically charged cabaret hall. Two white vinyl strips on the floor run from underneath two whirring treadmills; the strips reveal ground filmed during the duo's walk – gravel, grass, brickwork, woodland. Rosie and Ildikó walk on the treadmills, bringing the footsteps of 1945 and 2015 to 2017. They are walking through the footage of 2015, but the textures are timeless. The digital artwork persistently throbs through the performance, devouring all possible surfaces. Snaking between colour schemes and animation, the images serve to illustrate the narrative of the performance, set the scene and disclose secrets beyond the performance text (Figure 7.8).

End-to-End

The performers are consumed in the illustration, the digital beast responding without hesitation to their descriptions, anecdotes, stories and jokes.

Figure 7.8 Zoo Indigo, *No Woman's Land* rehearsal shot (2017). Photographer: Tom Walsh.

And bursting through this visual cacophony, there are screenings; moments from Ildikó and Rosie's walk, archival images and interviews. In these moments, the media is in control of the pace; the digital pulse slows down; and the past is brought to the present with room to breath. Uli Zeitz is on the screen; she joined the walk in 2015 for three days. The filmed footage shows her in a café, talking about her grandmother's plight across a war-torn Europe. A man is laughing loudly behind her over his lunch, and a waiter nudges her as he passes. The past and present are dining together. Uli struggles to describe her grandmother's journey; too much was never dared said aloud. Uli reaches her own conclusions – and right there in the café, she chokes on her words, catches her breath, wipes her tears before she continues. In another moment there are archival images of tired-looking women and small children in heavy winter coats. Later there is a picture of a woman staggering at a roadside in men's trousers, her face bloodied and swollen from a beating. Then Lucia as a grandmother, laughing and fussing over her grandchildren. Back to Rosie and Ildikó dancing with wild exhaustion in the Polish woodlands. The text and digital image are carefully woven together to guide the audience between tensions, times and territories. The digital media is intense, the emotional journey gruelling, the performers are exhausted and the treadmills are droning. This is Lucia's walk:

> We are tired. The performance is demanding, and we just do not have the training to stave off the heavy breathing. We are sweating; our beards are a little smudged, but we are close to the end. We clock the mileage that we have walked on the treadmills during the evening's performance. There is a whoop from the audience. *This is now*. But this distance was just a glimpse of Lucia's walk; she has not even reached her first crossing at the River Neisse yet. *This is then*. The piano stops playing, the lights fade, the treadmills cease their whirring, the breathing slows. And finally the projections snap off. We are left in the dark with just a white timeless set in a black-box theatre space. Transportation over.

No Woman's Land
Performers and devisers: Ildikó Rippel and Rosie Garton
Live music and composition: Matt Marks
Media design: Barret Hodgson
Film documenter: Tom Walsh

DRIES VERHOEVEN: THE NETHERLANDS

Guilty Landscapes (2016)

Background

Dries Verhoeven is a Dutch theatre maker and visual artist.

Verhoeven is internationally renowned for creating installations, performances and happenings in a multitude of locations, often large-scale public spaces in cities as diverse as Rio de Janeiro, Berlin, Vancouver, Oslo, Riga and Amsterdam. His work is difficult to categorise as he is always experimenting with form and audience reception. There is also a resistance to overt political or social commentary, as his website states: 'In his work, Verhoeven highlights aspects of the common social reality in which we live. He is not concerned with conveying a statement about reality, but mainly about unbalancing the visitor in order to evoke a shared vulnerability between the viewer and the viewed work.' Recent productions have included *Homo Desperatus* (2013–), a contemplation of human suffering through forty-four lifelike scale models inhabited by colonies of ants, and *Phobiarama* (2018), a full-sized theatrical ghost train inhabited by live performers, which questions the hysteria of contemporary political rhetoric on race and immigration.

Only Doubt Can Save Us

(Translated from Original Dutch by Sophie Redman)

In an attempt to relate to the unclear, incomprehensible and sometimes frightening world, we are constantly attempting to create stability. We decide how everything functions, what our position is with respect to what we see or hear, what is desirable and undesirable. We fill up Wikipedia. We make rules. We make sense. We draw boundaries. Our thinking is a continuous manufacture of stability. Only through such self-negotiation can one sleep at night.

Oh, were we just a worm, then we wouldn't have to relate! Then we could work our way consuming and copulating to our finality. But worms we are not. Most of us have at least heard one clock chime about ruthless natural phenomena, about the finality of our body, about injustice in the world. And behold, the tragedy of the conscious organism we need to do something about.

We live in a time when a multitude of perspectives reach us daily. And that does not always lead to changing our opinions. Rather, we have seen this continuous confrontation of alternative voices as an attack on world views which we created in the carefree fin du siècle of the twentieth century. Our grip collides with those of others, and as a result, we don't always question our ideas, or not thoroughly or genuinely enough, and our manufactured truths become dogmas. We pull ourselves back into our own bubble.

The question that has been puzzling me for twenty years is how to disarm the viewer, how to turn the viewer into a mollusc, soft and receptive to doubt. In times of increasing polarisation, that need only becomes stronger. I am convinced that when we are regularly thrown off balance, we can confront the social debate in a more sensitive and less didactic and binary manner. It's not up to the artist to bombard the spectator with yet another truth. But instead, I hope to work on a periphery of a debate, to question and shake up belief systems. I believe in the subtle breaking down of boundaries: the boundaries of the axioms in the mind of the observer and the boundaries of assumed decency. The most lasting memories I have as an observer are those when I felt like a child who had to conclude with wet eyes that his puzzle had just fallen apart. Uncertain, I had to try to put the puzzle back together again.

That questioning of certainties lies at the heart of what I hope to do: I regularly change disciplines and mediums of expression. A few years ago I was a scenographer, then a theatre director and now a visual artist, or maybe I'm still all three, or something in between. Sometimes an idea in my head manifests itself as an object, at other times as a happening or portable installation. I derive a childish joy in changing the playing field; a new creation must be a leap in the dark. It is also a strategy to keep the visitor uncertain. I think spectators approach a work unconstrained if they cannot directly link it to a previous work, or better still, if what they see does not immediately appear as a work of art.

I love to blur the lines between real and unreal. For example, I like to place work on the street, where it becomes unclear if it is staged or not. In recent years, I regularly use the Internet as a means of engaging the spectator. I am fascinated by this 'new' public space and the extent to which it influences our perspective and behaviour in the analogue world. The deceptive promise of the Internet as a representation of the non-digital world makes it the ideal place to let the spectator doubt about fact and fiction.

By the way, it is not yet a sinecure to stay ambiguous in form and content. With every presentation again there appears a small army of marketing staff, journalists and academics ready to define the gesture. While I think that gestures are most valuable when they bring us into imbalance, and thus preferably unexpected and unnamed in form, part of the art world benefits from identification and clarity. How should a work be described in the seasonal brochure if it is not clear whether it is an installation or a film? Why would an art collector buy a piece that looks nothing like a successful earlier piece? And who determines and pronounces what is a success? The need to value something is the polar opposite of my own desire to be inestimable. Valuation is something for fifty years down the line, for the art historians who live then.

If I manage to avoid an applause moment, then please let it be so. The artificial time limit between the proposed world and reality often gets in the way. I would rather see a visitor cautiously enter the outside world, not sure if what he has just experienced continues, infiltrates the world we call our reality.

It is for this same reason that I like to make work for the visitor who is free to roam and move at his own pace. In a museum or in public space, the viewer determines himself when he has finished looking. In a sense he is complicit in his experience. When you do not mention the duration of a piece, nervousness grows in the visitor's body. Has he looked well enough? Is there anything more going to happen? Is there perhaps another meaning that the viewer only discovers if even more attention to the work is exerted? Or has one been standing for minutes watching the emperor's new clothes? It's a more uncertain viewing situation than that of the theatre seat; we're more cautious with our verdict.

In 2016, I made *Guilty Landscapes*. What I hoped to do was to confuse the news images, to let the viewer look again at what is so often and clearly presented as problematic. Some see it as the artist's task to show misunderstandings in society. A task at least as valuable, I think, lies in offering value-free viewing. Artists are not the messengers of correct thinking, not servants of decency.

Of course, it is worrying if we are unaware of problems in the world. But equally worrying is if we are going to live by those concerns, if we view the protagonists of the news bulletins only as victims. Precisely in a world where information about the lives of others does not come to us through first-hand experience, but mostly from the media devices that surround us everywhere, it is important to be modest in our assumptions.

Guilty Landscapes is a series of four video works. The visitor enters a gallery room, the door closes, he is alone. On a wall he sees a video projection of a problematically assumed place in the world; in the first episode, a clothing factory in Hangzhou, China. The sound of weaving machines is overwhelming. The visitor sees on the screen that one of the factory workers, a young Chinese woman, stops her work and begins to imitate the visitor's movements. If the visitor holds up his hand, the factory worker will do the same. The moment of mimesis confirms the good old narrative of the globalised market economy in which our behaviour in the West influences people's behaviour in distant places around the world. Does the notion of postcolonialism and imperialism accompany these kinds of environments? Does it get in the way of adopting an unconcerned attitude? Does the visitor dare to do a lambada dance to see if the Chinese woman does it too, or does the environment put them in anticipation of a debt-conscious position?

But then the woman stops imitating. She puts on noise-muffling headphones and the machine sounds become muted. The woman crawls over the factory floor and lies under one of the weaving machines. She motions to the visitor to lie on the gallery floor. The roles are reversed. Woman and visitor crawl closer to each other, both closer to the screen, the only thing that separates them. The Chinese woman stretches out her hand, when the visitor does the same and touches the projection screen, he seems to be in touch with someone far away. The boundary between film and reality seems broken down. Digital becomes analogue. Not much later, the woman is behind her weaving machine again, the noise returns in the gallery room. Many visitors remain staring unsure at the screen for a few minutes. Have they just been through a Skype connection with an unknown person in China? Or was she just an avatar in a clever computer simulation? The visitor will not get an answer (Figure 7.9).

The protagonists (or their media appearances) seem to be aware of the fact that we, gallery visitors/TV viewers from the West, are watching them. They are witnesses to our witnessing. It shows the Internet as a medium built on reciprocity, it exists by the grace of an upload and a download. Perhaps refugees also read *The Guardian* on their phones. But how that thought further influences your daily life is up to you. One critic said in a review: 'What does Verhoeven want to do exactly with *Guilty Landscapes*? Am I allowed to know that?' No, sorry, I have no message for you. I cannot tell you if we should commit ourselves to the closure of Chinese factories and sweatshop labour. No matter how much I understand that there is a need for a new stability, the value of the art for me lies in the disorder, nothing more. Only doubt can save us.

188 *Intermedial Theatre*

Figure 7.9   Dries Verhoeven, *Guilty Landscapes* (2016). Photographer: Willem Popelier.

JAMES YARKER: ARTISTIC DIRECTOR, STAN'S CAFE THEATRE COMPANY, UK

Time Critical (2016)

Background

Stan's Cafe, based in Birmingham in the UK, was founded in 1991 by James Yarker and Graeme Rose. Graeme and James agreed to form the company during an impromptu meeting at Stan's Cafe, just off Brick Lane in the East End of London, hence the name, which in the English tradition is pronounced 'caff'. James Yarker has been the artistic director from its inception and the company has garnered an international reputation for experimental theatre practice which has encompassed large scale installations using rice as a medium (*Of All the People in All the World*), epic durational work (*Twighlightofthefreakingods, 24 Hour Scalextric*) through to intimate solo audience experiences (*It's Your Film*) alongside scores of theatre productions for small and medium scale venues across the world.

The chess clock had been left on the shelf. I had picked up the clock online in a burst of amorous excitement, imagining all the fun we could have together counting down the seconds to midnight, but that had been years ago and we'd never really got anything going between us. This isn't unusual for me, formal ideas for organising theatre shows need to be paired up with compatible content and making that match can often be a waiting game.

2016 was upon us, twenty-five years spent marrying form with content needed to be celebrated, and if Stan's Cafe was to celebrate its anniversary with a party, that party needed to have art at its heart. It was agreed: we would make a new show for the event. Now, whilst the hubris of making a show overtly about ourselves was unconscionable, this was nevertheless our anniversary party, and it was difficult to imagine what else the show could be about. 'Well', we supposed, 'there is the rest of the world and what they've been up to for the last twenty-five years'.

This tension between us as acting as heroes of our own narrative whilst simultaneously playing total nonentities in any global tale felt like material for a show. We could pitch our story, in all its parochial detail, against the vast import of wars and famine, elections and inventions, stock market crashes and geographical tsunamis. It could be us versus the world, a minute per year for us, a minute per year for the rest of the world, twenty-five plays twenty-five; if only we had a chess clock.

Time Critical is edited rather than written. With all personal and global events jockeying for position as possible content, 'what to leave out' was always going to be the crucial question and our decisions would inevitably form part of the subject of the show; we see the world from where we stand, you would have made a different show and maybe if the show were made in South America we wouldn't recognise it at all.

Craig Stephens, our Associate Director, made the first edit, he scoured chronologies of world events on the web in order to tabulate a '(very) long list' of possible world elements to include and in the column set out a parallel history of the company's shows, it's personnel changes and notable landmarks in the lives of company members (Figure 7.10).

Craig's 'long list' shortened with each iterative pass of the editors' pen and we started to investigate how historical events could be restaged with our frugal cast of two in order to prevent the show descending into a lecture format. We used the web to pull out original texts and archive footage of political speeches; treaties and court room drama; mission control chatter and public pronouncements and started performing fragments of these texts with enough accent or gesture to hint at their sources. We invented fictional versions of private or lost moments such as President Gorbachov's house arrest in 1991. We scripted incidents from or own history from memory, giving them a spin

Figure 7.10 Stan's Café, *Time Critical* (2016). Performers: Rochi Rampal and Craig Stephens. Photographer: Graeme Braidwood.

for comic or dramatic effect and exposing this spin by having one performer contest the accuracy of the script.

In order to counterpoint our wealth of documentary material we scoured Stan's Cafe's archives for moments from our old shows that could be restaged efficiently with simple gesture or prop and provide a feel of the spirit or atmosphere of that show. 'Art and its relation to Life' was to be another subject we hoped *Time Critical* would address and so we looked to include world events which had inspired these shows, played out in parallel with them or contrasted strongly with them: *Ocean of Storms* (1996) and the Challenger Disaster; *Canute The King* (1993) and the relationship between Charles and Diana etc.

With a chess clock playing a prominent role in the performance, the use of a chessboard in the show felt obligatory and using the movement of the chess pieces on, off and around the board quickly became a useful visual analogue for the comings and goings, birth, deaths and unions in Stan's Cafe circle.

The chessboard lay on a table placed centre stage. Rochi Rampal sat stage right playing for the world, facing her stage left Craig playing for Stan's Cafe. Upstage, pinned to a flat, a world map used to helping place events in a geographic context. Initially this was a standard world map with a wipe-clean surface so the performers could scribble on it but poor visibility under the theatre lights prompted us to get our own map printed for subsequent retours of the show. Using paper with a matt finish we were able to ensure pen marks were clearly visible. Having our own maps printed meant we could have them customise for the show, they now indicate the locations of most all the incidents referred to in the show and as such have embodied the rather esoteric idea of a script in map form.

Downstage of the table and stage right stands an Elizabethan flip chart borrowed from *The Anatomy of Melancholy* (2013), this indicates the year currently being performed. Downstage left a monitor carries a live video relay of the chess clock in close up as, on the up stage edge of the table, it is hammered each time the show flips from being about the global to being about the local.

Of course occasionally the local becomes the global we find ourselves impacted by or implicated in someone else's grander narrative. Zagreb's first Gay Pride march in 2002 coincided with Stan's Cafe performing *It's Your Film* (1998) in the city. These moments are useful for the show – as indicated above. Here the performance logic of the show is tested and contested onstage, whose precious time allocation should the event's depiction be performed in: Rochi's world time or Craig's personal time?

We have used Google Images to search for protest banners linked to the stories we're relating, one comes from Zagreb, translated it reads 'Gays to the camps'. The performers can be spiky with each other 'This isn't me! I'm being a fascist in the crowd; who do you take me for?' They can critique each other's editorial decisions 'why are you wasting your time on this?' or 'don't you want to talk more about that?' They perform in each other's scenes and so can waste each other's time sabotaging each other's chances of delivering all their proposed script in the time available.

In the show's preset both sides of the chess clock can be seen reading 25 minutes to midnight and the show starts with one side of the clock being punched and it starting to count down.[2] Although shown in close up for audiences on a large monitor down stage right via a live video feed, the clock is not a focal point for much of the performance. There are occasional references to the time and squabbles about its allocation (as indicated above) but it is only as the end of the show starts to loom that the twin mutability and inexorability of time come into focus.

The performance is structured to inevitably contain more material than there is time for it to be delivered. Time is measured out steadily and impartially by the twin clocks, so the performers are forced to relate events in ever-greater compression. With the performers abbreviating their material evermore ruthlessly events start to flash by evermore quickly and perceived time appears to accelerate mimicking our experience as we grow older and the years click by ever faster.

As historic moments start to flash by in the show we become increasingly aware of the cyclical, or perhaps more accurately spiralling nature of our news: elections, World Cups, bombs and peace treaties come round again and again with an inevitability that is only ever tempered by the knowledge that we are all ultimately always finally and irrevocably going to run out of time.

The performers grow evermore acutely aware they are going to run out of time with material left unperformed. Much of the acceleration described above is scripted but in the final few pages the performers are on their own, they have to fall back on their experience of the show and knowledge of their material to decide what to cut and what to keep as they try to deliver as much material as possible whilst attempting to deliver the concluding moment of action in the last second of the show before midnight falls and the lights go out.

CRAIG VEAR: PROFESSOR OF DIGITAL PERFORMANCE (MUSIC)

De Montfort University UK

Background

For more than two decades Professor Craig Vear has established himself as an internationally recognised composer of experimental music with technology, and recently as a scholar of digital performance and music. His research transects music, performance, artificial intelligence, gaming and embodiment, and was shortlisted for European Research Council Starting Grant in 2017. He has received numerous awards for his research including an Olivier award for theatre. His research monograph *The Digital Score* was published by Routledge in 2019.

Gravities, Trajectories and Postcards: The Heard Space in Intermedial Performance

As this is a short essay, I will get straight to the point. In doing so I expose that fact that I am audile,[3] and believe that sound is a significant part of the audiovisual contract of live performance. Actually, I would argue it to be more foundational than that: 'A head space in which the seen bathes' (Chion, 1994).[4] However, considering sound to be of such a foundational influence (*the heard space*) in intermedial performance (*in which the seen bathes*) presents significant challenges to those wishing to incorporate it in their work. This is particularly relevant to composers/sound artists wishing to engage with intermedial performance, and intermedial performance makers wishing to include sound-based media in their works. The challenge for both of these performance makers is there is no sound-specific intermedia model with which to discuss and apply the affect[5] and inter-effectivity of sound media on experience within intermedial performance. This essay, therefore, introduces my conceptualisation of how we can get to grips with the affectual qualities of sounds within the audiovisual contract of a live performative experience.

In Vear (2016) I present *Gesamtkomposition* as a conceptual means of understanding 'the compositional intent to evoke streams of sensation through the careful presentation and organization of media within the performance' (Vear, 2016). Within this 'fragmented streams of mental imagery – real, imagined, emotion, sense data – evoked by media affection (e.g. mixed- and intermedia) metaphorically correspond to individual instrumental parts which are organised within a polyphonic whole.' (idem). Using *Gesamtkomposition* as a ground-floor construct for this essay, I will focus on the operativity of sound and music in intermedial performance by conceptualising them as polyphonic objects-of-affect travelling through the time and space dimension of *my* experience.

To achieve this I have found it useful to describe such operativity of the *Gesamtkomposition* by using a poetics influenced by terms found in gravitational physics. In this, the relativities of these sound-media objects interact with *my* experience as a consequence of their properties and movements through space and time. At the centre of a dimensional space is *my* experience, in this sense *I* am the centre of a media system unique to each work. The *Gesamtkomposition* is defined by the library of sound media, their organisation in time, and their potential interactivity through time and space of each work. It is the consequence of their affect upon *me*, through their journeys in the here and now of performance that offer us the insight this essay seeks to clarify.

To achieve this we must understand each sound-media operational within a given *Gesamtkomposition* from the perspective of their affectual densities, mass and gravities (discussed below). And as orbits with relative relationships, attractions, radiation, and distorting systems through fields and resonances within the time and space of live performance.

These defined media elements might have equivalent properties throughout their duration of the work for example their operational properties may not change throughout their existence. Equally, they might have a harmonic weight and an influence upon each other – adding additional meaning and affect through proximity within the live experience. Also, depending on how they operate in the dimension of *my* experience they might effect *my* gravity within this system thus shifting where I thought I was, or who I think I am within the context of a particular work.

As these media elements orbit around the work, incoming or outgoing media fragments can distort the gravitational affect of other elements. With this in mind, something with a massive gravitational weight, density or mass (such as a familiar song sung by a live performer, or a recorded pop song) will have a bigger gravitational pull on the 'conductor' of *my* mind, and therefore will shift, alter, twist perception of the ongoing experience. Alternatively something with small mass on a distant orbit, for example a background electro-acoustic texture, might have a subtle influence upon *me* as the distant moon pulls on the tides in neap.

I will apply this poetics onto *Postcards* (2017), an intermedia composition created in collaboration between myself (as composer) and Anne La Berge a virtuoso on flute and electronics. The piece incorporates a media library of found materials (listed below), a laptop hosting a bespoke Artificial Intelligent music scoring system (Music-AI), a constant stream of generative poetry between co-located Raspberry Pi's, and a large projection screen showing processed images of the intermedial interactions as a super-fast collage of machine thinking.

The role of the Music-AI laptop is to actively compose the intermedia system using embedded aesthetic parameters developed through the collaboration of myself and La Berge, and notions of the *Gesamtkomposition*. In practice the laptop generates a score for the performer integrating sounds and images from a library of predefined elements of media. During the performance, the Music-AI makes decisions about what images to present on the laptop screen for the performer to consider as a visual score, and which sounds to present into the aural realm. A Kyma sound-computation engine is also controlled by the Music-AI system and chooses which effects to apply onto the aural realm of the live performance. The libraries of the media consists of:

A. Images: an English translation of a selection of letters sent between Gustave Flaubert and George Sands, a selection of letters sent between Elizabeth Bishop and Robert Powell, and the streaming poetry between the Raspberry Pi's generating new phrases from the Flaubert Sands and Bishop Powell letters.
B. Sound media containing recorded voices reading each letter; a 1982 recording of La Berge performing her first composition, and a bank of processing effects in Kyma.

All of these elements underpin a poetic narrative driving this composition, which is dealing with interrupted communication dislocated across time and geographic place, and drawing attention to:

- Relationships that could only survive through correspondence.
- What writers and poets say to one another through distant communications.

- Sexuality and how it effects relationships and artist's lives.
- The grey areas between sexualities and genders.

These libraries of media, the embedded aesthetics in the Music-AI, the potential inter-effectual media relationships, and their formal organisation of time are the *Gesamtkomposition* of this work. It's operational dynamics coupled with the sensorial affect upon the listening minds of the performer and the audience are the consequential intermedial relativities of their properties and movements through space and time, and can be defined by the following poetics:

a) Dimensional media space (DMS) – this is the realm that the intermedia composition constructs through the relationships and connections across, within, between and emergent from the media-system library and determine the identity of each composition. In *Postcards* the DMS can be considered as the wholeness[6] of the piece, or the metanarratives, dramaturgies and mediaturgies that are formed from the coalescence of the disparate elements including the live performers. The DMS is a poetic realm of potential: the potential for one media to interact or coalesce with another. As such, determining or developing the following factors are essential to defining the feel and sensation of the overall DMS and therefore the feel of the *Gesamtkomposition* in performance:

   i. Density – each media element will have density that can be understood in terms of its affectual power. For example, the words of Flaubert's letters to Sands naturally have more concrete semiotic value than a sound effect from the Kyma system, because they are words. Written on the screen or spoken by La Berge they will draw the mind into a preformed world through language. As such, it has the potential to pack more punch, to draw attention to itself and evoke more 'meaning'.
   ii. Mass – mass is different from density: density is about multiplicity and layers of indexical meaning, whereas mass is about pure affective weight. The word 'Love' compared to the word 'sometimes' has a different semiotic punch. The written word 'Love' and the spoken world 'Love' again have different masses, as does the sung word 'Love'.
   iii. Gravities – the gravity of a media element relates to its potential to draw attention to itself, and to effect a change in the ongoing spaciotemporal[7] signatures of affect that the performance is evoking. A distorted loud sound effect on the live voice smashing into the mix, for example, would immediately disturb the affectual balance of the ongoing performance, and draw attention to its qualities and our minds understanding of what is going on.

b) Operational dynamics – during performance media elements converge, interrupt, coalesce and relate. Time is a significant factor in this section of the poetics as it deals with relativity and relationships through experience and across time. The following factors help us define the relative relationships of densities, mass and gravities across time, and their coalescence in experience:

   i. Orbits – a media element in orbit is clearly within the realm of actual experience through performance. Its potentials within the defined DMS has become manifest and it is operational with a phenomenology of experience for the audience and performer(s) and the intermedial relationships with other media elements. For example a melodic line on the flute in combination with the words 'Paris' projected on the large projection screen are going to communicate something to the audience and the performer and take their minds somewhere. These elements may be coalescing into other trains of thought or generating individual responses with mind images. If the flute melody occurred first then this might establish a specific response, modified later by the inter-orbit relativity between the emerging word 'Paris'.
   ii. Trajectories – as one media element relates to another, meaning is changed and is dependent on their trajectories over time. When a new media element emerges into the performance, it signifies the start of its trajectory. Does it converge with the existing intermedial fusion? Does it draw attention away from this fusion due to its inherent mass and gravity? Is its trajectory an outer universe orbit, remaining small and quiet, but present enough to make some small changes to perception?
   iii. Attractions and repellents – When media elements are present in the dimensional space of the live, their relationships across such space, time and perception have the effect of drawing each other in, or repelling each other. The orbit, gravity, mass and densities of each element helps to define which are attracted/repelled to what. For example, a small sound effect in Kyma and an equally small vocal utterance might be drawn together in a harmonious fusion of texture. If this Kyma sound grows in intensity – loudness, density of timbre, harmonic distortion for example – it will start to repel the small live sound and gain a significance of its own. If at this point a collage of images is also presented on the screen with qualities more alike the small live vocal sound, these will attract the live voice and repel the distorted sound. Attractions and repellents alert the mind to perceptual harmonic distance between media elements and it's emergent affectual space.

iv. Radiation and distortion – like attraction and repellents these factors are emergent from the affectual space between media. Sounding media elements can emit radiation independent of its attraction or repellent to other media. This emission can colour meaning-making of the intermedial fusion between media elements. Similarly is can distort our perception of such relationships. Radiation and distortion are coefficient with all the other parameters of this framework, and across time. They are unstable and may be quantum, in the sense that they can be both at the same time to other discreet media. Significantly they are fleeting in existence.

I'm sure this essay evokes more questions and problems than it answers. I will attempt to address these in future. But from the perspective of a practicing composer and intermedial performance maker, this poetics is the most cogent way I know to describe what goes on in my mind when I'm creating works from an audile perspective. I feel it is no longer good enough to merely apply sound and music as an effect or afterthought onto performance. In fact I would push for an approach that starts with sound and music first, and to understand the 'heard space in which the seen bathes' as a matter of priority in any performance work. Once we acknowledge and understand this from the perspective of experience can we then augment this with other media and how their densities and gravities, trajectories and orbits affect experience.

DAVID PLEDGER: ARTISTIC DIRECTOR, NOT YET IT'S DIFFICULT, AUSTRALIA

v: Hotelling (2016)

Background

Not yet it's difficult is one of Australia's seminal interdisciplinary arts outfits. It has a unique presence in Australia's arts culture as a research unit, a producer of cultural development programs and a maker of contemporary artworks and events.

Our mission is to make critically engaged artworks of high artistic and discursive quality that arise out of ideas that reflect contemporary life. Our objective is to develop artworks that incite narratives of enquiry in the minds of our publics, to engage them viscerally, intellectually and humorously about ideas, politics, art and the human condition.

v: Hotelling

To hotel, to play, to lose oneself, to tell the hotel

One of the organising principles of our art making is the establishment of context and an understanding of our complicity in that context. At times we find ourselves in situations in which the politics are clear, uncluttered. Other times we find ourselves in a context in which we have less agency than we at first imagined, and so complicit in a structure, a program or a circumstance that is in conflict with our values as artists, as citizens, as human beings.

Today this configuration has been in my mind as I launched the second edition of an annual 'happening' I curate that takes place in the city of Gold Coast in Queensland where I've been working on various projects since 2013, a year or so after I returned from living and working in Brussels.

In the cultural imaginary of Australia, the Gold Coast is a two-bit town run by a white-shoe brigade of urban developers for whom real estate is a bottom line on a balance sheet. In every cliché there is truth, and development on the Gold Coast is an ongoing contest between those who see only monetary value in the land and those who see land as inhabiting a complex of social and cultural values.

As an artist my curiosity lies in the latter elements of the equation. For me, the Gold Coast is a strip city pressing hard against the coast, compressed into a surfers' paradise at the northern end, unravelling in a series of villages the further south you go. On one side is the ocean, on the other is a hinterland so immersive and luxurious it is another world. This concatenation of sea air, forest air, ocean, estuary, river, tide and current is unique. The Gold Coast revolves around the 'lived experience' of this evolving axis of water and air, and the interplay with the land is an alchemy of story, place and space.

The land holds some fascination for me both as a repository of knowledge and culture communicated to me by my First Nations friends and as a brutal architectural fact communicated by the tract of land called Surfers Paradise. Surfers Paradise is a confounding vista of hotels, around 150 of them depending on where you set your boundaries. Heading north from southern Gold Coast you meet them as a façade, a front, a barricade. They're arranged as if to defend the indefensible, the appropriation of land for the recreation of human beings. Development and hospitality, the primary drivers of life in paradise.

Many locals bemoan the aesthetic onslaught of Surfers' Paradise and the multiple social and cultural meanings that underlie its creation. It is an inherently conflicted space. As a visitor, I can see the hotels as a strength of the local culture, an opportunity to reimagine the whole idea of culture through the prism they offer. I offered up an idea to 'write' a story in which a Surfers Paradise hotel was the protagonist in the landscape rather than the antagonist. My initial provocation to the local arts ecology was much grander, to occupy a '100 Hotels' with art, all at once. But, sometimes, one must take a step at a time...

I've had various hotel projects in mind over the years. Hotels intrigue me. They're like mini societies. They reinvent themselves on a daily basis. The chemistry of the guests, visitors, staff, the weather, location and the hotel's activities are just a few of the dizzying factors that determine the kind of society created on any given day. It's an irresistible environment for an artist to play in because hotels are essentially mercurial social spaces.

Under the moniker *Hotelling*, I made the first of three annual 'happenings' in 2016, in QT, a highly idiosyncratic hotel driven by a vernacular built on the demonstration of cultural hospitality. I think of QT as a high-functioning playground in which its respective recreational and functional indoor and outdoor spaces interact like well-placed gym equipment. On every floor, as you step out of the elevator, itself adorned by nostalgic images of recreation, you meet a bench designed in the style of a surfboard. The hotel's strong design aesthetic is carried through to the staff, who are costumed as 'players' in the QT game. It's very Gold Coast, showy, colourful. It's also very stylish and sensual, not so Gold Coast. It's in this interplay that the elements of architecture and design, of living and working, are balanced like perfectly manufactured confectionery (Figure 7.11).

This was our artistic canvas which we proceeded to severely fuck up.

Taking our cues from the interior and exterior design, the hotel's location at the quieter northern end of Surfers' Paradise, the ironically orchestrated workplace culture and the overarching sensibility of permissiveness that dotted the *i*'s and crossed the *t*'s of guest, visitor and staff behaviour, we sought to amplify all that was present and all that was implicit by creating worlds that were familiar and others that were strange and otherworldly.

Conference rooms were reimagined as sound chambers, swimming pools as projection surfaces, neighbouring buildings as collaborators, audiences as interactors and performance spaces as interconnecting. Hotel rooms transformed into sites of spiritual possession and banal human experience; tennis courts became cabaret spaces; and a penthouse apartment, a wing of the palace of Versailles. These decisions were made in direct response to the architectural integrity of the building and its relational aspect to its surrounds.

The frame of these experiences was to go down the rabbit hole, from the penthouse to the tennis courts and swimming pool, and back up again, on a rollercoaster ride, a 'trip', an Alice in Wonderland–styled adventure which crossed adult entertainment with contemporary art, cabaret with sport, theatre with surveillance, and installation with climate change. In unpacking the architectural and design integrity of the building and riffing off its workplace and visitor culture, a kind of organised chaos revealed itself as the best way to turn

Figure 7.11 Not yet it's difficult, *v:Hotelling* (2016). Photograph: Bleached Arts Ltd.

the hotel into an agent of its own story, a genuine protagonist in the broader cultural and physical landscape it inhabited.

There were multiple kinds of audience for this story, punters who bought a ticket for the whole adventure; guests and visitors who directly encountered performances in the hotel corridors, elevators and foyer; those who experienced incidental encounters through the opening-and-closing frame of an elevator door or the rear window of an EK panel van parked in the hotel's drive-through or the floor-to-ceiling glass separating the lobby from an outdoor, heavy metal yoga class. One evening, three kids under the age of ten, who were house guests, spent two hours looking for the mythical rabbit we called Monty who traversed the twenty-four floors of the hotel, via elevator and corridor, carrying a dark and mysterious briefcase.

The various ways in which our audience engaged with *Hotelling* takes me full circle to our organising principles of context and complicity.

Before I resolve the circle, I'd like to note that it is a shape that's intrinsic to my dramaturgy as an artist. Lines are not always visible to me as an artist or a citizen. Art, society, human behaviour – they're all fluid, and I've not discovered merit in keeping things separate. I believe in the interconnectedness of things, at all times, in all circumstances. It is why I like circles. Circles are lines that resolve. And when resolved, they tend to emanate rather than demonstrate. Vibration rather than static silos. It is why I consider my dramaturgy to be 'amplified', as it emanates outwards from the circle of artistic practice to cultural and social circles.

So, my intention with *Hotelling* is to take down the silo of the hotel and build an entity that emanates through the local community so that it can take ownership of a space that for all intents and purposes is private. To publicise the private space of a hotel is a political act. To occupy. To take over. To alter the narrative, however briefly.

It is, however, a complex and nuanced presenting space which attracts various levels of complicity, of which I would like to mention two.

Entering the world of a hotel, you are entering a corporate space, even one with an emphasis on cultural hospitality. So the idea of expending the public funds of local government on an event in a private space needs to be declared. My view (which has changed over the last ten years as our cultural politics changed under neo-liberalism) is that, in this instance, the corporate nature of the space is little different to the presenting context of an arts centre or a major arts festival, entities governed by boards that are risk averse, artistically conservative and most mindful of income streams. I would describe this as the general context of a project such as *Hotelling*, one which would operate in many Western societies.

The more specific context is that of the city of Gold Coast itself, where the development issue rotates on a simple axis of pro and anti. In proposing *Hotelling*, the question must be considered: does a project that illuminates the possibility of hotels, a contentious manifestation of urban development, support new building of hotels, or does it encourage citizens to 'take over' the local space it occupies and demand greater access to its facilities and ownership of its iconography? The way to navigate this question – which, to be clear, was perceived as implicit by myself and my fellow artists, but which was never directly proposed by others – is to maintain the artistic integrity of the project by insulating it against the government's rhetoric of 'cultural tourism' and any attempt to editorialise the artistic content that arose from that rhetoric, of which there were a number of instances.

The complicity of the artist in this context needs to be assessed at all times and often requires deliberate and tactical 'pushing back' against interests that tend to see art as an instrument of commerce. It is a tricky space to play in but once established can provide artistic parameters that offer considerable freedom.

As today I launched *Hotelling*'s second edition – which will take place in a luxury hotel and operate as a metaphor for the rise and fall of the Western empire – I am very aware that the maintenance of such parameters requires constant vigilance.

The story continues . . .

Bibliographies

1 THEATRE (AND YOU) AS MEDIUM AND INTERMEDIUM: MARK CROSSLEY *WITH CONTRIBUTIONS FROM LARS ELLESTRÖM*

Alston, A. and M. Welton (eds) (2017) *Theatre in the Dark Shadow, Gloom and Blackout in Contemporary Theatre*. London: Bloomsbury, 20.
Bateman, J., Wildfeuer, J. and Hiippala, T. (2017). *Multimodality: Foundations, Research and Analysis – A Problem-Oriented Introduction*. Berlin: De Gruyter Mouton.
Bay-Cheng, S. et al. (eds) (2010) *Mapping Intermediality in Performance*. Amsterdam: Amsterdam University Press.
Bazin, A. (1967) *What Is Cinema? Volume 1*. Berkeley, Calif.: London: University of California Press.
Bell, P. (2000) Dialogic media production and inter-media exchange. *Journal of Dramatic Theory and Criticism*, 14, no. 2, pp. 41–55.
Bolter, J. D. and Grusin, R. (1999) *Remediation: Understanding New Media*. Cambridge, Mass.: London: MIT Press.
Bordwell, R. and Thompson, K. (2013) *Film Art: An Introduction*. New York: McGraw-Hill.
Chapple, F. and Kattenbelt, C. (2006) Key issues in intermediality. In F. Chapple and C. Kattenbelt (eds), *Intermediality in Theatre and Performance* (pp. 11–25). Amsterdam: Rodopi.
Cousins, M. (2011) *The Story of Film: An Odyssey*. DVD Music Box Films.
Dundjerović, A. (2007) *The Theatricality of Robert Lepage*. London: McGill-Queens University Press.
Ellestrom, L. (2010) The modalities of media: A model for understanding intermedial relations. In L. Ellestrom (ed.), *Media Borders, Multimodality and Intermediality* (pp. 11–48). Basingstoke: Palgrave Macmillan.
Ellestrom, L. (2014) *Media Transformation: The Transfer of Media Characteristics among Media*. Basingstoke: Palgrave Macmillan.
Etchells, T. (2008) 'Spectacular' programme note by Tim Etchells. *Forced Entertainment*. Retrieved from https://www.forcedentertainment.com/notebook-entry/spectacular-programme-note-by-tim-etchells/.
Forceville, C. J. (2011) Book review: Media borders, multimodality and intermediality. *Journal of Pragmatics*, 43, no. 12, pp. 3091–3094.
Gardner, L. (2003) Review: The watery part of the world. *The Guardian*. 28 June. Retrieved from https://www.theguardian.com/stage/2003/jun/28/theatre.artsfeatures.

Georgi, C. (2014) *Liveness on Stage: Intermedial Challenges in Contemporary British Theatre and Performance (Contemporary Drama in English Studies)*. Berlin: Walter de Gruyter.
Giesekam, G. (2007) *Staging the Screen*. Basingstoke: Palgrave Macmillan.
Halliday, M. A. K. (1978) *Language as Social Semiotic: The Social Interpretation of Language and Meaning*. Baltimore, Md.: University Park Press.
Heinrichs, J. and Spielmann, Y. (2002) Editorial. *Convergence*, 8, no. 4, pp. 5–10.
Higgins, D. (1965) Intermedia. *Something Else Newsletter*, 1, no 1. New York: Something Else Press. Retrieved from http://www.primaryinformation.org/product/something-else-press-newsletters-1966-83/.
Higgins, D. (1984) *Horizons, the Poetics and Theory of the Intermedia* Carbondale, IL: Southern Illinois Univ. Press.
Ingham, M. (2017) *Stageplay and Screenplay: The Intermediality of Theatre and Cinema*. New York: Routledge.
Jensen, A. P. (2007) *Theatre in a Media Culture: Production, Performance and Perception since 1970*. Jefferson, N.C.: McFarland.
Kattenbelt, C. (2006) Theatre as the art of the performer and the stage of intermediality. In F. Chapple and C. Kattenbelt (eds) *Intermediality in Theatre and Performance* (pp. 31–41). Amsterdam: Rodopi.
Kattenbelt C. (2008) Intermediality in theatre and performance: Definitions, perceptions and medial relationships. *Culture, Language and Representation, Cultural Studies Journal of Universitat Jaume*, 6, no. 1, pp. 19–29.
Kerouac, J. (1998) *On the Road*. London and New York: Penguin Books.
Klich, R. and Scheer, E. (2012) *Multimedia Performance*. Basingstoke: Palgrave Macmillan.
Kostelanetz, R. (1970) *The Theatre of Mixed Means*. London: Sir Isaac Pitman and Sons.
Kottak, C. (1994) *Window on Humanity: A Concise Introduction to General Anthropology*. New York: McGraw-Hill Humanities/Social Sciences/Languages.
Krämer, S. (1998) Das Medium als Spur und als Apparat. In S. Krämer (ed.), *Medien, Computer, Realität* (pp. 73–94). Frankfurt/Main: Suhrkamp.
Kress, G. and Van Leeuwen, T. (2001) *Multimodal Discourse*. New York: Bloomsbury Academic.
Kress, G. (2012) What is a mode? *YouTube*. Retrieved from https://www.youtube.com/watch?v=nt5wPIhhDDU.
Lavender, A. (2014) Modal transpositions toward theatres of encounter, or, in praise of 'media intermultimodality. *Theatre Journal*, 66, no. 4, pp. 499–518.
Lavender, A. (2016) *Performance in the Twenty-first Century: Theatres of Engagement*. London: Routledge.
Lehmann, H. T. (2006) *Postdramatic Theatre*. London: Routledge.
McLuhan, M. (1964) *Understanding Media: The Extensions of Man*. Cambridge, Mass: MIT Press.
McLuhan, M. (1967) *The Medium Is the Message: An Inventory of Effects*. New York and London: Penguin Classics.

Merleau-Ponty, M. (2002) *Phenomenology of Perception*. London: Routledge.
Nelson, R. (2010) Introduction: Prospective mapping and network of terms. In S. Bay-Cheng et al. (eds) *Mapping Intermediality in Performance* (pp. 13–23). Amsterdam: Amsterdam University Press.
Quick, A. (May 2011) *Personal interviews*.
Rajewsky, I. (2005) Intermediality, intertextuality, and remediation: A literary perspective on intermediality. In P. Despoix and Y. Spielmann (eds) *Intermédialité – Historie et théorie des arts, des lettres et des techniques*, 6, Special Issue: Remédier/Remediation, pp. 43–64.
Röttger, K. (2008) F@ust vers. 3.0: A (hi)story of theatre and media. *Culture, Language and Representation, Cultural Studies Journal Of Universitat Jaume*, 6, no. 1, pp. 31–46.
Saussure (1998) *Course in General Linguistics*. Open Court reprint.
Sindoni, M. G., J. Wildfeueur and K. O'Halloran (eds) (2016) *Mapping Multimodal Performance Studies (Routledge Studies in Multimodality)* Routledge.
Stevenson, J. (2009) Juliet Stevenson: The power of storytelling. Retrieved from https://www.theguardian.com/stage/2009/may/09/juliet-stevenson-acting-career.
Sontag, S. (1966) Film and theatre. *Tulane Drama Review*, 11, no. 1, pp. 24–37.
Tseng, C.-I. (2017) Analysing narrativised space in moving images: a multimodal discourse approach to narrative complexity and transmedial comparison. *Multimodal Communication*, 6, no. 1, pp. 61–82.
Wagner, R. (1849) *The Art-Work of the Future*. University of Nebraska Press.
Wagner, R. (1849) *Art and Revolution*. Cybraria LLC.
Wolf, W. (1999) *The Musicalization of Fiction: A Study in the Theory and History of Intermediality*. Amsterdam: Rodopi.
Wolf, W. (2011) (Inter)mediality and the study of literature. *Comparative Literature and Culture*, 13, no. 3. Retrieved from https://doi.org/10.7771/1481-4374.1789.
Woycicki, P. (2014) *Post-Cinematic Theatre and Performance*. Palgrave Studies in Performance and Technology. London: Palgrave Macmillan UK.

2 TWENTY-FIRST-CENTURY INTERMEDIALITY: ANDY LAVENDER

Bolter, J. D. and Grusin, R. (1999) *Remediation: Understanding New Media*. Cambridge, Mass.: MIT Press.
Chapple, F. and Kattenbelt, C. (2006) Key issues in intermediality in theatre and performance. In C. Kattenbelt and F. Chapple (eds) *Intermediality in Theatre and Performance* (pp. 11–25). Amsterdam and New York. NY: Rodopi.
Djonov, E. and Zhao, S. (2014) From multimodal to critical multimodal studies through popular discourse. In E. Djonov and S. Zhao (eds) *Critical Multimodal Studies of Popular Discourse* (pp. 1–14). New York and London: Routledge.

Elleström, L. (2010) The modalities of media: A model for understanding intermedial relations. In L. Elleström (ed.) *Media Borders, Multimodality and Intermediality* (pp. 11–48). Basingstoke and New York: Palgrave Macmillan.

Elleström, L. (2014) *Media Transformation: The Transfer of Media Characteristics Among Media*. London: Palgrave Macmillan.

Fernandes, C. (2014) *Multimodality and Performance*. Newcastle upon Tyne: Cambridge Scholars Publishing.

Howden, D. and Fotiadis, A. (2017) Where did the money go? How Greece fumbled the refugee crisis. *The Guardian*, 9 March. Retrieved from https://www.theguardian.com/world/2017/mar/09/how-greece-fumbled-refugee-crisis.

Jewitt, C. (2014) An introduction to multimodality. In C. Jewitt (ed.) *The Routledge Handbook of Multimodal Analysis* (pp. 15–30). London and New York: Routledge.

Kress, G. and Van Leeuwen, T. (2001) *Multimodal Discourse*. New York: Bloomsbury Academic.

Kress, G. (2014) 'What is mode?' In C. Jewitt (ed.) *The Routledge Handbook of Multimodal Analysis* (pp. 60–75). London and New York: Routledge.

Lavender, A. (2014) 'Modal transpositions towards theatres of encounter, or, in praise of "media intermultimodality"', *Theatre Journal*, 66: 4, 499-518.

Manovich, L. (2001). *The Language of New Media*. Cambridge, Mass.: MIT Press.

Müller, J. E. (2010) Intermediality and media historiography in the digital era. *Film and Media Studies*, 2, pp. 15–38.

Nelson, R. (2010) Prospective mapping. In S. Bay-Cheng, C. Kattenbelt, A. Lavender and R. Nelson (eds), *Mapping Intermediality and Performance* (pp. 13–23). Amsterdam: Amsterdam University Press.

Norris, S. (2013) Multimodal (inter)action analysis: An integrative methodology. In C. Müller, A. Cienki, E. Fricke, S. H. Ladewig, D. McNeill, S. Tessendorf (eds) *Body–Language–Communication: An International Handbook on Multimodality in Human Interaction* (Vol. 1; pp. 275–286). Berlin and Boston: De Gruyter Mouton.

Rajewsky, I. (2010), Border talks: The problematic status of media borders in the current debate about intermediality. In L. Elleström (ed.) *Media Borders, Multimodality and Intermediality* (pp. 51–68). Basingstoke and New York: Palgrave Macmillan.

Williams, R. (1987) Conventions. In V. Lambropolulos and D. N. Miller (eds) *Twentieth-Century Literary Theory: An Introductory Anthology* (pp. 185–190). Albany: State University of New York Press.

3 THE PERFORMER IN INTERMEDIAL THEATRE : JOANNE SCOTT AND BRUCE BARTON

1927. (2011). *The Animals and Children Took to the Streets* (live performance). [Cottesloe–National Theatre London, 22 December 2011).
1927. (2015). *Golem* (live performance). [HOME Theatre, Manchester, 8 October 2015].
Auslander, P. (1997) *From Acting to Performance–Essays in Modernism and Postmodernism*. London and New York: Routledge.
Auslander, P. (2008). *Liveness: Performance in a Mediatised Culture* (2nd edn). Oxon and New York: Routledge.
Barad, K. (2007). *Meeting the Universe Halfway: Quantum Physics and the Entanglement of Matter and Meaning*. Durham, N.C. and London: Duke University Press.
Barton, B. (2009). Paradox as process: Intermedial anxiety and the betrayals of intimacy. *Theatre Journal*, 61, no. 4, pp. 575–601.
Baumann, Franziska. (2017) Solos. Retrieved from http://www.franziskabaumann.ch/en/solos/.
Blast Theory. (2001) *Can You See Me Now*. Video retrieved from http://www.blasttheory.co.uk/projects/can-you-see-me-now/.
Blast Theory. (2009) *Ulrike and Eamon Compliant*. Video retrieved from http://www.blasttheory.co.uk/projects/ulrike-and-eamon-compliant/.
Blast Theory. (2012) *I'd Hide You*. Video retrieved from http://www.blasttheory.co.uk/projects/id-hide-you/.
Brown, A. and Sorensen, A. (2009) Interacting with generative music through live coding. *Contemporary Music Review*, 28, no. 1, 17–29.
Bryon, E. (2014) *Integrative Performance: Practice and Theory for the Interdisciplinary Performer*. London and New York: Routledge.
Complicité/McBurney, S. (2016) *The Encounter* (live performance). [HOME Manchester–Theatre 1, 19 April 2016].
Cooke, G. (2010) Start making sense: Live audio-visual media performance. *International Journal of Performance Arts and Digital Media*, 6, no. 2, pp. 193–208.
Derrida, J. (1978) Structure, sign and play in the discourse of the human sciences. (Trans. A. Bass). *Writing and Difference*. London: Routledge and Kegan Paul.
Derrida, J. and Kamuf, P. (1991) *A Derrida reader: Between the blinds*. London and New York: Harvester Wheatsheaf.
Fischer-Lichte, E. (2008) *The Transformative Power of Performance: A New Aesthetics* (Trans. S. I. Jain). Oxon and New York: Routledge.
Gade, R, & Jerslev, A., (2005) *Performative realism: interdisciplinary studies in art and media*. Museum Tusculanum Press, Copenhagen, Denmark.
Garner, S.B. (1994). *Bodied Spaces: Phenomenology and Performance in Contemporary Drama*. Ithaca, N.Y., and London: Cornell University Press.
Giannachi, G., Kaye, N. (2011) *Performing Presence: Between the Live and the Simulated (Theatre: Theory, Practice, Performance)* Manchester University Press.

Giannachi, G., Kaye, N. and Shanks, M. (eds) (2012). *Archaeologies of Presence*. New York and Oxon: Routledge.
Hayles, N. K. (1999) *How We Became Posthuman: Virtual Bodies in Cybernetics, Literature and Informatics*. Chicago, Ill., and London: University of Chicago Press.
Heap, I. (n.d.) Gestural Music Ware by Imogen Heap. Retrieved from http://www.imogenheap.co.uk/thegloves/.
imitating the dog. (n.d.) Details retrieved from http://www.imitatingthedog.co.uk/portfolio/hotel-methuselah/.
imitating the dog. (2011) *Hotel Methuselah*. Video retrieved from http://www.imitatingthedog.co.uk/portfolio/hotel-methuselah/.
imitating the dog. (2013) *The Zero Hour*. Video retrieved from http://www.imitatingthedog.co.uk/portfolio/the-zero-hour/.
Kozel, S. (2007) *Closer: Performance, Technologies, Phenomenology*. Cambridge, Mass., and London: MIT Press.
Lavender, A. (2006) Mise en Scene, hypermediacy and the sensorium. In F. Chapple and C. Kattenbelt (eds) *Intermediality in Theatre and Performance* (pp. 55–66). Amsterdam and New York: Rodopi.
Lavery, C. and Finburgh, C. (eds) (2015) *Rethinking the Theatre of the Absurd: Ecology, the Environment and the Greening of the Modern Stage*. London: Bloomsbury.
Lehmann, H. (2006) *Postdramatic Theatre* (Trans. K. Jürs-Munby). Oxon: Routledge.
Mitchell, K. (2006). *Waves*. Video trailer retrieved from https://www.youtube.com/watch?v=YDTPw6OMJy8.
Mitchell, K. (2007) *Attempts on Her Life*. Video trailer retrieved from https://www.youtube.com/watch?v=kdK_dIucZdY.
Mitchell, K. (2008) . . . *Some Trace of Her*. Video retrieved from https://www.youtube.com/watch?v=8Mg3_WI5YH8.
Nelson, R. (2010) Prospective mapping. In S. Bay-Cheng, C. Kattenbelt, A. Lavender, and R. Nelson (eds) *Mapping Intermediality in Performance* (pp. 13–23). Amsterdam: Amsterdam University Press.
Nelson, R. (2013) *Practice as Research in the Arts: Principles, Protocols, Pedagogies, Resistances*. Basingstoke and New York: Palgrave Macmillan.
Noe, A. (2004) Précis of Action in Perception, Psyche 2006: Volume 12 Issue 1.
Power, C. (2008) *Presence In Play: A Critique of Theories of Presence in the Theatre*. Amsterdam and New York: Rodopi.
Prager, K. J. (1995). *Guilford series on personal relationships. The psychology of intimacy*. New York: Guilford Press.
Troika Ranch. (2006). *16 [R]evolutions*. Video retrieved from http://troikaranch.org/portfolio-item/16-revolutions/.
Scott, J. (2016) *Intermedial Praxis and Practice as Research: 'Doing-Thinking' in Practice*. London: Palgrave Macmillan.
Varela, F. J., Thompson, E. & Rosch, E. (1991) *The Embodied Mind: Cognitive Science and Human Experience*. Cambridge, Mass.: MIT Press.

Wilson, A. (2017) Interview with J. Scott on 16 May. Salford. [Recording in possession of author].
Woods, N. (2017). Interview with J. Scott on 4 April. Salford. [Recording in possession of author].

4 TIME IN INTERMEDIAL THEATRE: JOANNE SCOTT

1927. (2011) *The Animals and Children Took to the Streets*. [Cottesloe–National Theatre London, 22 December 2011).
Barker, T. (2012) *Time and the Digital: Connecting Technology, Aesthetics, and a Process Philosophy of Time*. Hanover, N.H.: Dartmouth College Press.
Chaouchi, H. (2013) *The Internet of Things: Connecting Objects*. [Online]. London: ISTE/ Wiley. Retrieved from https://books.google.co.uk/books?id=EGNm4iT8TC8C&printsec=frontcover&dq=internet+of+things&hl=en&sa=X&ved=0ahUKEwi5vN O7ldHUAhWkK8AKHfPzC1YQ6AEIOTAD#v=onepage&q=internet%20of%20 things&f=false.
Chapple, F. and Kattenbelt, C. (eds). (2006) *Intermediality in Theatre and Performance*. Amsterdam and New York: Rodopi.
Complicité/McBurney, S. (2016a) *The Encounter*. London: Nick Hern Books.
Complicité/McBurney, S. (2016b). *The Encounter* (live performance). [HOME Manchester–Theatre 1, 19 April 2016].
Couzens, D. (2009). *The Time of our Lives: A Critical History of Temporality*. Cambridge, Mass.: MIT Press.
Elam, K. (2002). *The Semiotics of Theatre and Drama* (2nd edn). London and New York: Routledge.
Elleström, L. (ed.) (2010). *Media Borders, Multimodality and Intermediality*. Basingstoke and New York: Palgrave Macmillan.
Fischer-Lichte, E. (2008). *The Transformative Power of Performance: A New Aesthetics* (Trans. S. I. Jain). Oxon and New York: Routledge.
garageCUBE (2014) *Modul8 website*. Retrieved from http://www.modul8.ch.
Gee, H. (2001) *Deep Time: Cladistics, The Revolution in Evolution*. London: Fourth Estate.
Giesekam, G. (2007) *Staging the Screen: The Use of Film and Video in Theatre*. Basingstoke and New York: Palgrave Macmillan.
Gil de Zuniga, H., Garcia-Perdomo, V. and McGregor, S. (2015) What is second screening? exploring motivations of second screen use and its effect on online political participation. *Journal of Communication*, 65, no. 5, pp. 793–815.
Hansen, M. (2004) *New Philosophy for New Media*. Cambridge, Mass., and London: MIT Press.
Hansen, M. (2009). Living with technical time: From media surrogacy to distributed cognition. *Theory, Culture and Society*, 26, no. 2–3, pp. 294–315.
Hayles, N. K. (2012) *How We Think: Digital Media and Contemporary Technogenesis*. Chicago, Ill., and London: Chicago University Press.

Honoré, C. (2010) *In Praise of Slow: How a Worldwide Movement Is Challenging the Cult of Speed*. London: Orion.
Mancewicz, A. (2014) Looking back at the audience: The RSC and The Wooster Group's *Troilus and Cressida*. *Multicultural Shakespeare: Translation, Appropriation and Performance*, 11, no. 26), pp. 65–79.
Mason, P. (2015) *Postcapitalism: A Guide to Our Future*. Retrieved from https://books.google.co.uk/.
Oxford University Press. (2017). Definition of vertiginous. Retrieved from https://en.oxforddictionaries.com/definition/vertiginous.
Phelan, P. (1993) *Unmarked: The Politics of Performance*. London and New York: Routledge.
Pike, C. (2013) Listen up! Binaural sound. BBC Research and Development Blog. Retrieved from http://www.bbc.co.uk/blogs/researchanddevelopment/2013/03/listen-up-binaural-sound.shtml.
Rabey, D. I. (2016) *Theatre, Time and Temporality: Melting Clocks and Snapped Elastics*. Bristol and Chicago, Ill.: Intellect.
Royal Shakespeare Company/Wooster Group. (2012) *Troilus and Cressida* by William Shakespeare. [Riverside Studios, London–30 August 2012].
Scott, J. (2016). *Intermedial Praxis and Practice as Research: 'Doing-Thinking' in Practice*. London: Palgrave Macmillan.
Señor Serrano, A. (2017) *Birdie*. [HOME Manchester–Theatre 2, 6 April 2017].
Señor Serrano, A. (n.d.) *Birdie* dossier. Retrieved from https://www.srserrano.com/productions, 22 June 2017.
Troika Ranch. (n.d.) *loopdiver* Description. Retrieved from http://troikaranch.org/portfolio-item/loopdiver/.
Troika Ranch. (2009) *loopdiver*. Video retrieved from http://troikaranch.org/portfolio-item/loopdiver/.
Ubersfeld, A. (1999) *Reading Theatre* (Trans. F. Collins). Toronto and London: University of Toronto Press.

5 TECHNOLOGY AND INTERMEDIAL THEATRE : ROSEMARY KLICH

Baugh, C. (2005) *Theatre, Performance and Technology: The Development and Transformation of Scenography*. Basingstoke: Palgrave Macmillan.
Berry, D. (2015) The postdigital constellation. In D. Berry and M. Dieter (eds) *Postdigital Aesthetics*. Basingstoke and New York: Palgrave Macmillan.
Berry, D. and Dieter, M. (2015) 'Thinking postdigital aesthetics: Art, computation and design. In D. Berry and M. Dieter (eds) *Postdigital Aesthetics*. Basingstoke and New York: Palgrave Macmillan.
Causey, Matthew. "Postdigital Performance." *Theatre Journal*, vol. 68 no. 3, 2016, pp. 427–441.

Clarke, A. C. (1973) *Profiles of the Future: An Inquiry into the Limits of the Possible.* New York: Harper and Row.

Cramer F. (2015) What Is 'Post-digital'? In D. M. Berry D.M., M. Dieter (eds) *Postdigital Aesthetics.* London: Palgrave Macmillan.

Dawood, S. (2017) How the RSC brought theatre to life through its digital production of *The Tempest. Design Week 30*, 22 December 2016. Retrieved from https://www.designweek.co.uk/issues/19-25-december-2016/ow-rsc-brought-theatre-life-through-digital-production-the-tempest/.

Elleström, L. (2010) The modalities of media: A model for understanding intermedial relations. In L. Elleström (ed.), *Media Borders, Multimodality and Intermediality* (pp. 11–48). Basingstoke: Palgrave Macmillan.

Emerson, L. (2014) *Reading Writing Interfaces: From the Digital to the Bookbound.* Minneapolis and London: University of Minnesota Press.

Hemmings, S. (2017) A spellbinding tempest at the Barbican. *Financial Times*, 7 July 2017. Retrieved from https://www.ft.com/content/7f411eea-630d-11e7-91a7-502f7ee26895).

Ive, Jony (2010) Video launch of iPad. Retrieved from https://www.youtube.com/watch?v=2l6gXMi_ht8.

Kittler, F. (1995) There is no software. *CTHEORY*, October 18. Retrieved from http://www.ctheory.net/articles.aspx?id=74.

Latour, B. (2007) *Reassembling the Social: An Introduction to Actor-Network Theory.* New York: Oxford University Press.

Lewis, C. S. (1947) *The Abolition of Man.* New York: Macmillan.

Manovich, L. (2008) Introduction to info-aesthetics. In O. Enwexor, N. Condee, T. Smith (eds) *Antinomies of Art and Culture: Modernity, Postmodernity, Contemporaneity* (pp. 333–344). Durham, N.C., and London: Duke University Press.

Manovich, L. (2013) *Software Takes Command.* New York: Bloomsbury.

Manovich, L. (2014a) Postmedia aesthetics. In M. Kinder and T. McPherson (eds) *Transmedia Fictions: The Digital, the Arts, and the Humanities* (pp. 34–44). Oakland: University of California Press.

Parikka, J. (2015a) *A Geology of Media.* Minneapolis and London: University of Minnesota Press.

Parikka, J. (2015b) A geology of media and a new materialism: Jussi Parikka in conversation with Annika Richterich. *Digital Culture and Society*, 1, no. 1. Retrieved from http://digicults.org/files/2016/11/V.1-Parikka-Richterich_New-Materialism-interview.pdf.

Paulson, M. (2017) At this tempest, digital wizardry makes rough magic. *New York Times*, 4 January 2017. Retrieved from https://www.nytimes.com/2017/01/04/theater/at-this-tempest-digital-wizardry-makes-rough-magic.html.

Runcy, Charlotte (2016), 'How Andy Serkis is bringing holographic magic to Shakespeare's *The Tempest*', *The Telegraph*, 20 February 2016. Retrieved from http://www.telegraph.co.uk/theatre/what-to-see/how-andy-serkis-is-bringing-holographic-magic-to-shakespeare/.

Taffel, S. (2016) Perspectives on the postdigital: Beyond the rhetorics of progress and novelty. *Convergence*, 22, no. 3, pp. 324–338.
Taylor, P. (2016) *The Tempest*, Royal Shakespeare Theatre, Stratford-upon-Avon, review: Simon Russell Beale in the most profoundly moving performance of his career. *The Independent*, 18 November 2017. Retrieved from http://www.independent.co.uk/arts-entertainment/theatre-dance/reviews/the-tempest-royal-shakespeare-theatre-stratford-upon-avon-simon-russell-beale-gregory-doran-a7424881.html.

6 THE AUDIENCE IN INTERMEDIAL THEATRE: GARETH WHITE

Bourdieu, P. (1977) *Outline of a Theory of Practice*. London: Cambridge University Press.
Complicité/Simon McBurney. (2016) *The Encounter*. London: Nick Hern Books.
Johnson, M. (2007) *The Meaning of the Body: Aesthetics of Human Understanding*. London: University of Chicago Press.
Kittler, F. (1992) *Discourse Networks 1800/1900*. (Trans. Michael Metteer & Chris Cullens). Stanford, Calif.: Stanford University Press.
Kittler, F. A. (1999) *Gramophone, Film, Typewriter*. (Trans. Geoffrey Winthrop-Young & Michael Wutz). Stanford, Calif.: Stanford University Press.
Marquez, G. G. (2007) *One Hundred Years of Solitude*. Harmondsworth: Penguin.
Massumi, B. (2002) *Parables for the Virtual: Movement, Affect, Sensation*. London: Duke University Press.
Sale, S. and Salisbury, L. (2015) *Kittler Now: Current Perspectives in Kittler Studies*. Cambridge: Polity Press.
Thompson, E. (2007) *Mind in Life: Biology, Phenomenology, and the Sciences of Mind*. London: Belknap Press.
White, G. (2013) *Audience Participation in Theatre: Aesthetics of the Invitation*. London: Routledge.
Zunshine, L. (2012) *Getting Inside Your Head: What Cognitive Science Can Tell Us About Popular Culture*. Baltimore, Md.: Johns Hopkins University Press.

End Notes

1 THEATRE (AND YOU) AS MEDIUM AND INTERMEDIUM

1. In the mid-twentieth century, 'media essentialism' was one of the dominant theories, contending that art forms had distinct and discreet traits, but gradually this was countered by writers who highlighted the hybridity and transmedial qualities of art forms, notably Susan Sontag in her 1966 analysis of film and theatre hybridity in *The Tulane Review*. Since this period many writers have explored the intermedial and intermodal discourse between media, including Sybil Krämer (1998), Gunter Kress and Theo van Leeuwen (2001) and Lars Ellestrōm (2010, 2014), amongst others.
2. Modalities – the terms *modality* and *mode* were notably utilised and defined by Gunter Kress and Theo van Leeuwen in *Multimodal Discourse* (2001). The terms are also adopted by Ellestrōm (2010, 2014).
3. Semiotics, or sign systems, are discussed in detail in the discussion of Lars Ellestrōm's multimodal and intermedial theory within **Representation: Decoding the Divorcee and the Cowboy**.
4. Ellestrōm's theorisation of media and intermedia (2010) was significantly cited in *Mapping Intermediality in Performance* (2010), a major text developed by the Intermediality Working Group of the International Federation for Theatre Research (IFTR) and referenced by many writers in the field of intermediality (e.g. Claudia Georgi [2014]) since it was initially written.
5. Within this chapter any new term defined by, or of key significance to, Lars Ellestrōm's theories will be denoted in **bold italic** and then *italic* after that point.
6. *Media product* is the phrase Ellestrōm uses to describe the 'intermediate stage' that enables the transfer of ideas or information (what he refers to as 'cognitive import') from a producer's to a perceiver's mind. It is *that which needs to materialise* in order for the exchange from creator to recipient to occur. *Qualified media* may be comprised of multiple media products: image, sound, text and so on.
7. Singular notions of time and space become problematic when discussing contemporary performance, as digital technologies enable a multitude of 'space-times' to inhabit the stage. However, we as audience members can only occupy one space-time at any given moment but can recognise and interpret the collapsing and expanding of many fictional space-times in front of us. The focus of this book is the combination of live performance bodies with other media, so for now an emphasis is on the shared space-time in this context. Hans-Thies Lehmann succinctly defined this dynamic: 'Theatre means the collectively spent and used up lifetime in the collectively breathed air of that space in which the performing *and* the spectating take place' (2006, p. 17).

8   Elleström's concepts of *basic and technical media* resonate with my earlier definition of a medium as a means of realisation (distinct from communication) because *basic and technical media* (unlike *qualified media*) function without interpretative processes.
9   Source: *Modelling Human Communication: Mediality and Semiotics* (2017, In: Meanings & Co.: The Interdisciplinarity of Communication, Semiotics and Multimodality / [ed] Alin Olteanu, Andrew Stables, Dumitru Borţun, Cham: Springer, 2018, p. 7–32.
10 This distinction (or fluidity) between actor and performer is explored further in **Chapter 3 – The Performer in Intermedial Theatre**, Suffice to say for now that either term is sufficient to describe a live, physical body on a theatrical stage.
11 See Chapter 2, 'Twenty-first-century Intermediality', for further analysis of *mode*.
12 Watch 'What Is a Mode?' ('Kress and van Leeuwen on Multimodality') at http://newlearningonline.com/literacies/chapter-8/kress-and-van-leeuwen-on-multimodality for a fuller explanation of *mode* by Gunter Kress.
13 Presemiotic – as something exists outside of human interpretation: before the decoding and interpretation begins.
14 My emphasis in bold and italics.
15 Organs such as the eyes and ears house a range of specific, small receptors – for example, the eye engages with visual data via the lens, iris and retina.
16 It is important to flag up that our sensorium is very broad and includes our sense of heat (thermoception), pain (nociception), our body in relation to itself (proprioception) – all of which are potential tools for crafting theatre – but for simplicity at this stage, I confine the sensory terms to the principle *modes* of sight and hearing (incidentally touch, smell and taste).
17 In *The Story of Film: An Odyssey* (2011), Mark Cousins notes that early in the history of film, film-makers realised that they could create a sense of 'and then', or alternatively 'meanwhile', in a narrative by how they edited from one shot to another.
18 *Signifier* and *signified* are terms created originally by Saussure and first published in *Course in General Linguistics* in 1916. (1998).
19 See also 'Intermediality: The everyday kind'.
20 These shifts in semiotic signification, influenced by changes in social processes (politics, power dynamics, tastes, class, gender etc.), are acknowledged and analysed in Michael Halliday's concept of 'social semiotics' (1978). These elements are also reflected in Ellestrőm's *qualifying aspects*.
21 The impact of this 'theatricalisation' is discussed further in 'Theatre as Hypermedium: When Is a TV Not a TV?'
22 Cinema, for example, initially borrowed certain conventions from theatre, such as an exaggerated nineteenth-century gestural style appropriated from melodrama, until it founds its own practices and forms that exploited the emergent possibilities of film, such as the close-up or the long shot. For further reading on the relationship between film and theatre, take a look at, amongst many others, Andre Bazin's *What is Cinema* or Greg Giesekam's *Staging the Screen* (2007).
23 Ellestrőm's definitions of remediation and transmediation are also considered under the subheading 'Transformation'.

24 Depending on your level of sophistication, clothes may be classed as the *qualified medium* of 'fashion' with its associated cultural codes and shifting conventions.
25 Phenomenology – the study of our lived experience and consciousness, how we engage with and comprehend the world around us.
26 Occurring prior to reflection or rational thought.
27 The term *gesamtkunstwerk* was first used by the German writer Karl Trahndorff in 1827 and then by Richard Wagner, who proposed the unification of all artworks through theatre, in two essays from 1849 entitled *Art and Revolution* and *The Artwork of the Future*.
28 It is worth noting that Victorian burlesque often took the form of a parody (a type of remediation) of well-known operas, plays and ballets from the period.
29 The term *intermediality* has been coalescing since the early nineteenth century. The writer Samuel Taylor Coleridge referred to the *intermedium* in 1812 in reference to the style of the sixteenth-century poet Edmund Spenser, whilst in 1908 Edward Carpenter wrote *The Intermediate Sex*, a book that explored his views on homosexuality, a state that he referred to as 'uranism'.
30 This definition of intermediality by Rajewsky is one that accords with Werner Wolf's (2011).
31 Klich and Scheer (2012) refer to Parker and Jordan's (2001) five characteristics of computer-based multimedia: *integration, interactivity, hypermedia, immersion and narrativity* (2001).
32 Andy Lavender was one of the original editors of *Mapping Intermediality in Performance* (2010) along with Sarah Bay-Cheng, Chiel Kattenbelt and Robin Nelson.
33 See also Chapter 3, 'The Performer in Intermedial Theatre', for further analysis of The Wooster Group's performance strategies.
34 It may be noted that in such practice, there are resonances with the second logic of Bolter and Grusin's 'double logic' of remediation, which they refer to as 'hypermediacy' (1999, p. 70), the intention of which is to make the perceiver or audience aware of the mediating process, a kind of 'honest' revelation, in pursuit of what Bolter and Grusin refer to as the 'real', by which they mean it would 'evoke an immediate (and therefore authentic) emotional response' (1999, p. 53).
35 Apologies to those readers who are unfamiliar with the British TV 'institution' that is *Dr Who*, a sci-fi series starring a 'Timelord' (the eponymous Dr Who) that has been played by a male actor since its inception in 1963, until now (as of spring 2019). In my defence, the programme has a rather large global following, of which you might be aware, or indeed a Whovian yourself.
36 For more analysis of this theatrical phenomenon, you may wish to read *Theatre in the Dark Shadow, Gloom and Blackout in Contemporary Theatre* (Alston and Welton, 2017).
37 This festival at the Odyssey Theatre was partly inspired by the 1998 summer season at London's Battersea Arts Centre, entitled *Playing In the Dark*, conceived by the director Tom Morris.
38 Benshi were originally performers who provided live narration for silent films in Japan in the early twentieth century.

End Notes   215

2   TWENTY-FIRST-CENTURY INTERMEDIALITY

1 The modalities and modes are given in tabular form on page 36 of Elleström's essay. See Lavender (2014) for a fuller discussion of Elleström's account of modalities and of multimodality more broadly.
2 See Chapter 1 for further analysis of Ellestrom's modalities.
3 Katia Arfara, 'Fast Forward Festival 4', http://www.sgt.gr/eng/SPG1801/. All links in this essay were live at 22 November 2017.
4 ITI Deutschland, http://www.theaterderwelt.de/en/tdw/.
5 See Akira Takayama, 'FFF4 | Piraeus/Heterotopia' (2017, 2–14 May) Onassis Cultural Centre, http://www.sgt.gr/eng/SPG1900/, and 'Tokyo, Heterotopia', 21 November 2013, http://portb.net/en/archives/119. For details of Takayama's company, Port B, see >http://portb.net/en/. I followed the tour in Piraeus on 8 May 2017.
6 'Refugee Crisis Puts Athens on the Brink' (2015, 2 October) DW, http://www.dw.com/en/refugee-crisis-puts-athens-on-the-brink/a-18757016; see also Daniel Howden and Apostolis Fotiadis, 'Where Did the Money Go? How Greece Fumbled the Refugee Crisis' (9 March 2017) *The Guardian*, https://www.theguardian.com/world/2017/mar/09/how-greece-fumbled-refugee-crisis.
7 For details, see Hikaru Fujii, FFF4 | Piraeus / Heterochronia (2017, 2–14 May), http://www.sgt.gr/eng/SPG1901/.
8 For details, see Daniel Wetzel and Rimini Protokoll (2017, 3–8 May), http://www.sgt.gr/eng/SPG1905/ and Daniel Wetzel, 'Evros Walk Water1&2', Rimini Protokoll, http://www.rimini-protokoll.de/website/en/project/evros-walk-water-1-2. I attended the piece on 8 May 2017. Rimini Protokoll's website is at http://www.rimini-protokoll.de/website/en.
9 See, for example, Nikolaj Nielsen, 'Fortress Europe: A Greek Wall Close Up' (2012, 21 December) eu*observer*, https://euobserver.com/fortress-eu/118565.
10 See Chim↑Pom, Kenji Kubota, Eva Mattes, Franco Mattes and Jason Waite, FFF4 | Don't Follow the Wind (2017, 2–14 May) Onassis Cultural Centre, http://www.sgt.gr/eng/SPG1899/, and Chim↑Pom, 'Don't Follow the Wind' (n.d.), http://chimpom.jp/project/dfw.html for details of the project, and https://frieze.com/article/dont-follow-wind for Philip Brophy's review, 'Don't Follow the Wind' (2015, 21 October) for the art magazine *Frieze*. I visited the piece on 9 May 2017. See http://chimpom.jp for Chim↑Pom's website.
11 For details, see Brett Bailey, FFF4 | Sanctuary (2017, 3–7 and 9–10 May) Onassis Cultural Centre, http://www.sgt.gr/eng/SPG1903/, and ITI Deutschland, http://www.theaterderwelt.de/en/artists/artist/artist-5852.html. I visited the installation on 9 June 2017. For details of Third World Bunfight, see http://thirdworldbunfight.co.za.

3 THE PERFORMER IN INTERMEDIAL THEATRE

1. Derrida, through the concept of *différance*, proposes that 'the signified concept is never present in and of itself' and 'is inscribed in a chain or in a system within which it refers to the other, to other concepts, by means of the systematic play of differences' (Derrida in Derrida and Kamuf, 1991, p. 63). Auslander uses this concept to point to the 'play of differences' he perceives in the actor's work, which negates the notion of a stable and preceding self which can be revealed or demonstrated through the performance.
2. Stanton B. Garner Jr. employs the term 'presencing' to cast presence in performance as 'multiply embodied, evoked in a variety of experiential registers, refracted through different (and sometimes divergent) phenomenal lenses' (1994, p. 43), an active, constructed characterisation of presence which resonates with the perspectives explored here.
3. A live coding event involves performers 'writing and modifying computer programs that generate music [or images] in real time' (Brown and Sorensen, 2009, p. 17).
4. Grayson Cooke describes live audiovisual performance as 'the live and improvised performance of audiovisual media' (2010, p. 194). These modes of intermedial practice involve performers activating and manipulating audiovisual media 'on the fly' to generate diverse experiences, events and environments.

4 TIME IN INTERMEDIAL THEATRE

1. Throughout this chapter, I refer to intermedial theatre and performance. Though all the pieces to which I refer took place on stages in theatre venues, intermedial practices as I have experienced them are more usefully positioned under a broader field of performance-making, which encompasses live and performance art and site-based and ambulatory works as well as hybrid practices such as live animation.
2. Binaural sound is created through 'a sound production technique that mimics the natural hearing cues created by our head and ears to create the impression of three-dimensional sound when listening on headphones' (Pike, 2013). Often the recording of the sound is done in relation to a 'dummy head' so that the two microphones mimic the position of the right and left ears, and we hear the sound in three dimensions. In the performance, McBurney played with activating live and recorded sound in relation to a binaural head onstage, so we could both hear and see the sound source moving around our 'head'.
3. Though many practitioners and theorists still refer to pieces that employ media in their construction and presentation as 'multimedia', I always return to the distinction drawn by Greg Giesekam (2007) between multimedia and intermedial. Giesekam states that in the latter, 'more extensive interaction between the performers and various media reshapes notions of character and acting, where neither

the live material or the recorded material would make much sense without the other, and where often the interaction between media substantially modifies how the respective media conventionally function and invites reflection on their nature and methods' (p. 8). As such and according to this definition, I consider both *The Encounter* and *Birdie* to be intermedial pieces of performance.

4 In his 2015 book, Paul Mason claims that 'the long-term prospects for capitalism are bleak' (Introduction, para. 6) and that, as a system, it has 'reached the limits of its capacity to adapt' (para. 24). As such, he proposes 'post-capitalism' as a way of 'reshaping the economy around new values, behaviours and norms', claiming that this 'has started' (para. 30) because of the power of information technology, goods and production in the digital age and the 'mismatch between market systems and an economy based on information' (para. 14).

5 As Robin Nelson points out, the term 'intermedia' was 'coined by Coleridge in 1812 for works which fell between established disciplines', before 'Dick Higgins' use of it to describe interdisciplinary arts practices' in the 1960s. Only since the 1990s, Nelson outlines, has intermediality become current 'within performance and within cultural discourse to describe a set of practices across (notably, but not exclusively, digital) media' (quoted in Scott, 2016, p. x).

6 'Second screening' is the term given to the practice of using 'a digital device (i.e. smartphone or laptop) while watching television to access the Internet and social network sites in order to obtain more information about or discuss the program they are watching' (Gil de Zuniga, Garcia-Perdomo and McGregor, 2015, p. 793).

7 Aneta Mancewicz's article, analyzing the critical responses to this divisive piece helps to position why certain UK critics responded so negatively to the Wooster Group's 'avant-garde performance practices' (Mancewicz, 2014, p. 66).

8 I deliberately place inverted commas around the word 'new' here. Though 'new media' and 'new technologies' are fairly well-accepted terms (Hansen, 2004), and indeed the whole field of new media studies attests to this, there are clearly some issues with trying to define newness, particularly in a world where technologies and their capacities are changing so quickly.

9 The 'Internet of things', or 'IoT', is a term used to describe the networking of everyday objects or 'things', so that 'computing . . . [is] embedded everywhere and programmed to act automatically with no manual triggering', resulting in 'connected machines or objects/things' (Chaouchi, 2013, Section 1.2, para. 1–2). Current examples of these types of connected objects are smart fridges, TVs and heating systems.

10 Live animation is a subset of intermedial performance-making. It involves practices where live performers animate static objects, puppets, models and drawings, often with that action filmed live and projected. Notable practitioners who engage in live animation are Paper Odyssey http://thepapercinema.com, Hotel Modern http://www.hotelmodern.nl and Agrupación Señor Serrano https://www.srserrano.com.

11 In this chapter, I consider *The Encounter*, particularly paying attention to its temporal play and the layers of time intermedially activated and represented. In Chapter 6, Gareth White returns to this piece, specifically focusing on the headphone and

audio technology employed, which he argues positions the audience as a node in the network of the performance. These two views of the same intermedial practice are worth reading together, as they provide complementary perspectives of this complex event.

12   The term 'vertiginous' means 'very high and steep' or 'relating to or affected by vertigo' (Oxford University Press, 2017). I use it in my depiction of *The Encounter* to evoke the feeling the piece created for me of standing on the edge of a vast and unfathomable sense of time, which is akin perhaps to the actual experience of curling your toes over the edge of a cliff and viscerally feeling the drop below.

13   Modul8 is designed for 'real time video mixing and compositing' (garageCUBE, 2014) and allows for prerecorded and live footage to be activated, layered and manipulated in a variety of ways. There are also a number of other pieces of software, available to download, which fulfil a similar purpose.

7   PRACTITIONER CASE STUDIES

1   This is a text in which Benjamin amusingly contrasts 'book' with 'harlots'. For example, he writes, 'Books and Harlots: footnotes in one are as banknotes in the stockings of the other' amongst twelve other similar tenets (Benjamin, 1979 [1933], p. 68).

2   For the show's revival in 2017, an additional minute was added to each side of the clock, and the show's content extended to include events since the show's premiere. This process is expected to continue for as long as the show continues to be performed.

3   An audiophile is a person in whose mind auditory images, rather than visual or motor images, are predominant or unusually distinct.

4   There is a reason why we sit in an auditorium and are called the audience.

5   By 'affect' I mean the mind's connecting response between sensorial input of external events with the internal perception of causation such as emotion or feeling, through time.

6   Discussed in detail in Vear (2014), adopting a phenomenological stance that acknowledges how the physical, computational, performative, interactive and aesthetic qualities of a work amalgamate with an understanding that 'thought, imagination, memory and fantasy coalesce with the "polyphony of the senses" and articulates our "sense of being in the world" that, existentially, strengthens our "experience of self" (Pallasmaa, 2005, p. 41). As such, it is the sense of self that is taken to the worlds within each of these compositions, placing *I* at the centre of this experience.' (Vear, 2014).

7   A term adopted from Elleström (2010) that 'covers the structuring of the sensorial perception of sense-data of the material interface into experiences and conceptions of space and time' (2010, p. 18).

Chapter Authors and Contributors

Mark Crossley is Senior Lecturer in Performing Arts at De Montfort University, UK, specialising in intermedial devising practices and applied theatre. His work on intermediality has been published in a range of journals including the *International Journal of Performance Arts and Digital Media* and *Research in Drama Education* (RiDE). Currently he is on the editorial board of RiDE and co-edited the special edition 21.3 – *Responding to Intermediality* in 2016. Recently he co-authored a book entitled *Devising Theatre with Stan's Cafe* (Bloomsbury Methuen, 2017), written with the company's artistic director James Yarker. His next book project is another text for Palgrave Macmillan, entitled *Education as Drama: A journey across the UK* (pub. 2020). His applied theatre research includes a major collaborative project between Indian and UK partners, exploring the mental health and resilience of migrant workers in India through the use of community theatre.

Lars Ellestrom is Professor of Comparative Literature, Linnaeus University, Sweden. Ellestrom has written and edited several books, including *Divine Madness: On Interpreting Literature, Music, and the Visual Arts Ironically* (Bucknell University Press, 2002), *Media Borders, Multimodality and Intermediality* (Palgrave Macmillan, 2010) and *Media Transformation: The Transfer of Media Characteristics Among Media* (Palgrave Macmillan, 2014). He has also published numerous articles on poetry, gender, irony, semiotics, and in particular intermediality. Ellestrom leads the Linnaeus University Centre for Intermedial and Multimodal Studies (IMS) and chairs the board of the International Society for Intermedial Studies (ISIS).

Andy Lavender is Professor of Theatre & Performance at the University of Warwick, UK, and Head of the School of Theatre & Performance Studies and Cultural & Media Policy Studies. Recent writing includes the monograph *Performance in the Twenty-First Century: Theatres of Engagement* (Routledge 2016) and articles for *Contemporary Theatre Review*, *Studies in Theatre & Performance* and *Theatre Journal*. Andy co-edited a special issue of *CTR* on digital theatre and performance and is co-editor of *Making Contemporary Theatre: International Rehearsal Processes* (Manchester University Press, 2010) and *Mapping Intermediality in Performance* (Amsterdam University Press, 2010). He is an associate editor for *Theatre, Dance and Performance Training*, a member of editorial board of the

International Journal of Performance Arts and Digital Media, and a member of the UK Arts and Humanities Research Council's Peer Review College.

Joanne Scott is a live media practitioner-researcher and lecturer in performance at the University of Salford, UK. Her research explores the creation, activation and experience of events created through live media modes of practice. Jo has presented her live intermedial practice as research at various events and symposia, including live sets in 2015 for the Sonic Fusion Festival at MediaCityUK, Salford, and the EVP Sessions in Shoreditch Town Hall. She is currently working on a project, exploring the relationships between place, autobiography and live intermedial practice and her first monograph, a Palgrave 'Pivot' publication titled *Intermedial Praxis and PaR*, was published in 2016.

Bruce Barton is a performance maker and research/creation scholar located in Calgary, Alberta. His stage and radio plays have been produced across Canada, celebrated with regional and national awards, and anthologised. He works extensively as a director, playwright, dramaturg and designer with numerous devising and intermedial performance companies across Canada and internationally. He is also the artistic director of Vertical City, an interdisciplinary performance hub. Recent Vertical City projects include *2YouTopia* (Toronto's Nuit Blanch, 2014), *All Good Things* (Toronto, Vancouver, Halifax, 2013–14), and the award-winning *Trace* (Toronto 2014). Publications inc. "Intimacy." *Mapping Intermediality in Performance*. Ed. Sarah Bay-Cheng, Chiel Kattenbelt, Andy Lavender, and Robin Nelson. Amsterdam: Amsterdam UP, 2010. 46.

Rosemary Klich is Professor and Director of Research at East 15 Acting School in the UK. In 2007, she moved from Sydney, Australia, to the UK to find out for herself what theatre was like on the other side of the world. After more than seven years, there remains much to see. Her research interests include multimedia theatre, performance spectatorship, public performance interventions, media installations and the connection of bodies and technology in performance. She is also interested in the manipulation of the senses in performance and the immersive, visceral and participatory potential of performance. Rosemary is a member of the Intermediality in Theatre and Performance working group of the International Federation for Theatre Research (IFTR).

Gareth White is Reader in Theatre and Performance at Central School of Speech and Drama, University of London, UK. His research focuses on questions of participation and aesthetics. Publications include *Audience Participation in Theatre: Aesthetics of the Invitation* (Palgrave Macmillan, 2013), *Applied Theatre: Aesthetics* (Bloomsbury Methuen, 2015) and 'On Immersive Theatre' in *Theatre Research International*, October 2013. As a practitioner Gareth has specialised in work with community groups and in educational settings, and continues to explore his research interests through performance making at Central.

Index

1927   75, 79, 80, 84, 91

actor   1, 2, 7, 8, 10, 11, 13, 15, 18, 30, 35, 38, 41, 66–69, 73–74, 87, 94, 97–98, 103–105, 121–122, 146, 148, 159, 171–178
agency   53, 59, 66, 68–70, 75, 124, 145, 156, 172, 198
Agrupación Señor Serrano   95, 107–111
Apple   117–119
Athens   47–54, 58
audience   xi–xiii, 2, 3, 9–11, 20, 30, 33, 36–42, 46–48, 57, 60–64, 70–85, 90–91, 94–98, **136–160**
Auslander, Philip   67, 74, 172, 216

Barton, Bruce   **62–89**
Bay-Cheng, Sarah   23–24, 67, 214, 220
Birdie (2017)   95, 102–111
Blast Theory   63, 70, 73–76, 81–82, 84, 116
Blossom, Roberts   67
Bolter, Jay and Richard Grusin   3–4, 24, 214
borders   20, 25–28, 48, 161, 180–181
Brecht, Bertolt   32, 172–173
Brooks, Pete   161–162, 175–179
burlesque   24, 214

Cage, John   37, 50
camera   12, 49, 62, 76, 81–91, 102, 107–110, 121, 128, 132, 156, 178–179
Chapple, Freda   19, 24, 43–44, 112, 172–173
choreography   38, 79, 87–91, 109, 115, 128–135

cinema   12, 29–31, 38, 70, 126, 176–178, 213
cognition   65, 147–148
convergence   24, 26–27, **28–32**, 34, 37–41, 162
contrast   27–29, **32–34**
co-presence   20, 78
Crossley, Mark   xi–xiii, **1–42**, 93, 112, 119, 137, 139–140, **161–163**
Cunningham, Merce   37–38
cyclorama   171

Derrida, Jacques   64–65, 216
disembodied   55, 129, 141, 145–147, 155
DIY technology   131
dreamthinkspeak *Absent* (2015)   20, 163–171
Don't Follow the Wind (2017)   52–56
Doughty, Sally   36
Dundjerović, Sasha   29

Encounter, The (2015)   xi, 94–95, 101, 104–110, 115, 120, 125, 129–137, 151–155, 217
Ellestrőm, Lars   xii, **1–42**, 44–45, 94, 100–104, 124–125, 130, 212–215, 218
embodied   xiii, 22, 140, 142–144–149, 165, 191, 216
enculturation   15, 139–141
Evros Walk Water (2017)   50–56
Etchells, Tim   36, 74

Fast Forward Festival   47
Fewster, Russell   162, 171–175
film-space   12

Fischer-Lichte, Erika   73, 91
Foley   105–107, 126, 131, 151, 159
Forced Entertainment   36, 42
Forkbeard Fantasy   32

Garton, Rosie   **179–184**
Georgi, Claudia   5, 18–19, 23, 32
Gesamtkomposition   162, 193–195
Gesamtkunstwerk   23, 214
Giannachi, Gabriella and Nick Kaye   74, 78
Giesekam, Greg   25, 29, 32, 213, 216
Google   96, 99, 138, 191

habitus   139–142, 148
Hansen, Mark   98–100, 217
headphones   48–51, 94–95, 105–109, 117, 126, 136–160, 187
Higgins, Dick   22, 24, 217
hybrid / hybridity   xi–xiii, 19–34, 39–40, 44, 80, 97, 101, 104, 134, 157, 212, 216
hypermedium   xi, 18–26, 31–32, 112, 173

imitating the dog   20, 29–30, 34, 63, 71–74, 80–81, 162
imitating the dog   *The Zero Hour* (2013) & *A Farewell to Arms* (2014)   **175–179**
immersive   23, 54, 57, 116, 154, 163, 171, 198
Improvisation   xi, 92, 164
Ingham, Michael   32
interactivity   25, 43, 78, 82, 97, 175, 193, 214
invitations   139–141
intermultimodality   23–28, 39
International Federation of Theatre Research (IFTR)   24, 43, 212, 220
intimacy   xii, 19, 40, 63–72, 77–78, 129, 134, 153
intramediality   4

Kanwar, Amar   30–31, 34, 41
Kerouac, Jack   21
Kiss and Cry (2017)   120, 128–133
Kittler, Friedrich   123, 136, 154–157
Kitson, Daniel   120, 125–132
Klich, Rosemary   xiii, 25, 31, **116–135**
Kneehigh Theatre   29, 34–35
Kress, Gunter and Theo Van Leeuwen   8, 45, 60

Lavender, Andy   xii–xiii, 23, 26, 28, 38–39, **43–61**, 67, 162, 214–215
Lehmann, Hans-Thies   67, 73
Lepage, Robert   29, 35, 173
loop   33, 55, 68, 73, 81–83, 95, 100, 105, 109, 111, 114, 123, 126, 131
live-feed   76, 81, 83, 109
live filming   88, 102, 110, 114

magic   116–135, 162, 173
Manovich, Lev   44, 119, 123
Massumi, Brian   136, 148–149
McBurney, Simon   81, 94–95, 101, 104–109, 120, 126–129, 131–132, 151–154
McGuire, Davy and Kristin   30
McLuhan, Marshall   3, 4, 22, 28
media (basic-technical-qualified)   7
media representations   15, 34–38, 42
media transformations   36
Mercuriali, Silvia (*Macondo*)   136–137, 146, 150
Merleau-Ponty, Maurice   21–22, 140
migrants/migration   47–49, 51, 59, 95, 107–110, 162, 180, 184
mind-reading   147
mobile phones   40, 153, 156, 159
modality (material-semiotic-sensorial-spatio-temporal)   8–10
mirroring   84, 87, 92, 109, 114, 171
mode   8–12, 15–40
Mitchell, Katie   81, 85
multimedia   25–26, 95, 179, 214, 216

multimodality 4–5, 9, 11, 23, 26, 28, 39–40, 43–46

narrative 7, 12, 16, 20, 28–31, 38, 49, 52, 108, 126, 131, 151, 158, 163, 171–178, 189–191, 194–197, 200
Nelson, Robin 4, 26, 44, 63, 67, 214, 217
networks 44, 65, 140, 156
Not Yet Its Difficult v: HOTELLING (2016) 162, 197–201

participation xiii, 36, 46, 73, 116, 139, 141, 144
performativity 65
performer **62–89**
performer-technician 68, 85
Piraeus Heterotopia (2017) 48–56
Pledger, David 162, **197–201**
Popescu, Petru (*Amazon Beaming*) 104–105, 152
post-dramatic 57, 65, 67
postdigital xii, 130–131
Prager, Karen J. 72
precarity 34, 68, 71–72
prerecorded 68, 70, 74–75, 79–84, 90–95, 101–107, 109, 114, 126–127, 144, 218
pre-semiotic 13, 26, 31, 3, 37
presence xiii, 14, 18, 20, 33, 54–55, 59, 62–63, 68, 71, 73–78, 85–86, 94, 107, 125, 127, 129, 142–143, 149, 173–177, 197

qualifying aspects (contextual-operational) 16–20, 27–33, 36, 162
Quick, Andrew 161–162, 175–179

Rajewsky, Irina 24, 28, 59, 214
Rauschenberg, Robert 37
refugees 48–53, 181, 187
remediation 3, 4, 17, 22–24, 35–36, 42, 54, 213–214

representation 10–15, 17, 26–27, 31, 34–38, 42, 45–47, 60, 66, 73, 82, 85, 98, 100–104, 109–112, 143, 162, 165, 176–179, 186
Remote London (2016) 136–139, 141–143, 148–154
Rimini Protokoll 50–51
Rippel, Ildikó **179–184**

Sanctuary (2017) 57–59
scenography 18, 23, 29–30, 38, 119–122, 176
Scott, Joanne **62–89, 90–115**
scrim 171–174
Shakespeare, William 7, 30, 35, 97–98, 120–121
Sharp, Tristan 161–171
sign (signifier/signified) 4–19, 27, 41–42
site-responsive 163, 171
site-specific xi, 48, 54, 57, 163
Sound and Fury 36
spectatorship vii–viii, 17, 55, 92, 136, 220
Stan's Cafe 20, 162
Stan's Cafe *A Translation of Shadows* (2015) 38–39
Stan's Cafe *Time Critical* (2016) **188–192**
Stevenson, Juliet 2

Takayama, Akira 48
technology **116–135**
telematic 68, 114
The Tempest (2017) 120–124
Theater der Welt festival 47
Third World Bunfight 57
temporality 11, 18, 20, 33, 38, 54, **90–115**
time **90–115**
transformation 19, 23–28, 33, **34–37**, 39–42, 162, 177, 180
transmediation 4, 20, 34–35, 45

Vandewalle, Benjamin and Yoann Durant 37
Vear, Craig 161–162, **192–197**
Verhoeven, Dries -161, *Guilty Landscapes* (2016) **184–188**
virtual/virtuality 11, 13, 18, 31, 33, 37–38, 62, 67, 77–78, 85, 88, 103, 119–122

walking 8, 21, 48–49, 56, 97, 113, 126, 136, 138, 141, 167–169, 174, 179–184
Walter Benjamin — A Life in Translation (2016) 171–175

Wetzel, Daniel 50–52
White, Gareth **136–160**
Williams, Raymond 56–57
Wilson, Anna 63, 70, 74–75
Wilson, Robert 32
Wolf, Werner 5–6, 24, 214
Woods, Niki 63, 70–71, 73, 76, 84
Wooster Group 32, 97, 103, 130, 217

Yarker, James 162, **188–192**

Zoo Indigo *No Woman's Land* (2017) **179–184**
Zunshine, Lisa 142–144, 147

www.ingramcontent.com/pod-product-compliance
Lightning Source LLC
Chambersburg PA
CBHW071831300426
44116CB00009B/1508